P9-CFW-747

Third World Coups d'État and International Security

Third World Coups d'État and International Security

STEVEN R. DAVID

THE JOHNS HOPKINS UNIVERSITY PRESS

Baltimore and London

321.09
D28T

© 1987 The Johns Hopkins University Press
All rights reserved
Printed in the United States of America

The Johns Hopkins University Press
701 West 40th Street
Baltimore, Maryland 21211
The Johns Hopkins Press Ltd., London

(∞)

The paper used in this publication meets the minimum re-
quirements of American National Standard for Information
Sciences—Permanence of Paper for Printed Library Materials,
ANSI Z39.48-1984.

Library of Congress Cataloging-in-Publication Data

David, Steven R.
  Third World coups d'état and international security.

  Bibliography: p.
  Includes index.
  1. Coups d'état—Developing countries.   2. Security, Inter-
national.   I. Title.
JC494.D39   1987   321.09   86-45451
ISBN 0-8018-3307-8 (alk. paper)

To Maureen and Sarah Rose

Contents

Preface

In this book I examine the international dimension of coups d'état. Instead of viewing third world coups exclusively as internal affairs, of interest only to those concerned with the countries in which they take place, I consider the way coups affect outside states and the steps those states can and do take to determine their outcome. I am less concerned with how and why coups occur than with what countries have done to maximize their own interests, given the prevalence of coups in third world politics.

This book grew out of the conviction that the outcome of many third world coups was simply too important to be left to the vagaries of domestic politics. Because coups have international repercussions, they are likely to generate outside international involvements. The temptation to try to determine the outcome of coups to protect friendly regimes from hostile interests or to replace unfriendly regimes with more pliable leaders sometimes seems too great for many countries to resist. This appears to be especially true of the superpowers. The interests of the United States and the Soviet Union in the third world have already been strongly affected by coups. Just how their positions in the third world have been affected and what the superpowers have done (and might do) to manipulate coups seems to be a subject worthy of examination and analysis.

Studying the international dimension of coups has proved particularly attractive because so little attention has been paid to it. There has been a fair amount written on the broader implications of revolutions, rebellions, and wars. Despite their central role in third world politics, the international implications of coups d'état have not received commensurate attention. This, even though coups arguably have had a greater impact on the third world and on states with interests in the third world than any other type of political violence. By examining the international dimension of coups, I hope that this gap in the national security literature will be partially filled, and that this book will stimulate additional works in this neglected but critical field. Despite its policy implications, this work is not an exercise in policy analysis. The specifics of American coup policies or the difficulties these policies encounter in the United States' government and military are not addressed. Insofar as policy implications are considered, they are raised in connection with the need to enhance policy makers' awareness of international involvements in coups, suggesting broad directions in which the United States can move to meet the challenges coups pose.

It is also important to stress that this work rests mainly on secondary sources. In part this is due to the breadth of the study. It would be virtually impossible to examine and analyze the over three hundred successful and unsuccessful coups that have taken place historically by relying on primary sources. (As used in this work, a coup refers both to a successful overthrow of a government and to an unsuccessful attempt to do so. At times, I will use the words "coup attempt" to highlight the fact that a coup did not succeed.) More important, primary sources have not been emphasized here because they are not helpful in a study of this kind. The contribution to be made by this work lies not in unearthing previously undisclosed information but in analyzing known data in an original way. Thus, for example, the Sudanese coup of 1971 is shown to be significant not because the role of Egyptian forces in protecting the regime from a coup is revealed (a fact well known to students of the Sudan). Rather, its significance is demonstrated by linking the role of these Egyptian forces to similar actions undertaken by (among others) the East Germans in South Yemen, and the Cubans in Angola and the Congo.

The book is divided into six chapters designed to present an examination and analysis of the international dimension of coups and their impact on the United States. Chapter One focuses on explaining what coups are, why they occur so frequently in the third world, and how American interests can be affected by such coups. Chapter Two considers America's experiences in deterring, defeating, and initiating third world coups. Chapter Three examines the same questions with regard to Soviet experiences with third world coups. Chapter Four focuses on the suppression of third world coups by outside states and the lessons such efforts have revealed. Chapter Five presents an overview of foreign-backed coups, including various methods outside states have employed for supporting coups. The book concludes with an examination of future challenges likely to confront the United States with regard to the international dimension of coups, and it examines possible American responses to these challenges.

Portions of Chapter One, Three, and Four have appeared previously in *International Security*, the *Washington Quarterly*, and in a Harvard University Center for International Affairs' monograph, *Defending Third World Regimes From Coups d'État*. I would like to thank the editors of the two journals and Harvard University for permission to include the material in this book.

A great number of people have offered advice and encouragement to me during the completion of this work. I would like to acknowledge especially the assistance of Samuel Huntington, Walter Laqueur, and Michael Nacht for their helpful comments and criticisms. I am also grateful to Harvard University's Center for International Affairs and Georgetown University's Center for Strategic and International Studies for their financial support. Most important, I would like to thank my wife, Maureen, whose patience and support were especially noteworthy because the birth of this book coincided with the birth of our daughter, Sarah Rose. Final responsibility for the views and facts presented here rests with myself.

Third World Coups d'État and International Security

Introduction

Coups d'état traditionally are thought of as purely domestic occurrences with little or no foreign involvements or effects. The persistence of this conception is easy to understand because the overwhelming number of coups do indeed fit this description. They arise from internal causes, are carried out without assistance or interference from outsiders, generate few changes in foreign policy, and occur in countries of minor strategic significance.

Because the causes and effects of coups are usually confined to the countries in which they take place, the study of coups has normally been carried out by country specialists and by scholars concerned with political development. Most of these studies of coups focus on a specific country or region, or on the coup itself. They seek to understand why coups occur, the motivations for coups, why so many coups are launched and why so many succeed, the likelihood of coups continuing to dominate the politics of the third world, and how regimes installed by coups compare with governments that have assumed power through more traditional means of succession.[1]

These areas of inquiry (which received the most attention during the 1960s) are certainly worthy, but they neglect the critical international dimension of coups. A significant number of coups have been deterred, suppressed, or backed by outside states that have a significant stake in their outcome. Far from being isolated, internal events, coups are often instruments of foreign policy for outside states seeking to expand or preserve their interests. Therefore, the study of coups belongs as much to students of international politics and national security affairs as it does to its more traditional adherents.

Just how important is the role of foreign involvement in coups? From 1945 to mid-1985, there have been 183 successful and 174 unsuccessful coups d'état in the third world.[2] Of this total, foreign involvements played a significant role in support of at least twenty-four coups and in efforts to suppress fourteen coups.

Because they make up only a little more than 10 percent of the total number of coups, those with significant foreign involvement would appear to play only a minor role in third world politics. This impression is misleading on several counts. The involvement of foreign states in thirty-eight coups either to topple or to defend third world regimes should not be ignored, however insignificant it is statistically when compared to the overall number of coups. The frequency of coups involving foreign participation is several times that of all revolutions, and (depending on definitional criteria) is at least as common as the frequency of invasions and insurgencies.

Equally important, the figure of thirty-eight coups understates the degree of foreign involvement in coups. It includes only those coups where public, credible evidence that foreign involvement played a major role has surfaced. The most successful cases of foreign involvement in coups, particularly those cases involving Soviet bloc countries, cannot be persuasively documented. Moreover, as will be made clear, this figure only counts foreign involvement in coups narrowly defined. Outside efforts to defend regimes from internal threats that are not defined as coups and outside attempts to overthrow regimes by actions other than coups have not been included. In addition, this measure also excludes foreign-backed plots that do not culminate in actual coups. A vast number of coups have been successfully deterred by foreign states. The count also excludes the role of outside actors in fomenting subversions that have led, eventually (but not directly), to coups. When these and other such factors are included, it becomes clear that the importance of foreign involvement in third world coups is far greater than a simple statistical accounting can demonstrate.

The reasons for foreign involvement in third world coups are many. For third world leaders, controlling the outcome of any coup is important because coups are a dominant influence in the politics of the third world. In regard to coups launched against their own regimes, the concern of third world leaders is obvious. They are also concerned, however, with coups occurring elsewhere in the third world. Successful coup policies, that is, bringing about the coups you want and preventing those you don't, hold out the promise of enabling third world leaders to protect friendly regimes and to undermine hostile ones. By controlling the coups launched by others, third world leaders can protect their states against outside aggression and can extend their influence over other countries. In short, an effective coup policy can be an important asset to the foreign policy of a third world state.

This is all the more true because of the difficulties third world states face when they attempt to use force to assert their interests. Many third world countries lack the military capabilities to project their forces much beyond their own borders. Problems of logistics, command and control, and the fear of internal repercussions make protracted military interventions difficult to undertake. Norms against interference in the internal affairs of other countries further complicate plans for coercive, overt involvements. Although these norms are often violated, the risk of censure by the world community and especially by regional organizations (e.g., the Arab League, the Organization of African Unity) can deter states from undertaking such aggressive actions.

Manipulating the outcome of coups, on the other hand, is attractive because such manipulations are less subject to considerations of capability and more immune to the influence of international norms. In some ways similar to the state support of terrorism because it is both inexpensive and deniable, involvement in other countries' coups can be an effective instrument of foreign policy. It takes very little in the way of military strength to assist foreign groups seeking the overthrow of their own governments. For example, Libya's armed forces would have a difficult time reaching, much less conquering, the Sudanese capital of Khartoum. This weakness has not prevented Libya's Muammar Khadaffi from sponsoring several coup attempts against Sudan's Gaafar al-Numeiry, some of which were nearly successful. The ability to hide or plausibly to deny efforts to overthrow other regimes also increases its appeal. Defensively, many third world states have the capability to help neighboring regimes suppress the usually low-level military threat posed by most coups. Moreover, intervening to defend a foreign regime from a coup does not violate international norms and is fully consistent with the right of an existing government to request outside assistance to help ensure its survival. When Senegal sent troops into Gambia to protect it from a 1981 coup attempt, the Organization of African Unity and virtually all African states applauded the intervention.

Major powers also have a strong interest in determining the outcome of coups. Although they are not as weak militarily as many third world countries, the major powers too face difficulties in projecting force beyond their borders. The increasing expense of conventional conflict, the political constraints against using force that exist in many states, and the developing military power of third world countries themselves make military intervention far more difficult and consequently more infrequent than has been the case historically. The erosion of international hierarchy and the presence of international norms against intervention always complicate foreign military adventures. No longer is it the case that "the strong do what they have the power to do and the weak accept what they have to accept."[3] Rather, all states are presumed on some level to be "equal" and state sovereignty (defined by whomever is in power) is not easily challenged by outsiders. In such a world, it is little wonder that major powers will seek to safeguard their interests covertly by ensuring that friendly leaders emerge in key third world countries. With friendly leaders in power, the overt use of military force can be avoided, or, if it becomes necessary, it can come at the request of the existing government.

None of this is meant to suggest that backing and suppressing foreign coups will ever replace more traditional state exercises of force. States are likely to continue to rely on conventional warfare and defenses to assert and protect their interests. Nor do the benefits of manipulating coups imply that this is always an effective policy tool. As the high number of coups that have failed despite foreign backing indicates, this is a very sensitive policy area with no guarantees of success. But while large-scale conflicts continue to engage the world's attention, more subtle forms of coercion and defense persist whose implications are no less great for their being less obvious.

Even leaving aside international participation, coups also produce international effects. While it is true that most governments that have come to power following a coup have not fundamentally altered the foreign policies of their predecessors, this is not always the case. New leaders of new regimes often change the foreign policy directions of their countries. They do so out of ideological conviction, the desire to distinguish themselves from the governments they have overthrown or in response to new international opportunities opened up by the coup. As we will see in chapters two and three, a great number of realignments from one superpower to the other have come about as a result of coups.

There are many examples of coups bringing to power leaders who then produced important changes on an international scale. Nasser of Egypt, Khadaffi of Libya, Pinochet of Chile, and Mengistu of Ethiopia all came to power through coups d'état. All dramatically changed the foreign policies of the regimes they represented, generating worldwide repercussions. Other coups have resulted in important changes occurring on a more regional scale. Idi Amin's seizure of power in Uganda eventually led to a war with Tanzania. The entire politics of the Middle East has been strongly influenced by Haafez el-Assad, who came to power in Syria following a coup in 1970. Coups in Somalia (1969) and in Ethiopia (1974, 1977) exacerbated the conflict in the Horn of Africa, eventually leading to war and to the political realignment of both states.

The world's interests and the interests of neighboring states are frequently affected by coups d'état.

The international dimension of coups exists because outside states can effectively promote or advance their interests by maintaining influence over a small leadership elite in a third world country. In many third world countries, all of the foreign policy decisions affecting the interests of outsiders are made by a single individual or at most a small group. In essence, the sovereignty of these third world states is invested in this small elite. Gaining influence over states that are controlled by this kind of small elite, regrettably, does not mean responding to the needs of the people or of the country as a whole. It is instead reducible to the relatively simple task of convincing the elite that their needs would best be served by following the suggestions of a foreign power.

For these elites, no need is greater or more pressing than staying in power. This is not because third world leaders are any more ambitious · or megalomaniacal than other heads of state. Rather, they face a greater likelihood of being overthrown, and graver consequences if they are overthrown, than is the case elsewhere. Confronted with the reality that the loss of power can mean the loss of life, it is not surprising that third world leaders will respond positively to those outside states that can best help to ensure their survival.

Because the greatest threat (by far) to most third world leaders comes from coups, the ability to help determine the outcome of coups puts foreign powers in a central position to influence the politics of third world states. This remains true whether the outside state seeks to protect the leadership from coups, seeks to threaten them with a foreign-backed coup, or (perhaps most effectively) to do both simultaneously. Moreover, because it is only necessary to defend or threaten a small elite group, foreign involvements in third world coups are within the operational capabilities of most states.

If the weaknesses of third world states tempt outsiders into foreign involvements, the strengths of third world states provide added reasons for such involvements. Replacing leaders by means of coups would be pointless if the new leaders could not deliver, in some form, the states they head. Before the emergence of the modern bureaucracy, civil servants in the third world owed their loyalty to a particular individual, ethnic group, or family. If the leadership were overthrown, especially by outsiders, the new leaders would be confronted with the difficult task of ruling the state without the support of this attendant bureaucracy. The development of a modern bureaucracy in the third world that is loyal to whomever is in power has greatly modified this concern. So long as any leader of a state inherits the levers of power that control the state, the potential benefits and temptations of a coup are greatly enhanced.[4]

Another strength of third world states that helps to explain the international dimension of coups comes from the fact that, although a country's sovereignty may rest with only a small elite, the benefits and protections of full state sovereignty do nevertheless become embodied in that elite. The international community is usually less concerned with the way a leader assumed power or is maintained in power than with the reality that he does indeed hold power. Attempting to challenge any existing regime violates international norms against interfering in the internal affairs of another state. An outside state can exploit the weaknesses of third world sovereignty by placing sympathetic people in power, and then it can rely on international norms against interference with any sovereignty to make certain that they stay in power.

Coups are likely to persist in the third world as long as power is concentrated in a narrow elite that succeeds in denying meaningful political participation to the people. As long as coups exist as a means of seizing power, outside states will seek to determine their outcomes as a way of extending their influence. Third world states will vary in their vulnerability to foreign penetration, and outside states will vary as to their willingness and capacity to affect the outcomes of coups. For many developed and developing states, determining the outcome of coups in other countries has become (to paraphrase Clausewitz) a continuation of politics by other means.[5]

1

The Coup d'État and American Interests

A successful coup d'état is the sudden, forcible overthrow of a government by a small group. In its simplest form, a coup consists of a few individuals who conspire together, who try to remove the head of state from power, and, if they are successful, who then assume leadership of the country. A coup d'état usually also involves the active participation of a limited number of military troops. This type of coup carries with it the familiar imagery of the Presidential Palace being surrounded by tanks.[1] Once the government inside agrees to relinquish power, the coup has been successfully completed.

It is useful to distinguish a coup from other acts of political violence. A coup differs from a revolution in that the latter is a mass-based movement for radical change. A coup is neither mass-based nor does it necessarily lead to radical change. While some successful coups do change the nature of the society in which they take place (Khadaffi's rule in Libya is a good example of this), most coups do little to change everyday life. In a civil war, large elements of the armed forces compete for power in a protracted struggle. Coups take place in a much shorter time period with a smaller number of troops (if troops participate at all). A coup is also not an internal rebellion. Internal rebellions aim not to displace the state but to establish some autonomous or independent region within the state.[2]

Several characteristics define the coup. First, the attempt to overthrow the government must be carried out quickly. Most coups are over in a matter of hours, and none should take more than a few days. Second, violence or the threat of violence must be present. In a successful coup, the incumbent regime must leave office unwillingly and against established procedures. Third, for a coup to succeed the government must actually be replaced by the leaders of the coup or by individuals they designate. Forcing a regime to behave in a specified manner by means of behind-the-scenes threats or blackmail does not constitute a successful coup. Nor can a coup be equated with an assassination, provided that neither the assassin nor his backers take power. Moreover, only a small number of participants are typically involved in the implementation of a coup. Although there is no precise quantitative limit to this condition, actions involving more than a few hundred individuals would not generally be considered to constitute a coup. Finally, coups are characterized by having as participants those who already enjoy some political power in the system they seek to lead. Former leaders, exiled groups, and regular political opponents may attempt to topple a government, but such efforts are usually not considered coups unless they are in some way actively supported by elements of the existing power structure.[3]

Motivations for Coups d'État

Understanding what motivates people to undertake coups must begin with the military, which is behind virtually every coup. By virtue of its superior organization, discipline, centralized command, and monopoly of arms, the military is the most powerful institution in many third world countries, including the government itself.[4] Understanding what motivates people to try coups, therefore, means understanding what convinces some elements in the military to seek the overthrow of the government they are supposed to serve.

Motivations for which military personnel undertake coups vary. In some cases the military intervenes to protect what it sees as the national interest. The military overthrows the regime, in effect, to protect the state. This is especially the case when the government is widely seen to have lost its legitimacy.[5] The military may also launch a coup because it sees itself as different from—and better than—the society in which it originates. Frustrated with a lack of social order and discipline, the armed forces acts to bring society up to what it sees as its own standards.[6]

Preserving the position of the armed forces against encroachments by civilian leaders also often forms a major reason for the military to launch a coup. If the regime tries to interfere with the autonomy of the military by (for example) establishing a rival militia, the military will often act to supplant the government.[7] Differences in ethnic or tribal origins between the ruling elite and the military also frequently account for coups. If the leadership of the state comes from a different class or region or ethnic group than the military, conflict can result, leading to attempts to overthrow the regime.[8] Military coups can also of course stem from the pursuit of individual self-interest. Soldiers are driven to coups by a wide range of considerations, from the desire to increase their personal wealth to the ideological goal of launching a revolution from above.[9] Military intervention against the government may also be brought about because the military exists in a society lacking effective political institutions for moderating political action. The military can launch a coup because it believes that that is virtually the only way it can make its influence felt.[10]

In sum, the range and variety of the military's motivations for launching coups are virtually limitless. While some of these factors are partially subject to the control of the third world regime in question, many are not. What all the coup makers have in common is the belief that they stand a good chance of being successful.

The Coup d'État and the Third World

The coup d'état is by far the commonest form of extralegal regime change in the third world. Over two-thirds of the states in the third world have by now experienced successful or unsuccessful coups.[11] For many third world states, leadership succession by means of a coup has become the norm rather than the exception. Why coups have succeeded in dominating the political life of much of the third world can best be explained by examining the political conditions that encourage coups and the extent to which those conditions pertain in the third world.

One of the most important preconditions for a successful coup d'état is a lack of meaningful political participation by the civilian population in the state in which the coup takes place. Because a coup is usually carried out by only a small group, it cannot succeed in the face of mass opposition. Even if the military could take control of the government physically, it would not want to have to deal with the continuing unrest a politically active and resistant population would create. In societies where the people are politically mobilized, involved, and powerful, there is not much chance of a coup occurring against the wishes of the people.

Another factor that promotes coups is a weak public commitment to civilian institutions. If the people in a state do not have strong independent trade unions, political parties, and voluntary associations, there will be very little standing in the way of successful military coups. This becomes all the more important if the civilian government must depend on the military for defense and for the suppression of civilian unrest.[12] Keeping the military out of politics requires at the very least that there be meaningful political institutions in a country aside from the armed forces.

The absence of a strong sense of the legitimacy of the existing government also increases the likelihood of coups. A government that must rule by force because its exercise of power is not accepted as being just by broad segments of the society is likely to be overthrown as soon as some group can muster superior force against it. Similarly, coups become more probable when there are no generally agreed-upon political succession procedures. When brute strength is the sole determinant of the government, politics will be little more than the outcome of internal military struggles.

Rapid social change within a state can increase the likelihood of a coup. When change cannot be channeled effectively into established institutions, instability results. Sudden surges of wealth in ruling groups produce corruption, modernization creates bitter conflicts between Western and traditional values, and industrialization is often accompanied by painful social dislocations. Sudden decreases in wealth are especially destabilizing, because various groups then move to protect their existing assets. These kinds of instabilities are likely to prompt the military to intervene, both because military leaders face the same anxieties and temptations as the rest of the society and because they also are undergoing the difficult transition to a modern way of life.[13]

These conditions that encourage coups d'état are found in varying degrees throughout the third world. Despite the rise of nationalism, most third world states have very low levels of meaningful political participation. The relatively brief historical existence as independent entities of the vast majority of third world countries has frustrated the development of these states' self-consciousness. Moreover, their arbitrarily drawn colonial borders have created linguistic, ethnic, and cultural divisions within these states that have inhibited political participation further. Especially in the emerging states of Africa, the political life of these states is concentrated in a narrow elite located in the capital city. Even in the more developed states of Latin America and the Middle East, public opinion is often neither coherently organized nor politically influential. Consequently, in much of the third world fear of an adverse public reaction would not deter the initiation of a coup d'état.

In many third world countries, civilian institutions hardly exist or they do not inspire the public commitment necessary for them to play a significant role in politics. This lack of civilian institutions reinforces the tendency of the people to direct their energies and loyalties toward ethnic and regional leaders and issues. This promotes both political apathy and political divisiveness, leading to chronic political instability.

Furthermore, a general conception exists in much of the third world that social change is impossible within a constitutional framework. Because the military in many third world countries is the only enduring national symbol, and because they believe that only the military can bring about real change, coups are often welcomed by the people as their sole hope for a better life.

Third world governments generally do not have high levels of legitimacy either. In part this stems from their relatively brief tenure in power; most third world states achieved independence well after World War II. The absence of political legitimacy also reflects a lack of national consciousness. Where people owe their primary allegiance to ethnic groups or regions, as they do in much of the third world, the state (whose boundaries were often arbitrarily established by former colonial masters) is little more than an abstraction. If it is difficult for the people to achieve a consensus on what constitutes the state, it is equally difficult for them to agree on what constitutes legitimate authority in that state.

Legitimate procedures for establishing a peaceful political succession have not been set up in most third world countries. Changes in regimes that take place according to constitutional or legally sanctioned rules are the exception rather than the rule in the third world. The result is an atmosphere of continual uncertainty and crisis, frequently culminating in a military coup.

Rapid social and economic change is characteristic of some third world states, which increases the prospects for coups. Especially in the Persian Gulf, societies are feeling the strains of a huge influx of wealth—which in the 1980s suddenly turned into a decline—accompanied by myriad attempts at modernization. The Iranian revolution bears eloquent testimony to the instabilities generated by such changes. While the Arab Persian Gulf states are not culturally similar to Iran, neither are they politically developed societies. Inasmuch as coups are a far likelier result of such instability than are revolutions, the Iranian experience serves as an ominous warning of the great probability of coups in the newly wealthy Arab states of the third world.

The extent to which the conditions that facilitate coups d'état exist in the third world varies greatly from state to state. For India, Mexico, Venezuela, and possibly Argentina, for example, political participation, civilian institutions, and political legitimacy have been developed to the point where a coup is unlikely. In the Sudan and North Yemen, however, as opposing examples, political participation is weak, civilian institutions are impotent facades, and political legitimacy is absent. For these countries, the coup d'état can become the principal means of regime change.

Launching a successful coup merely involves the relatively simple task of neutralizing those few individuals who constitute the current leadership of the country. These "coup-prone" states make up much of the third world.

Coup-Prone States

Coup-prone states can be divided into five categories. First, there are states that exist at very low levels of economic, social, and political development. These states tend to be political entities only in an abstract, legalistic sense. The presence of the government is strongly felt only in the capital and perhaps in a few other cities. The population identifies not with the state (of which they may not even be aware), but with a tribe, community, or region. Most of these countries are in Africa; Chad, Zaire, and Rwanda are examples of this category of states.

The second category of coup-prone states comprises those with traditional political systems. Their governments are usually feudal monarchies (or they have recently emerged from being feudal monarchies), exercising power over many different tribes in a manner not very different from what had been the norm for centuries. A greater sense of nationhood and state consciousness exists in these states than in the first type, but the level of modern political penetration and development remains low. These states are located predominately in the Middle East, and many of them have lately experienced rapid economic growth on the basis of oil revenues. Their strong sense of tradition makes them resistant to new forms of government. This can be seen in the lack of movement towards democracy in Saudi Arabia, Kuwait, and the United Arab Emirates, and equally in the lack of movement toward totalitarianism in South Yemen and Afghanistan.

The third type of coup-prone state involves very small countries (i.e., countries with populations of less than one-half million) with relatively low levels of political development. Because of their size, these "micro" states can achieve greater modern political penetration than can other types, but their smallness creates a sense of fragility about these regimes that is not easily overcome. These tiny states are found throughout the world, including especially the South Pacific (Micronesia), the Indian Ocean (the Seychelles), and, most significant for the interests of the United States, the Caribbean and Latin America (Grenada, Suriname).[14]

The fourth set of coup-prone countries are countries that have achieved moderate levels of political and economic development, but because of a lack of legitimacy on the part of their governments and the absence of a tradition of civilian rule, they maintain regimes that offer little resistance to military control. These countries are ruled either directly by the military or through a civilian leadership that governs at the sufferance of the military. While substantial levels of political participation often exist in such countries and the authority of the government is felt throughout, no real constraints operate in them to deter periodic military coups. Often the lack of a consensus within the military itself precludes the possibility of setting up a stable (albeit military-controlled) political rule, which exacerbates the lack of civilian opposition to the military's involvement in politics. This type of country is found mostly in Central and South America. Guatemala, Honduras, and Bolivia are some of the more prominent examples.

Finally, virtually any third world state (and some states not in the third world) can become coup-prone at certain points in their historical development. Even third world states with high levels of political participation, strong attachments to civilian institutions, and a well-developed sense of governmental legitimacy can lapse into instability and vulnerability to coups d'état. Lebanon was often cited as an "island of stability"—the "Switzerland" of the Middle East—until its devastating civil war began in 1975. Even if the fighting stops, the threat of a coup d'état will persist in Lebanon for a long time. Mexico's record of political stability for the past half-century is indeed worthy of admiration. Should falling oil revenues or some other factor precipitate domestic unrest, however, the possibility of Mexico reverting to a coup-prone condition (especially as memories of the horror of civil war fade) cannot be ruled out. Thus, while some states are inherently coup-prone, no state in the third world is so stable that changing conditions cannot render it vulnerable to the possibility of a coup.

Types of Coup

Just as third world states differ in their susceptibility to coups, so do coups differ in relation to the motivations of their makers and their effects. Understanding these differences is especially relevant in terms of the interests of outside states, because a knowledge of these differences can help predict whether a new regime, emerging as a result of a coup, will adopt policies different from its predecessor. Of the many different ways to categorize coups, six basic types stand out.[15]

"Traditional" coups occur in relatively simple oligarchical societies. Usually a high-ranking officer together with some supporters will seize power. Although a new regime is established, no real change takes place in the direction or scope of governmental authority or national life. Life goes on as before, with much of the population unaware that a coup has taken place. Traditional coups occurred frequently in Latin America during the latter part of the nineteenth century. They are now most common among the newly emerging states of Africa. This type of coup usually does not bring about any changes in foreign policy, and it is consequently of little interest to outside states.

In "breakthrough" coups, however, the military overthrows a traditional elite and establishes a radical or "progressive" regime. This kind of coup is usually carried out by middle-level officers because the senior commanders are often part of the establishment being overthrown. Breakthrough coups are also distinctive for placing individuals with middle-class or foreign views in power. After taking control, the military make no promises about restoring power to the civilians because they believe that only they can bring about the fundamental societal changes that are necessary. Breakthrough coups are of particular concern to outside countries because they often produce major foreign policy realignments. Examples of breakthrough coups include Nasser's coup in Egypt (1952), Kassem's in Iraq (1958), Khadaffi's in Libya (1969), and Mengistu's in Ethiopia (1974, 1977).

"Guardian" coups are characterized by the intervention of the military into politics to preserve the existing order. They are brought about by the failure of the existing regime to govern effectively. The toleration of large-scale corruption by the civilian leadership, or of insurrections, or of serious public disorders often prompts this type of coup. The military come to power promising to "set things right," at which time they will agree to relinquish control to the civilians. The military often does eventually restore civilian control in these states, either because it has dealt with the problems that prompted its intervention, or because (what is more likely) it finds that governing is far more difficult than it originally had thought. Guardian coups normally do not result in major foreign policy changes. Nevertheless, guardian coups are sometimes encouraged by foreign powers such as the United States in the belief that a corrupt or ineffectual regime had better be replaced by a more effective government before a more radical opposition can take over. As we will discuss in Chapter Two, American efforts to instigate military coups in South Vietnam in 1963 and in Iran in 1979 were attempts to produce guardian coups.

"Veto" coups originate in societies where large new groups attempt to secure for themselves a share of political power against the wishes of the military. These groups usually come from the lower-class masses, and they are encouraged in their efforts by a government seeking to broaden its base of support. Fearful of losing influence, especially to communist-inspired movements, senior military officers overthrow the existing regime in order to deny the new actors political power. Veto coups are notable for their relatively high levels of violence and for the reluctance of the military to return power to civilians. The specter of communist takeovers that accompanies most veto coups sparks intense outside interest in their outcomes. The removal of Juan Bosch in the Dominican Republic (in 1963) and the overthrow of Salvador Allendé in Chile (in 1973) are examples of this type of coup.

"Radicalizing" coups occur in leftist regimes when extremist elements attempt to remove a leadership they see as being too moderate. The extremists launching the coup often originally gained access to power by means of a coup or by some other violent struggle, which replaced a traditional or colonial regime with one committed to a "progressive" path. Radicalizing coups are most likely to occur at the point when the leadership seeks to moderate its foreign policy or when it is judged to lack sufficient ideological fervor at home. The Soviet Union takes a special interest in radicalizing coups because they most frequently occur in countries within Moscow's sphere of influence. Examples of this type of coup include the 1971 coup attempt by communists to topple Numeiry in the Sudan and the 1977 coup attempt launched against Neto in Angola.

"Idiosyncratic" coups stem from personal grievances or the ambitions of small groups within the military. An individual soldier, able to mobilize a small following, simply takes power from the existing elite. The regime that results from this type of coup is entirely dependent on the individual or faction that assumes control. Idiosyncratic coups occur most frequently in relatively simple societies. They differ from traditional coups in that lower-ranking officers and even enlisted personnel are often the coup makers. Idiosyncratic coups usually do not provoke much outside concern (unless they occur in a vital third world state), since the new leadership rarely feels secure or competent enough to make significant foreign policy changes. The 1980 overthrow of the Liberian government by Sergeant Samuel Doe falls into this category.

In terms of American policy, guardian and veto coups are the most likely to tempt Americans to support dissident groups seeking to overthrow their regimes. Either because a leader resists American efforts to have him reform or because a regime proves unable to cope with leftist or other anti-American pressures, the possibility of an American coup-backing effort in such situations cannot be discounted. Guardian and veto coups can also provoke an American response in defense of a regime when American policy makers judge that the destabilizing consequences of a coup will be more harmful to U.S. interests than preserving the existing leadership. Breakthrough coups are also likely to provoke American efforts in defense of a regime when there is a high level of confidence that the coup makers will adopt policies hostile to the United States after seizing power. Since radicalizing coups are usually attempted by and against groups hostile to the United States, American involvement in them will be rare. Traditional and idiosyncratic coups will probably not arouse American concern unless they occur in a third world state of extreme importance. Even then, the estimation that the policies of the new regime would probably remain the same as the old would likely preclude American action.

American Interests in the Third World and Coups d'État

Although American interests are likely to change over time, it is safe to assume that the preservation or expansion of those interests will depend on the third world states in which they are often located. Because coups produce regimes that can be either hostile or friendly to the United States, the outcome of coups in such countries will be as important to Washington as are the American interests these third world regimes control.

One of the most important American interests is the United States' need for foreign petroleum. American dependence on third world oil, particularly oil from the Persian Gulf, was demonstrated by the 1973 Arab oil embargo and the 1979 oil price increases that followed the Iranian revolution. Although Persian Gulf oil accounted for only 2 percent of American energy requirements in 1982, the loss of that oil or its control by a hostile power would have serious economic and political effects in the United States.[16] The combination of huge oil price increases, spot shortages, and the fear of ever-worsening economic conditions would hurt the American economy. For America's allies in Europe and Japan, the situation could be even more serious. Because their dependence on Persian Gulf oil is so great (about 40 percent for Western European countries and nearly 90 percent for Japan), any long-term interruption of oil supplies would gravely threaten their economic life. The United States would also be affected because of its position as the leader of the Western world, its obligation to share oil supplies with its allies in the event of a shortage, and its need to compete with Europe and Japan for other remaining sources of oil. Despite a decline in OPEC's market share of oil in the mid-1980s, the long-term dependence of Europe and Japan on the Persian Gulf remains strong and could grow. Whether or not and to what extent the Western economies would survive the loss of Persian Gulf oil is impossible to determine. That such a loss would be devastating to American interests is a virtual certainty.

All of the Persian Gulf oil-rich states are coup-prone in that their present regimes are threatened as much by coups as by any other economic or political factor. Saudi Arabia is of special concern because it contains more oil than all the other Persian Gulf states combined. As acknowledged by the Carter Doctrine, Saudi Arabia's huge oil reserves make the defense of its pro-Western regime a vital interest of the United States. While the development of the United States' Central Command (formerly called the Rapid Deployment Force) has perhaps eased the potential threat to Saudi Arabia from regional or Soviet invasion (and questions about the effectiveness of the Central Command persist),[17] the prospect of a coup d'état against the Saudi monarchy remains a danger to U.S. interests.[18]

This danger is especially acute in light of the large number of groups that could be tempted to try to overthrow the Saudi regime. Fundamentalist religious groups, such as those who seized the Grand Mosque in 1979, could attempt to take over the government in order to correct what they see as a drift into Western decadence. Palestinians living in Saudi Arabia might instigate a coup in order to produce a more activist anti-Israel policy on the part of the government. Conflict within the ruling elite of Saudi Arabia (especially between the Jiluwi and the Sudairi factions) could spread to the military, precipitating a coup. In the armed forces themselves, officers unhappy with promotions, with pay, or with the level of corruption in Saudi society might seek to supplant the government.[19] Internal, ethnically based conflict similar to the Shi'ite uprisings in 1979 could create enough instability to prompt a military takeover to restore order. External threats from Iran or Iraq could also induce the armed forces to launch a coup, in the belief that a military government would be better able to defend the state. Should the price of oil continue to fall rapidly (as it has been falling in the 1980s), the desire of dominant groups to retain their wealth, combined with general societal instability, could well create the conditions for a coup. No matter what the cause of such a coup and no matter what group attempts it, any successor regime in Saudi Arabia is likely to be more hostile to the United States than the present one.

In addition to Saudi Arabia, other major third world suppliers of oil to the United States and its Western allies are susceptible to coups. Venezuela has been a working democracy since 1958, but falling oil prices, a large external debt, and domestic instability could cause it to revert to its coup-prone history. Similarly, Mexico's postrevolutionary tradition of democracy could be ended by a coup, if, for example, its oil wealth cannot keep up with the demands of an exploding population. Another major oil producer, Nigeria, already demonstrated the fragility of its democracy when its elected government was replaced by military coups on New Year's Eve, 1983, and again in 1985. Although the new leader-

ship did not change Nigeria's oil export and production policies, there
is no guarantee that such changes will not occur in the future. Wherever
the possibility of a coup exists, there is always the chance of a new regime emerging that might reverse the policies of its predecessor and em-
bark on a course hostile (or more favorable) to American interests.

Apart from oil, the United States has economic interests in other raw
materials found in the third world. In order to meet its industrial and
defense requirements, the United States must import many raw materials, most of which are to be found in the third world. A strong expression of this position is put forth by the revisionist historian Gabriel
Kolko: "The economies and technologies of the advanced industrial
nations, the United States in particular, are so intricate that the removal
of even a small part, as in a watch, can stop the mechanism. The steel
industry must add approximately thirteen pounds of manganese to
each ton of steel, and though the weight and value of the increase is a
tiny fraction of the total, a modern diversified steel industry *must* have
manganese."[20]

While this position is overstated here, Kolko is correct in pointing
out that the United States does have some dependence on raw materials
found in the third world. In addition to manganese, the United States
imports about 90 percent of its domestic consumption of chromium
(necessary for jet engine parts), cobalt (needed for high strength steel
alloys), and platinum (used in communications equipment and petroleum refining).[21] Western Europe and Japan are even more dependent
on these minerals than is the United States. Without access to adequate
supplies of these raw materials at reasonable prices, the Western economies would be severely hurt.

American concern about such dependencies is heightened because
many of the raw materials it needs most are concentrated in a few
southern African countries where coups are a distinct possibility. Zaire,
Zimbabwe, and Gabon are among the major producers of chromium,
cobalt, and manganese. Each of these countries has experienced serious
domestic turmoil, and Zaire and Gabon have already suffered coup attempts. Should regimes hostile to Western interests gain control of any
of these countries, U.S. interests would suffer. This remains true even if
over the long run substitutes, alternative suppliers, and conservation
mitigate the effects of American dependence on raw materials.

The United States also has an interest in preserving its security and its
assets from a direct attack by third world states. Many third world
countries are located in strategically important areas. Even with their
limited military capabilities, these countries can utilize sophisticated
weapons to strike at American interests and the interests of its allies.

Oman overlooks the Straits of Hormuz through which a large portion of the non-communist world's oil passes. If an anti-Western regime took power in Oman, it could (at least in the short term) halt much of the tanker traffic that passes so close to its shores. Similarly, U.S. interests would be adversely affected if the present government of Panama were to be replaced by a regime that sought to interfere with ships passing through the Panama Canal.

Moreover, a third world country need not be strategically located to be in a position to threaten American interests directly. As the 1983 invasion of Grenada illustrated, "unimportant" third world countries can suddenly gain added strategic significance when American lives are threatened. Coups are especially likely to provoke this kind of concern or response, because (as in the case of Grenada) they can quickly replace a relatively benign regime with one that might place U.S. citizens at risk. American investments in third world countries can also be affected by coups. Because the economic climate for U.S. firms depends on the leadership of the third world nations, a rapid change in governments can threaten U.S. investments or (as happened in Guatemala and Chile) a change may make such investments more attractive by removing a regime hostile to U.S. business interests.

Defeating terrorism is another U.S. purpose closely associated with the third world. Terrorism is unlikely to challenge directly the security of the United States and its allies. Nevertheless, terrorist attacks against American civilians, diplomats, and military installations abroad cannot be ignored. Terrorism interferes with American policy objectives, diverts political attention from more pressing substantive issues, and creates a climate of fear and outrage that demands a response. Many terrorist groups are supported by third world states whose leaders provide financing, arms, and training facilities for terrorists. Coups exacerbate the terrorism problem by placing in power leaders who sponsor terrorism (e.g., Khadaffi in Libya, Assad in Syria). Coups also represent a potential response to terrorism, threatening terrorists by overthrowing the leaders who support them.

America's interest in protecting itself and its allies from direct attacks by third world countries becomes especially critical should those countries possess nuclear weapons. Clearly, a nuclear strike against the United States or an area of importance to the United States (e.g., the Saudi oil fields) would have catastrophic consequences. Any use of nuclear weapons in the third world, either by accident or by design, would carry with it the possibility of conflict escalation and superpower confrontation. To prevent any such development, the United States has worked to prevent the spread of nuclear weapons to other countries and, even more frightening, to terrorist groups. While American efforts are laudable, a determined third world state might still develop a nuclear weapons capability. It is in U.S. interests not only to prevent nuclear proliferation but also to make certain that those states that do acquire nuclear arms do not use them.

Preventing the use of nuclear weapons by third world states is inextricably linked to the character of the third world regimes that might inherit such weapons, and thus it is linked with coups d'état. Many of the third world states most suspected of being close to having a nuclear weapons capability are also vulnerable to coups. These countries include Argentina, Brazil, Libya, Iraq, and Pakistan. If a third world state governed by a relatively responsible regime (e.g., Pakistan) acquired nuclear weapons, it would be in America's interest to defend that regime against irrational or bellicose elements attempting a coup. If a vehemently anti-American regime acquired nuclear weapons (e.g., Khadaffi in Libya), it might be in America's interest to assist in the overthrow of that government.[22]

Third world countries bordering on states critical to American interests are also of concern to Washington. Even without accepting the "domino theory," we can acknowledge that countries that share a common frontier are in a better position to undermine each other's security than are states farther away from each other. This is especially critical for the overwhelming majority of third world states, because those states lack the means to project force over long distances. Should one state seek to overthrow the regime in another through armed invasion (as in Iraq's attack on Iran and Iran's counterattack against Iraq), or by means of internal subversion (as in Khadaffi's numerous attempts to overthrow Sudanese President Numeiry), a common border could prove essential for taking such action and for its success. The United States has no vital interests in North Yemen. But the United States does have an interest in making certain that the North Yemeni regime does not fall to groups implacably hostile to the West because of the effects that eventuality would have on Saudi Arabia.

The United States also has an interest in ensuring the security of third world regimes that are essential for reaching some critical goal of American foreign policy. For example, since the creation of the state of Israel in 1948, a major foreign policy goal of the United States has been the establishment of peace between the Arab states and Israel. This purpose was intensified in the wake of the October 1973 war, which demonstrated that continual Middle East conflict ran the risk of provoking a U.S.-Soviet confrontation and the Arab use of the oil weapon against the West. In order for there to be a possibility of peace in the Middle

East, regimes must persist that remain more or less amenable to a political settlement. If such regimes (e.g., Mubarak in Egypt, perhaps Hussein in Jordan) are overthrown and replaced by elements opposed to any Arab-Israeli agreement, the likelihood of further wars and subsequent threats to American interests would be greatly increased.

The U.S.-Soviet rivalry provides the basis for another set of coup-related interests the United States retains in the third world. Since World War II, the United States has been committed to containing Soviet influence. The need for this containment in relation to vital third world countries (e.g., Saudi Arabia) is obvious. The United States, however, also has a pressing interest in protecting pro-Western countries of less strategic importance (e.g., the Sudan, Egypt, Thailand) from the threat of Soviet domination. If the Soviets succeed in maintaining their influence in enough countries, they might be able to control regional security to the point that new anti-Soviet governments and international alignments toward the West will become increasingly rare. With one "nonvital" country after another falling into the Soviet sphere of influence, a perception could emerge that the United States lacks the will and capability to protect its friends. Such a perception, combined with the reality of geographical isolation, could have an impact on countries in which the United States has more significant interests. An accommodation to Soviet designs and a dangerous lessening of American influence throughout the third world could result.

A third world under Soviet influence would have an adverse effect on the conventional superpower balance of forces. At least since the advent of nuclear parity in the late 1960s, the role of nuclear weapons has been confined largely to the role of a deterrence against the use of nuclear weapons.[23] As was demonstrated by the Cuban missile crisis, conventional weapons superiority is an important factor in determining the outcome of a superpower confrontation—even when the conflict revolves around nuclear weapons.[24]

The third world can help maintain the conventional balance of forces by providing military bases for one or the other of the superpowers. Military bases enable the United States and the Soviet Union to earn their "superpower" status by enabling them to project force throughout the world and to define the interests that are of greatest importance to them. Moreover, military bases are important because the superpower that maintains a unilateral military presence in a given region has a substantial deterrent advantage over its adversary. In the event of a superpower conflict or the threat of such a conflict, the decision to provoke a military response lies with the superpower without a presence in the region. It has to decide whether to provoke a further military confrontation (with its potential of uncontrolled escalation) with the super-power already in place geographically. Should a crisis develop in the Persian Gulf, for example, the superpower that can project its forces to the area of conflict first may determine the outcome of that conflict. Getting to the conflict first could very well depend on which super-power already has forces deployed in the area. And that depends on the nature of the governments in the area, all of which are subject to sudden replacement by coups.

The U.S.-Soviet competition in nuclear weaponry is also affected by the third world. Third world countries are an important element in helping the United States gather intelligence information about Soviet nuclear developments. Most of the United States' knowledge concerning Soviet nuclear forces comes from satellites that photograph weaponry and monitor missile tests from space. Although these intelligence-gathering capabilities are impressive, satellites cannot do everything. In particular, satellites have difficulty collecting information about the specific characteristics of Soviet missiles—the amount of weight the missile is capable of carrying—which can be gained only during the first few minutes of flight. This kind of information is crucial for determining what new kinds of missiles the USSR is testing, so that the United States can verify increasingly demanding arms control agreements and keep abreast of Soviet military developments. Obtaining this information requires land-based facilities, preferably bordering on the Soviet Union. These in turn necessitate the cooperation of certain third world regimes, such as the one in Turkey.

The third world nations may also be important to the superpower nuclear balance as potential bases for Soviet and American missiles. In the 1950s, before ICBM technology had been developed, the United States deployed intermediate-range ballistic missiles in Turkey, which greatly enhanced U.S. capability to strike at the Soviets. In 1962, the Soviets attempted to reach nuclear parity quickly with the then-superior United States by deploying intermediate- and medium-range ballistic missiles (which they had in great numbers) in Cuba to make up for their lack of an intercontinental striking capability. While the development of intercontinental ballistic missiles and submarine-launched ballistic missiles has dramatically lessened the importance of deploying nuclear weapons from the third world, advantages still remain in doing that. If the Soviet Union were to base nuclear missiles in Nicaragua, for example, the flight time of the missiles to their targets in the United States would be reduced from thirty minutes (for an ICBM based in the USSR) to about ten minutes. With so little warning time, American bombers could be destroyed on the ground, and, even more ominously, command and control centers could be destroyed before an order to retaliate could be issued.[25] This kind of threat is greater from land-based missiles than from those deployed in submarines because the former are much more accurate and therefore are better able to destroy protected targets, such as command centers.

Even without considering them as bases for nuclear weapons, third world countries could become critical to the U.S.-Soviet nuclear balance. The ability to hide or track ballistic missile submarines is already somewhat dependent on the existence of overseas bases. For example, by basing antisubmarine aircraft around the world, it becomes possible to search for submarines in areas of the ocean that might otherwise be out of range. With the development of highly accurate ballistic and cruise missiles, it may become possible for conventional weapons to threaten the nuclear arsenals of the superpowers. If this possibility should become a reality, the maintenance of military bases close to an adversary would then assume an importance unequaled since the advent of nuclear weapons.

Coups are a major cause of countries aligning themselves with one or the other superpower. Recognizing the importance of coups in the third world, the Soviets have developed impressive abilities to defend pro-Moscow regimes from pro-Western coups. The Soviets are also taking steps to improve their ability to back coups against pro-Western regimes. Both of these steps constitute a threat to American interests. By defending third world regimes against coups, the USSR denies the United States the opportunity to reap the benefits of coup-induced realignments. By overthrowing pro-Western regimes, the USSR can undermine U.S. interests and (if the Soviet influence is discreet), it can do so at virtually no risk to itself.[26]

The nature of the U.S.-Soviet competition provides another reason for renewed U.S. concern about coups. Both superpowers recognize that their abilities to initiate and also to prevent coups in the third world are important factors in determining their overall influence. The difference between the superpowers lies in the ways they use coups to threaten or defend third world regimes. For the Soviet Union, manipulating the security concerns of third world leaders (often by means of coups) represents the best way it can extend its influence in the third world. By making short-term security considerations paramount, the Kremlin is able to prevent the U.S.-Soviet competition for influence in the third world from moving into areas where the United States can capitalize on its strengths.

For the United States, meeting the short-term challenges presented by Soviet policies in regard to coups is necessary so that it can exploit its superiority in other areas of its competition with the USSR. Both the United States and the Soviets realize that competition in the economic sphere, for example, would greatly benefit the United States because of America's enormous advantages in aid and trade with the third world. Nevertheless, although the United States maintains long-term advantages over the Soviet Union, these advantages are rendered meaningless if Washington cannot protect friendly third world regimes from coups in the short term. Thus, being able to cope with the consequences of coups becomes an important element in superpower competition in the third world.

America's interests in the third world also stem from its role as a great power. Like all great powers, the United States seeks to shape a world that is hospitable to its dominant values. Such a world would satisfy the security concerns of the United States and at the same time instill confidence in the American people that their way of life is a viable and worthy one.[27] Establishing a congenial international environment does not mean that the United States must recreate the third world in its image. Rather, it suggests that, as a great power, there is much the United States can and would do to change things it finds unacceptable. Since the United States would not choose to live in a hostile world, it is likely that it would take steps to make certain it does not have to do so.

Of particular concern to the United States are third world countries located close to its borders. Although the days of a rigidly enforced Monroe Doctrine and a formal empire are largely past (the last surviving empire of any note is that of the Soviet Union), spheres of influence based on geographical proximity still have meaning. As a great power, the United States can tolerate with equanimity internal diversity among neighboring countries. It may choose not to tolerate the adoption by those countries of pro-Soviet/Cuban foreign policies in open defiance of American wishes. The reason for this is clear. If it is demonstrated that the United States cannot or will not ensure the absence of hostile regimes in country after country in its own region, third world governments elsewhere and policy makers in the United States itself may lose confidence in America's position as a great power.[28] Not all American administrations will react to this kind of "loss" of third world regimes with the same degree of concern. Nevertheless, no American leaders wish to see third world countries (especially those located close to the United States) turn toward the Soviet Union. Since coups are one of the likeliest ways that pro-Soviet regimes in neighboring countries could emerge, Washington's interest in the conditions that produce the potentials for such coups is clear.

Coups also threaten U.S. interests by placing in power regimes whose policies make them morally unacceptable to the American people. It is very difficult and sometimes impossible for the United States to back regimes that engage in gross violations of human rights. Even if a regime is pro-American and rules over a country important to the United States, U.S. opposition to brutal political practices can rule out American support for the regime. Under both the Carter and Reagan administrations, the United States made it clear that it would not tolerate a communist takeover in El Salvador. And yet, Washington usually will not be able to back a regime whose policies—though anti-communist—are repugnant to the people of the United States. If such a regime comes to power, even in a key country such as El Salvador, Washington may have no choice but to allow leftist guerrillas fighting the regime to triumph. It is precisely to avoid such an eventuality that the United States has worked to prevent coups fomented by right-wing elements led by Roberto D'Aubuisson against the moderate Duarte government in El Salvador.

Finally, Washington's concern with third world coups stems from the great difficulty that obtains in the United States in using direct force to achieve its objectives. Because of the American experience in Vietnam, the high costs of direct intervention (in human and economic terms), and the fear of a confrontation with the Soviet Union, it is highly unlikely that the United States would use large numbers of American troops in a protracted third world conflict for any but the most vital of its interests. Moreover, any direct protracted intervention for other than vital purposes (and even perhaps for vital purposes as well) would not be supported by the American people. As the Korean and Vietnam wars so painfully demonstrated, the American people and the U.S. Congress will no longer back a protracted American involvement in a third world conflict. As I will argue, however, the rapidity and narrow scope of a coup often makes a possible U.S. involvement in a coup neither protracted nor costly. Foreign involvements in coups represent a policy option that at times can be useful, even in a world in which the use of force has become constrained.

American interests in the third world are inexorably linked with coups d'états. Coups bring to power friendly regimes that support American interests and unfriendly regimes that threaten those interests. Whether coups are purely internal affairs or are influenced by outsiders, the United States often cannot ignore their implications. What happens in the third world usually affects the United States, and little of what happens there is more important than coups d'état.

2

The United States' Experience with
Third World Coups

Because of American interests in the third world, the United States has
attempted historically to ensure that friendly regimes remain in power
there and that hostile regimes are removed from power. At times by
relying on direct intervention and at other times by employing indirect
economic and security assistance, the United States has tried to determine the outcome of revolutions, insurgencies, and invasions, with de-
cidedly mixed results. While the debate over the effectiveness and justifiability of American policies toward these threats continues,
American experience with third world coups has been virtually ignored
by scholars and policy makers alike. This omission is significant, because coups are one of the most important factors affecting American
interests, they are likely to continue to be so, and they are often susceptible to American influence.

That coups have had a major impact on America's position in the
third world is indisputable. Coups have placed in power many leaders
who subsequently adopted policies hostile to the United States. In the
Middle East, a 1952 coup placed Gamal Abdel Nasser in power in
Egypt; his anti-Western policies antagonized the United States and delighted (at times) the Soviets for nearly twenty years. Libya's Muammar Khadaffi, who took power in a 1969 military coup, has taken
the lead in attacking American interests worldwide by his support of
terrorism, by implementing increases in the price of petroleum, and by
exacerbating the Arab-Israeli conflict. The United States lost its closest
friend and most reliable ally in Africa when Haile Selassie succumbed to
a virulently anti-American coup in Ethiopia in 1974. The Marxist military coup that overthrew Mohammed Daoud in 1978 helped transform
Afghanistan from a state merely within the Soviet sphere of influence
into a Soviet client state. Closer to American shores, military coups

have established pro-Soviet governments in Grenada (1979) and in Suriname (1980). A later coup in Grenada provoked the 1983 American invasion of that tiny but symbolically important island.

Coups have also brought to power pro-Western regimes in the third world. The overthrow of Prime Minister Mossadegh in Iran in 1953 removed a potentially anti-Western leader from a key Persian Gulf state. The military coup that overthrew President Arbenz in Guatemala the following year rid the United States of a regime that some thought was turning toward the USSR. Also in Latin America, the 1973 coup against Salvador Allendé removed a Marxist government from the area that the United States perceives as its sphere of influence. The 1965 *de facto* coup against Sukarno in Indonesia and the 1966 coup against N'krumah in Ghana similarly realigned those two important countries away from the Soviet Union.

Despite their political and strategic significance, the United States has not developed a consistent or even a coherent strategy for dealing with coups. In terms of overall American interests, coups in the third world have been seen (especially by policy makers) as a regrettable but virtually unchangeable fact of political life. When the United States (usually through the CIA) does attempt to determine the outcome of a coup, it does so with little regard for past experience. This reflects a prevailing American belief in the uniqueness of every coup and in the consequent need to treat each one solely in terms of the specific context in which it occurs.

The absence of an overall policy regarding coups should not obscure the fact that over time a distinctly American approach to third world coups has nevertheless emerged. This approach derives from broad American policies toward the third world that have not been designed in relation to coups, but whose impact nevertheless affects the outcomes of coups. In addition, American policies toward specific third world coups reveal a great deal about Washington's thinking about how to deal with coups in general. By extrapolating an American approach to third world coups from both the broad and the specific policies, the effectiveness of the United States in deterring, suppressing, and backing coups can be roughly determined.

The Impact of American Policies toward the Third World in Relation to Coups d'État

The United States for a long time has sought to develop policies that will foster the establishment of democratic regimes in the third world. From John F. Kennedy's Alliance for Progress to Ronald Reagan's Caribbean

Basin Initiative, U.S. presidents have used a mixture of security and economic assistance to promote democracies. Their reasons are not difficult to understand. Democratic governments generally tend to be supportive of American interests. They are far more likely to adopt pro-American policies than are their nondemocratic counterparts, and are less prone to rapid shifts of alignment. Third world democracies rarely, if ever, go to war with one another, which frees Washington from the need to make painful choices between them and promotes regional security. Mobilizing domestic support in the United States is also far easier in relation to democratic regimes than it is for authoritarian ones. Furthermore, as a great power, the United States naturally seeks a world with governments similar to its own.

The advent of a democratic form of government in a third world country holds out the promise of being able to protect such a third world regime from coups. Expanding popular participation, creating meaningful political institutions for channeling political conflict, ending extralegal succession struggles, and inculcating a noninterventionary ethic in the military can dramatically lessen the threat of coups in countries where it has been the norm. Where democracy is present in the third world—in India, Costa Rica, Botswana, Venezuela, and Mexico—the fear of coups has diminished.

Nevertheless, problems posed by third world coups will not be solved mainly through the advent of democracy. Despite some major gains in Latin America, the vast majority of third world states are not democratic and few show tendencies toward attempting or attaining democracy. Very few third world countries have the minimal levels of social, economic, and political development required for democratic institutions to take root. Even were such developments to take place, the traditions of Oriental despotism in the Middle East and Asia and the tradition of tribal rule in black Africa will preclude indefinitely the attainment of democracy in much of the third world.[1] Moreover, the leadership elites in many third world countries are not seeking to establish democratic regimes. These elites are far more concerned with protecting and expanding their own power than they are with dispersing it. The long-term benefits of democratic institutions for third world societies provide scant comfort to third world leaders facing short-term threats.

Nor can the United States do much to change their minds. Despite America's strength, democracy is not something that can be imposed on an unwilling society or its leaders. As much as U.S. policy makers want to see a democratic third world, they cannot avoid the realization that the attainment of this goal is not probable for the foreseeable future.

Even in instances in which the United States can be a guide to third world countries toward democracy, no guarantee ensues that coups will thereby be eliminated. The successful coups against the government in Nigeria (1983 and 1985) and the nearly successful coups in Gambia (1981) and Gabon (1964) demonstrate the vulnerability even of democracies to coups d'état.

Equally important, the United States has not been consistent in defending democratic regimes against coups. There have been times when Washington has stood firmly on the side of democracy against coups. During the early part of the Kennedy administration, for example, the United States maintained a policy "to deny diplomatic relations and economic aid to newly created military regimes, unless they offered firm assurances of restoring democratic rule within the foreseeable future."[2] After a 1962 coup in Peru, the United States followed this policy by suspending diplomatic relations and cutting off military and economic aid to that country.

This policy, however, proved short-lived. A more pragmatic approach replaced it, which sought to evaluate each individual coup in terms of American interests. This approach was enunciated by Assistant Secretary of State Thomas Mann in March 1964.[3] In a private speech, Mann told U.S. ambassadors in Latin America that the United States "would no longer seek to punish military juntas for overthrowing democratic regimes." The key determinant of U.S. policy was not to be the occurrence of a coup against a democratic government, but rather how the new regime behaved toward the United States. If the new coup-empowered leadership supported U.S. investments and opposed communism, then it would earn American support. Instead of pursuing a policy that unilaterally condemned all coups against democratic governments, Washington would judge each case individually on its merits in terms of American interests. It was not so interested in the survival of democratic governments.[4]

This case-by-case pragmatic approach has been demonstrated by the historical record. The United States is believed to have encouraged and supported coups against democratically elected regimes in Guatemala (1954), in Brazil (1964), and in Chile (1970, 1973). Moreover, other coups have been tolerated and even rewarded when they removed democratic regimes perceived to have been hostile to American interests (e.g., the coup overthrowing Juan Bosch in the Dominican Republic in 1963). As strong as general American support for democratic regimes against coups has been, it clearly is not considered predominantly germane in every case.

Economic assistance is also given by the United States to states in the third world, and the implications of this policy also extend to coups. From 1945 to 1979, the United States extended loans and grants to the third world amounting to over $107 billion (compared to $18 billion given by the Soviet Union).[5] American aid, channeled through such international agencies as the World Bank and the International Monetary Fund, provides additional needed resources to poor third world countries. Giving economic assistance to third world nations is motivated by a general desire to increase American influence in the third world and to benefit the U.S. economy by increasing American trade with the third world, and by humanitarian concerns.

Economic aid can also have an important impact on the outcome of coups. Many coups stem from social disruption caused by the inability of a regime to meet the economic needs and demands of its people. By providing economic assistance, the United States can help third world governments cope with economically induced problems before they generate political coups. Conversely, the denial of economic aid, combined with market exacerbations of a regime's economic problems, such as occurred in Chile from 1970–73, can provoke a coup.

The export of food is also an example of the way economic assistance or its lack can affect coups. As the world's leading exporter of food, the United States is in the best position to assist third world governments to feed their people. Aside from its humanitarian benefits, food aid is especially important because it allows third world regimes to spend scarce revenues on other problems and helps to prevent urban food riots that can themselves generate coups. Famine played a large role in the coup that overturned Haile Selassie in 1974. In contrast, American economic and food aid proved instrumental in stabilizing situations that threatened to lead to coups in Egypt in 1977 and in the Dominican Republic in 1983.

And yet, economic aid alone is often not an effective instrument for preventing coups. The motivations of people leading coups are too numerous and the influence of outside financial assistance is too diffuse for it to play a decisive role in deterring or preventing coups. Furthermore, economic aid can unwittingly increase the chances for a coup, by disrupting traditional forms of rule and creating social instability. This is not to suggest that economic aid is useless. American economic assistance can help certain regimes in specific situations deter or prevent coups, or it can work to encourage the armed forces to launch a coup. As long as the military is the prime force behind coups, however, economic aid alone will be unable to play a determining role in an American policy toward coups.

American security assistance programs also play a major role in

United States policies toward the third world and they also have important implications for third world coups. From 1950 to 1980, American security assistance amounted to over $100 billion, the overwhelming part of which went to the third world. These programs included credits for the purchase of U.S. weaponry, grants for military purchases, training at U.S. facilities for foreign military personnel, and economic support for countries of critical importance to the United States.[6]

As with economic aid, the purpose of American security assistance is to protect and expand U.S. interests rather than simply to prevent or provoke coups. By providing the United States with an opportunity to influence third world militaries, however, the security assistance programs can also affect the probability of those militaries launching coups. In a general sense, the prevention of military coups can be accomplished by inculcating in third world military establishments the belief in civilian supremacy and by teaching them a noninterventionary ethic. More specifically, American military assistance can be used as a reward or as a threat to induce third world armies to behave in ways supportive of U.S. interests.

There is no evidence that American military assistance has affected the overall propensity of third world militaries to attempt coups. Third world armies that have received foreign military aid seem neither less nor more likely to intervene in politics.[7] While the United States has enjoyed some success in transferring its weapons and military tactics to the third world, it has generally not been able to convince third world armies not to become involved in politics.

On a more specific level, however, American military assistance programs have been instrumental in affecting specific coups. Third world armies that are dependent on the United States for arms will often be reluctant to take action against the wishes of their American benefactors. The combination of a shrewd American aid policy and a dependent, controllable third world military force can often put the United States in a position to deter, suppress, or back a coup, in accordance with American interests. This combination has worked with some frequency in regions of strong American influence, such as Latin America and South Vietnam. Unfortunately for the United States, third world coups often do not reflect the interests of the military as a whole. Bureaucratic disputes, ethnic divisions, political ideologies, and individual greed can all precipitate a coup or help to prevent a coup that the United States wants to encourage. There is no guarantee that even a third world army that is dependent on the United States for arms will not launch an anti-American coup.

The limits of indirect influence force us to focus attention on the uses of American military forces stationed abroad to deter, prevent, or provoke third world coups. Because coups by definition involve small numbers of actors, the presence of a relatively modest number of American troops should be enough to serve as an effective countercoup or coup-backing force. Such forces theoretically would be able to safeguard governments against pro-Soviet or other anti-Western elements attempting a coup d'état.

Despite their theoretical potential for success in this regard, American troops stationed abroad have not in fact played a decisive role in countering third world coups. In part, this is because there are very few U.S. troops based in third world countries. Although approximately 500,000 American military personnel are stationed abroad, the overwhelming majority are in Western Europe and Japan. In countries that are vulnerable to third world coups, only South Korea (with 39,317 U.S. troops), the Philippines (with 15,414 U.S. troops), and Panama (with 9,616 U.S. troops) have a sizeable American presence.[8] These American forces are not deployed for a countercoup role in these countries, nor is such a role a likely possibility.

In South Korea, American troops are needed to provide protection from an invasion by the north. Any internal role for those troops would jeopardize this critical American mission. The lack of American reaction to a 1961 coup in South Korea reflected Washington's view that a successful coup was preferable to prolonged political instability, which might provoke a major war. American forces in the Philippines are stationed at Clark Air Force Base and the Subic Bay Naval Base. Both bases play a key role guarding American interests in east Asia and it is unlikely (although not impossible) that Washington would risk increasing Filipino opposition to their presence by using American troops in a coup-suppression effort, especially if the political orientation of the coup makers was not known. As for Panama, the vulnerability and sensitivity of the U.S. presence in the Canal Zone make it highly unlikely that the United States would become involved in any internal countercoup enterprises there. Elsewhere, American forces in Egypt, Liberia, Somalia, and the Sudan are too small even to play a countercoup role. In the final analysis, the power of third world countries to evict the forces of the United States following a botched countercoup attempt, combined with domestic constraints on U.S. involvement in the domestic affairs of other countries, makes the suppression of a coup using existing foreign-based American troops not very likely.

The presence of American forces in third world countries can, however, play a major role in the deterrence or backing of coups. Although the possibility of direct American countercoup actions might be remote, most coup plotters would want to be certain of American inaction (or support) before attempting to overthrow an existing regime. As has been demonstrated (e.g., in the Dominican Republic and in South Vietnam), the presence of American troops abroad can compel potential coup makers to sound out Washington's views on whether it wishes to see the present regime toppled. By showing that it would welcome or that it would discourage such an attempt, the United States can do much to determine whether a coup takes place.

Other security-related policies of the United States are also relevant to third world coups. The United States maintains an extensive training program for third world military officers and police forces. These programs, which are based in the United States as well as in the third world countries themselves, attempt to help security forces deal with internal challenges while instilling in them a pro-American ethos. The development of the United States Central Command presumably will provide the United States with the capability to intervene quickly to suppress coups. Shows of force by the U.S. Navy have already proven effective in deterring unfriendly coups and in bolstering weak regimes against anti-American threats.[9]

While they do sometimes benefit the United States by enhancing its ability to deal with coups, these measures are not in fact very effective. American training of third world military personnel has not guaranteed a pro-American political orientation, even when the direct recipients of that training assume power. For example, despite Mengistu's extensive military training in the United States, he adopted strident anti-American policies when he became the leader of Ethiopia. The United States Central Command has the potential to act against coups, except that its mission appears to be directed more against a Soviet or other major conventional attack. By focusing on transporting armor and large numbers of troops, the Central Command might not be prepared to act quickly enough to deal with the unique kind of political threat presented by coups. Finally, the effectiveness of the U.S. Navy in dealing with coups is constrained by the need for it to move rapidly anywhere in the world, and of course the navy needs there to be a coastline in the third world country that is threatened by a coup.

American policies toward the third world cannot help but have an impact on coups. The decision to bolster a regime, weaken a regime, or do nothing in the midst of political turmoil can mean life or death for third world leaders. The effectiveness of American policies in dealing with coups cannot, however, be judged solely in terms of policies designed to increase American influence in the third world and that only incidentally affect the outcome of coups. Only by examining how the

United States has acted toward specific third world coups can its policies be evaluated. This is best accomplished by examining American successes and failures in deterring, suppressing, and initiating coups.

Deterring Coups

Determining how well the United States has done historically in controlling the outcome of third world coups first requires an examination of American successes in deterring coups. Deterrence is a particularly difficult kind of condition to evaluate. It is impossible to be certain whether the absence of coups among a given group of states is due to American efforts or to other factors. This is especially true because the United States does not have a clearly defined countercoup policy. Claims made by American policy makers that some specific absence of a coup against U.S. interests is the result of American actions must be treated with skepticism.[10] Nevertheless, a broad measure of the effectiveness of the American deterrent can be taken by focusing on cases in which the United States has either taken specific actions to deter a coup or has explicitly warned against a coup being launched.

Convincing potential coup makers that the costs of launching a coup will exceed the benefits is no easy task. The speed at which a coup can succeed combined with the reluctance that the United States would have for overthrowing an existing government makes it difficult for the United States or for any outside power to deter a coup. At the very least, Washington has to be able credibly to threaten to defeat the coup or directly to undercut the regime that would emerge from a successful coup for its deterrence to be credible. These conditions are met only in places where the United States already exercises substantial control over the country where the coup is threatened.

Despite such difficulties, Washington has apparently succeeded in deterring coups in several countries important to American interests. These successes have occurred first where the United States has maintained a substantial military force in the country threatened by a coup. The deployment of large numbers of American troops in a third world country greatly complicates the task of the coup makers because direct American suppression of the coup attempt is always possible. Instead of just having to overthrow a small leadership elite, the coup makers must confront the existing and potential power of the United States.[11]

The United States has also apparently succeeded in deterring coups in countries that depend on Washington for a major portion of their military and economic aid. El Salvador is a case in point. Although in the early 1980s the United States maintained only some fifty military advisors in El Salvador, the El Salvadoran regime and military realized they could not long survive without U.S. economic and military assistance. While a military coup might succeed initially in overthrowing the government, the cut-off of American aid that would follow would certainly jeopardize the long-term viability of the new government. The acceptance of this reality, combined with timely U.S. warnings against military intervention in the government, almost certainly has deterred coups against the democratically elected Duarte regime.

In addition to deterring the initiation of coups, the United States has been successful in suppressing challenges to existing governments that have threatened to become coups. For example, following the U.S.-initiated coup in Guatemala against President Arbenz in 1954, Washington sought to preserve a stable pro-Western government in this strategically located Central American country. Washington became concerned when half the Guatemalan army revolted on November 13, 1960, against the U.S.-supported government of Mighuel Fuentes Ydigoras. Fearing that the revolt would lead to a coup that might interfere with the upcoming Bay of Pigs invasion (Cuban exiles were being trained in Guatemala), the United States sent several CIA-owned B-26 bombers, piloted by Cuban exiles, to Guatemala. President Eisenhower also sent naval warships, including an aircraft carrier, to the Guatemalan coast. Because of this American military action, the revolt was suppressed and the Ydigoras regime preserved.[12]

In the Dominican Republic, American policy during the 1960s centered on preventing a coup hostile to American interests. Following the assassination of the right-wing dictator, Rafael Trujillo, in May 1961 (an event welcomed by the United States because of Trujillo's repressive rule and his overtures to Castro), the United States sent a navy task force off the coast of Santo Domingo. Complementing this force were American warnings of direct U.S. intervention in the event of an attempted coup. The American presence and these threats succeeded in deterring potential coups, both from pro-Castro groups and from members of the Trujillo family.[13]

The United States decreased its support for the government of the Dominican Republic when the leftist leader, Juan Bosch, assumed the leadership of the country. Shortly afterwards, Bosch fell victim to a military coup in 1963. That the United States could have tried to deter the coup is indicated by the State Department's refusal to accede to a request by the American ambassador to the Dominican Republic to send an aircraft carrier to suppress the coup. The State Department's refusal was not based on an American incapacity to deter the coup, but on the grounds that the fall of the Bosch regime might serve American interests.[14]

The United States continued its policy of deterring Dominican coups after the suppression of the April 1965 revolt and the subsequent intervention of over twenty thousand American troops.[15] Following the revolt, the United States helped to establish a provisional regime under the leadership of President Hector Garcia Godoy. Washington was determined to use its troops deployed in the Dominican Republic to protect this regime from both left- and right-wing threats. It did not have long to wait. A week after Garcia Godoy took power, a general in the Dominican army and political opponent of Garcia Godoy, Elias Wessin Y Wessin, challenged the new government. General Wessin appeared to be preparing for a coup as he placed his troops on alert and ordered his tanks to the capital of Santo Domingo. American Ambassador Ellsworth Bunker quickly ordered the Inter-American Peace Force (made up mostly of U.S. troops) to stop Wessin. Once this was accomplished, General Wessin was flown under U.S. escort to Miami, where he was given a diplomatic post.[16]

Ambassador Bunker also played a pivotal role in deterring two other potential coups. In November 1965 he learned of a right-wing plot to seize the city of Santiago.* Before the plot could be carried out, the Inter-American Peace Force occupied Santiago's airport, while Bunker warned the Dominican military against supporting any coup. Heeding Bunker's warning, the Dominican military refused to cooperate with the conspirators and the plot never came to fruition. Two months later, a military rebellion succeeded in seizing the government radio and television stations. Bunker immediately had the Inter-American Peace Force protect the national palace and evict the army from the stations. Their success in doing this prevented a coup from developing and enabled U.S. troops to depart from the Dominican Republic in September 1966.

In May 1978, the United States again successfully deterred a coup in the Dominican Republic. National police units attempted to stop the counting of ballots in a general election when it became clear that a leftist candidate (Antonio Guzman) would become president. Suspecting that incumbent President Joaquin Balaguer was behind the effort to halt the election, the U.S. State Department threatened to suspend aid to the Dominican Republic. The American threat convinced Dominican military forces not to support the police, which induced Balaguer to allow

---

*A plot can be distinguished from a coup by being limited to plans to overthrow a regime. In a coup, an actual attempt to overthrow the regime takes place.

the election to proceed. Because of this American response, the police action collapsed and the Dominican Republic inaugurated a democratically elected (albeit leftist) government.

Although its jurisdiction is limited theoretically to the United States, the Federal Bureau of Investigation is credited with having defeated at least two plots before they could develop into actual coups. In April 1981, the FBI arrested ten American and Canadian mercenaries (some of whom were linked to the Ku Klux Klan) who were planning to overthrow the government of Prime Minister Eugenia Charles in the tiny Caribbean country of Dominica. The mercenaries planned to join black terrorists and disgruntled Dominican soldiers in the establishment of a drug and gambling haven. The FBI learned of the plot and arrested the coup makers in Louisiana the day of their departure for Dominica. The plotters had with them automatic rifles, shotguns, rifles, handguns, and dynamite.[17]

In November 1984, the FBI reported that it had foiled a plot to launch a coup against the regime of Honduran President Roberto Suazo Cordova. The right-wing coup makers planned to pay an FBI undercover agent to kill the Honduran president and then to exploit the ensuing unrest to take over the government. The leaders of the plot were senior military officials (including the former Chairman of the Joint Chiefs of Staff, General José Bueso-Rosa) who had lost their positions in March 1984. They were backed by Honduran businessmen living in Miami who planned to finance the coup by the sale of cocaine. The FBI learned of the plot in July, placed an undercover agent in the plot as one of the assassins, and kept the Honduran government informed about the case. The FBI finally arrested the Honduran businessmen, a pilot, and several others of the conspirators.[18]

The United States has also failed at deterring coups in the third world. These failures have become known when it was revealed (usually after the fact) that, despite American warnings, a coup was launched. During the 1960s several American attempts to deter coups against Latin American regimes proved largely ineffective. Despite warnings from Washington to the third world militaries involved, coups occurred in Argentina (March 1962), in Peru (July 1962), in Guatemala (March 1963), in the Dominican Republic (September 1963), in Honduras (October 1963), in Argentina (April 1964), in Bolivia (November 1964), and in Argentina (June 1966).[19]

American reactions to these coups varied markedly. In some cases (e.g., in Peru and Honduras), American military and economic aid were suspended and diplomatic relations with these countries were severed. After several months, however, both the aid and the diplomatic ties were restored in exchange for promises of "democratic" elections.[20] In other cases (as in Guatemala and the Dominican Republic), Washington was content simply to condemn the coups, while maintaining or even increasing aid.

Why did the United States not respond severely to military officers who ignored its warnings not to launch a coup? Once a coup had succeeded, overwhelming pressure was exerted in Washington to deal with the government in power. By punishing the regime, Washington risked losing whatever influence it retained. Moreover, other Latin American governments would not support the United States in issuing sanctions against regimes installed by coups. On the contrary, they saw American aid and diplomatic cut-offs both as unwarranted U.S. interference in the internal affairs of sovereign countries. Rather than compound the problem, the United States essentially accepted that its inability to deter these coups reflected the limits of American power.[21]

A more general failure of American deterrence of coups is evidenced by the large number of coups that have been launched against friendly third world regimes by anti-American groups. Since 1969, coups have replaced pro-Western governments with regimes hostile to U.S. interests in Libya (1969), in Benin (1972), in Ethiopia (1974), in the Seychelles (1977), in Grenada (1979), and in Suriname (1980). During this same period of time, several successful coups occurred in leftist or otherwise anti-American governments that resulted in new regimes that were even more anti-American or pro-Soviet than their predecessors. Examples include Somalia (1969), Afghanistan (1973 and 1978), and South Yemen (1978). This record is noteworthy both because of the number of coup-induced setbacks suffered by the United States, and because of the relatively timid reaction of the United States to Soviet gains that have come about through coups. The United States reacted quite mildly to the Soviets solidifying their position in Afghanistan through coups, in contrast to Washington's pronounced reaction when the Soviets invaded that country. A relatively high number of anti-American (compared to anti-Soviet) coups occurred during the 1970s as well.

Of the failures of American deterrence, the most critical was Ethiopia. In Ethiopia in 1974, the United States lost its closest friend in black Africa. For twenty-five years, Ethiopia had received more U.S. military and economic aid than any other black African state. At the time Haile Selassie was overthrown, several hundred American military personnel were present in Ethiopia. That an anti-American coup could have taken place under such circumstances, and that anti-American elements were able to solidify their position there over the next several years by means of additional coups and power struggles, demonstrated the inability or unwillingness of the United States to deter coups in a key country theretofore thought to be plainly subject to U.S. influence.

The United States has had mixed success in deterring coups. American military and economic strength has deterred many coups in the third world, coups that would have exacerbated political instability in those countries and increased the number of regimes hostile to the United States. Moreover, such gains have been achieved at little or no financial and political cost. Nevertheless, coups still represent a major threat to the U.S. position in the third world. Deterrence has not been effective with regard to states outside the U.S. sphere of influence (e.g., Afghanistan or Libya) or in places where the coup makers were not clearly seen as hostile to Washington's interests (e.g., Ethiopia in 1974). American deterrence policies (especially with regard to the defense of democratic governments) have also been hurt by the inconsistency of U.S. responses to coups. The unwillingness of the United States to punish coup makers once they have gained power over Washington's objections (as happened in Latin America during the 1960s) damaged Washington's ability to deter subsequent coups.

Suppressing Coup Attempts

The actual suppression of coups by U.S. forces is both a riskier and a more effective policy than deterrence. It is riskier because the United States must go beyond making threats to acting directly to defeat an ongoing coup attempt. This kind of action leaves the United States open to charges of unwarranted interference in the internal affairs of other nations, and it can place Washington in an awkward situation should the coup succeed. Once American personnel take the decision to act, however, the prospects for success are good. As the following examples of U.S. coup suppressions demonstrate, unambiguous signals that Washington supports the existing regime, that it would oppose a successor government, and that it is prepared to defeat the coup will often strengthen the resolve of indigenous defenders to resist the coup while undercutting the efforts of coup makers.

One of the first instances of the United States actually defending a regime from a coup occurred in Ethiopia in December 1960.[22] Elements of the Ethiopian Imperial Guard launched a coup against the pro-American leadership of Haile Selassie while the Emperor was abroad. The United States acted quickly and effectively to defeat the coup. The United States informed the Emperor of the attempted coup, provided him with a communications capability enabling him to speak with his generals from the safety of Liberia, assisted in the planning of countercoup operations, and may also have directly participated (with American military advisors already stationed in Ethiopia) in the military suppression of the coup. Largely because of this American involvement, the Emperor was restored to power, where he remained for the next fourteen years.

The threat of the use of American military power succeeded in defeating a coup in the Dominican Republic in January 1962. Having just expelled the principal Trujillo supporters and deterred a series of coups against the regime of Joaquin Balaguer, the United States was eager to promote the development of democracy in the Dominican Republic. It quickly became apparent, however, that Balaguer was more interested in remaining in power than in promoting democracy. Under intense American pressure, Balaguer was replaced by a seven-person council of state that promised to hold elections.

This process was interrupted by an attempted coup led by the commander of the military base in Santiago. Perhaps working with Balaguer, he attempted to overthrow the council and to replace it with his own "civil-military" junta. The United States then threatened implicitly to intervene by moving its ships closer to the shores of Santo Domingo, in order to restore the council. Faced with this show of strength, the coup collapsed and its leaders were sent into exile. The rescued council survived until free elections were held.[23]

In Laos, American diplomatic intervention helped defeat a coup against the neutralist regime of Prince Souvanna Phouma. Right-wing military officers launched the coup because they feared the prince would preside over a coalition government that would give too much power to the communists. From Thailand, the coup makers made their way to the Laotian capital, where they quickly succeeded in capturing several key buildings. They then attempted to convince the country's conservative military leadership to join their coup. At this point, U.S. Chargé d'Affaires, John Gunther Dean, intervened. Dean first hid the prince from the insurgents and then forcefully told the Laotian generals (whose army depended on the United States for aid) that Washington did not support the coup. Because of Dean's efforts, the coup makers were unable to secure the support of the Laotian military, which brought about the collapse of the coup.[24]

Bolivia presents another case where American diplomatic intervention helped to defend a regime from a coup. In 1980, a rare election placed leftist Hernan Siles Zuazo in the presidency. To prevent his being confirmed as president, the Bolivian military launched a successful coup. The new military junta could not rule, however, partially due to the Carter administration's suspension of diplomatic relations with them. In October 1981, a subsequent military coup replaced the junta with a more reformist government. A month later, the United States resumed diplomatic relations with Bolivia. This paved the way for new elections to be held in October 1982, which finally placed Siles Zuazo in the presidency that he had won two years before.

The presidency of Siles Zuazo marked the end of almost eighteen years of military rule in Bolivia. Despite his leftist orientation, the United States was committed to protecting Bolivia's new-found stability. So when another coup was launched against Zuazo, the U.S. ambassador played a central role in defeating it.

The coup began with the kidnapping of the president by armed men. The kidnappers then attempted to enlist the army's support by claiming the backing of the Reagan administration in their effort to overthrow the government. The claim had a certain plausibility, because the coup makers were part of a special antidrug task force trained and equipped by the United States. Their attempt failed because of the prompt action of U.S. Ambassador Edwin Corr. Within hours of Zuazo's abduction, Corr had telephoned military and political leaders telling them that the United States would oppose any coup. Corr's prompt action dissuaded the military from joining in the effort to overthrow the existing regime, which caused the coup to fail. Siles Zuazo was discovered unharmed and he resumed his duties as president. He publicly thanked the U.S. ambassador for his role in defeating the coup.[25]

The United States also failed to defeat a coup, after having made an attempt to do so. In May 1961, a military coup shook the elected government of John Chang in South Korea.[26] As soon as the coup began (with the takeover of civilian buildings in the capital of Seoul by some thirty-six hundred Korean soldiers), American personnel stationed in South Korea acted to defeat it. The American embassy issued statements of support for the "freely elected" government of Chang. Given the near-total dependence of South Korea on the United States, this declaration had been expected to have a major impact. More important, the Chief of the UN Command, General Carter B. Magruder, ordered the Korean officers to support the existing regime. Because General Magruder had operational command of the Korean army, disobeying him was tantamount to mutiny.

Despite these conditions, no significant resistance to the coup developed and the insurgents successfully overthrew the South Korean regime. A military government took its place, led by the South Korean Chief of Staff, General Do Young Chang. Within a short time, the alleged mastermind of the coup, General Park Chung Hee, became chief of state, pledging to continue South Korea's pro-American policies.

The American experience protecting third world regimes from coups is one of modest success. Because such a countercoup role for the United States is defensive, is supportive of sovereignty, and operates largely behind the scenes, the political drawbacks to this kind of policy have been slight. The United States has never had to resort to overt, direct military intervention to suppress a coup. This reflects the effectiveness of less drastic American policies in protecting third world regimes. More important, occasions for the United States to intervene directly to protect critical third world regimes from anti-American coups have not yet arisen.

Despite the generally high rate of success of American countercoup policies, actual efforts in this regard have tended to be confused and improvised. That they have proved to be so effective despite this demonstrates the importance of American support for defeating a coup. The lone U.S. failure (in South Korea) does not disprove this fact. In part, American involvement failed to suppress that coup because it had succeeded so quickly, because the existing regime commanded so little social or military support, and because the armed forces chose to obey their South Korean officers rather than their nominal American commander.

Most important, the United States failed to suppress the South Korean coup because it was never completely committed to its defeat. If Washington had acted quickly and forcefully to quell the coup, many observers believe it could have succeeded. But the main goal of the United States was not to reverse the coup, but to make sure that the whole affair ended quickly so as not to tempt a North Korean attack. Once it became clear that the coup makers had succeeded in bringing about a *fait accompli,* Washington refused its support to the former government. Thus, the South Korean case is less a case of the failure of American coup-suppression policies than it is an illustration of how Washington can view political instability as a greater danger even than the removal of a friendly regime.

As in the case with deterrence, American efforts to suppress coups have been limited to countries within its sphere of influence. Most American countercoup activities (both for deterrence and for the actual suppression of coups) have occurred in Latin America, where the United States enjoys a preponderance of economic and military power. Latin America is also a region where the United States can credibly threaten to take military action without fear of provoking Soviet retaliation (Cuba and perhaps Nicaragua being exceptions to this rule). The dependence of many Latin American regimes on the United States, in combination with a credible threat of U.S. intervention to prevent anti-American governments taking root in its own "backyard," has enabled Washington to work with existing Latin American regimes to prevent coups against U.S. interests with a degree of success unmatched in any other region. In particular, the presence of American troops in the Dominican Republic from 1965 to 1966 made it the focus of more countercoup activity than any other country.

These cases also demonstrate that the United States has defeated more coup threats from the right than from the left. In El Salvador, Honduras, the Dominican Republic, Bolivia, and Laos, the United States has acted to protect an incumbent regime from right-wing threats. The justification for the American decision to do so varied in each of these cases, but they all reflected the belief in the long-term benefits of stability and democracy over the short-term gains to be had from a friendly government coming to power.

American Efforts at Backing Coups

Before examining the record of America's backing of coups, it is necessary to clarify exactly what American backing of a coup means. As the definition in Chapter One shows, for a coup to occur, the coup makers must already enjoy some power in the political system they seek to forcibly replace, those launching the coup (or their backers) must actually try to take over the government, and this action must involve only a relatively small number of participants over a short time. The term American-backed coups, therefore, refers to efforts by the United States to initiate, assist, or encourage existing groups in third world countries to launch coups against their governments.

Not all American actions to overthrow third world regimes constitute U.S.–backed coups. Just as rebellions and invasions are not coups, U.S.–supported rebellions and invasions are not U.S.–backed coups. The United States' support for rebels in Indonesia (1958) and in Tibet (1959) consisted of actions designed to influence the policies of the existing regimes by means of a threat of large-scale military opposition. The American-backed invasion of Cuba in 1961 was designed to overthrow Castro by provoking mass opposition to his rule. In none of these situations was the principal purpose of the American action the removal of the leaders by means of a coup.[27] Similarly, American actions taken during the 1980s in support of the Nicaraguan "contras" and in support of the Afghan rebels have had as their goals the overthrow of anti-American governments. But because these rebels hope to gain power by means of widespread popular rebellion, American efforts on their behalf cannot properly be labeled American-backed coups.

Nor can Washington's efforts to remove third world regimes directly be called American-backed coups. In Grenada, for example, the American invasion overthrew the existing leadership and laid the groundwork for the pro-Western government that followed. Nevertheless, because the United States toppled the Grenadian government without working through indigenous intermediaries, and because large numbers of troops were necessary for this, the Grenada operation cannot accurately be described as an American-backed coup. American-backed assassination plots are also not the same definitionally as backing a coup. The United States government has been charged with having plotted the assassination of Fidel Castro, Rafael Trujillo, Salvador Allendé, and others.[28] Since these alleged assassination attempts were not combined with efforts to place specific individuals in power, they do not constitute American-backed coups.

One major difficulty in examining American-backed coups is obtaining reliable information. Few countries want to admit that they backed the overthrow of another country's government. This is especially true of a democracy like the United States, which takes pride in its superior morality and must remain accountable to its citizenry. When the United States backs a coup, it tries to act covertly. While some of these actions have subsequently become public, the most successful of them have not. Conversely, although the United States has sometimes succeeded in concealing its role in supporting a coup, it also must bear the burden of being charged with having backed coups in which in fact it played no role. Third world leaders know that raising the specter of U.S. involvement in coups can mobilize internal and external support, and that often makes such charges politically expedient even when they are not supported by the evidence.

The United States has backed successful coups against third world regimes in Iran (1953), in Guatemala (1954), in Vietnam (1963), in Brazil (1964), and (probably) in Cambodia (1970). In each of these cases, American support proved critical for mobilizing indigenous groups to launch a coup against existing leaders, to replace them with regimes more in line with Washington's wishes. Not all of these American efforts resulted in success. Despite its efforts, the United States failed to provoke coups in Chile (1970), in Iran (1979), and in Libya (1986).[29]

What these cases show when they are considered chronologically is declining willingness and capability on the part of the United States to become directly involved in backing coups against third world regimes, especially when such involvement may become public. The earliest coups, in Iran in 1953 and in Guatemala in 1954, were marked by

American leadership and control. In both cases, the United States financed, planned, and instigated these coups. That Iran and Guatemala were not critical to U.S. interests did not hinder American involvement. American influence in the world was at its peak and its covert actions were able to be kept secret.

American involvements in coups in Vietnam (1963 and 1965) and in Brazil (1964) were a good deal more limited and circumspect. In these coups, the United States did not become directly involved, but it approved of and (to a limited extent) supported the plans of the coup makers. These coups illustrated the maintenance of American influence, in that it was the dependence of third world militaries on U.S. aid that made the coup makers seek out American support before attempting to overthrow their respective governments. On the other hand, the lessening of American influence throughout the world (and the resistance to it in the third world) forced these American involvements to be indirect and dependent on the initiatives of indigenous third world actors. The United States was still prepared to back coups, but it was much more concerned that its involvements be kept secret.

During the 1970s, the successful alleged U.S.–backed coup in Cambodia and the unsuccessful efforts in Chile and Iran illustrate the declining willingness and capability of Washington to become involved in third world coups. Domestic norms against interference in others' affairs, combined with the mounting difficulty of keeping such operations secret, made direct American involvement more difficult to carry out.[30] In these cases, the United States' role was indirect and, at the most, advisory. When direct American involvement was requested as a condition for the coup to take place as it was in Iran in 1979, the United States chose to abandon the coup effort. Even in Libya (where the United States has openly said it wishes to overthrow Khadaffi) the thrust of American efforts has been to indirectly provoke a coup rather than to directly assist Libyan coup makers in toppling Khadaffi. In examining why the United States decided to back these coups, therefore, the key determinants seem to be not so much the interests involved, but the historical time during which they took place and the type of support demanded of the United States.

One of the first and most important of the American-initiated coups was the 1953 overthrow of Prime Minister Muhammad Mossadegh of Iran.[31] A charismatic nationalist, Mossadegh gained prominence through his efforts to nationalize British petroleum interests in Iran. His popularity forced the young shah (the nominal leader of Iran) to appoint him prime minister in 1951. As prime minister, Mossadegh skillfully exploited domestic unrest to gradually increase his influence, until he gained nearly absolute power in 1953.

The United States viewed these events in Iran with ambivalence. Washington was sympathetic to Mossadegh's demands for a greater Iranian share of oil revenues and recognized that Mossadegh was not a communist. Nevertheless, British pressure on the United States to topple Mossadegh and the growing political instability in strategic Iran caused officials in the Eisenhower administration to think seriously about supporting a coup. American concern heightened as Mossadegh moved further to the left and appeared unable or unwilling to halt the mounting unrest. The United States feared that in time the communists would take advantage of the turmoil by seizing power, either ridding themselves of Mossadegh or reducing him to a figurehead. To prevent such an occurrence, the United States agreed to a British request to overthrow the prime minister.

The CIA in cooperation with Britain developed a plan whereby the shah would depart the capital for a remote part of Iran. He would leave behind an order removing Mossadegh from office and replacing him with a shah loyalist. In addition, $100,000 in Iranian currency would be distributed among Tehran's poor by two Iranian agents of the CIA to ensure popular support for the shah's move. The shah agreed to the plan in August 1953, at which time the coup began.

The attempt to unseat Mossadegh very nearly failed. Instead of leaving office when ordered to by the shah, Mossadegh (who had been alerted previously to the shah's action) arrested the shah's supporters and publicly declared that he was suppressing a coup. Tehran was thrown into chaos as communist mobs shouted anti-American slogans and tore down the statues of the shah and his father. Believing all was lost, the shah traveled to Italy for what looked as if it would be permanent exile.

At this point, the Americans took charge. The American Ambassador to Iran, Loy Henderson, demanded that Mossadegh order the police and soldiers to protect American citizens. This resulted in the communists being removed from the streets by soldiers yelling pro-shah and anti-Mossadegh slogans. The following day, crowds organized by the CIA and paid for with the $100,000 took to the streets of Tehran, where they attacked government buildings while shouting their support for the shah and the United States. The shah's choice for prime minister, Fazollah Zahedi, who had been hidden by the CIA, was carried through the streets of Tehran by ecstatic crowds. The shah returned to power in triumph. He remained the leader of Iran for the next twenty-five years, until he was himself overthrown by the Khomeini revolution.

American involvement in the coup against President Jacobo Arbenz of Guatemala in June 1954 is a nearly flawless example of the way an external power can overthrow a third world leader.[32] Arbenz had incurred the displeasure of American policy makers from the time of his election to the presidency in 1950. While not a member of the Communist Party, Arbenz was suspected of harboring communist sympathies. These suspicions grew out of communist support for Arbenz, Communist participation in his government, and Arbenz's policies of land reform. The United States also objected to Arbenz's attempts to challenge the United Fruit Company by expropriating much of its land. Furthermore, Washington was concerned that an Arbenz-dominated Guatemala might one day pose a threat to the Panama Canal and other Central American regimes. These American concerns appeared to be validated in May 1954, when Guatemala received a shipment of arms from Czechoslovakia. At this point, the United States decided to implement already made plans to overthrow Arbenz.

The American plan to overthrow Arbenz focused on the Guatemalan military. In part this was because of a lack of other alternatives. There were not enough Guatemalan exiles to mount a successful invasion, even with U.S. assistance, and Arbenz's support among the lower classes precluded the initiation of general domestic unrest in the manner of Iran. More important, Arbenz's greatest weakness lay in the military. Arbenz had failed to set in place a new army loyal to him, and this factor, combined with the military's suspicion of his leftist policies and its fear of being supplanted by a "people's militia," made it susceptible to the idea of a coup. American policy makers believed that by undermining the remaining loyalty of the military, by convincing key officers that a coup was in their interests, and by making sure it would succeed, the United States could persuade the Guatemalan army to remove Arbenz.

The American plan called for a symbolic invasion of Guatemala by a small force of exiles and mercenaries based in Honduras. This force had been recruited, trained, and equipped by the CIA, in anticipation of the coup. In conjunction with the land invasion, American pilots would bomb and strafe targets in Guatemala. In addition, radio transmitters set up in Guatemala would spread disinformation and confusion concerning the progress of the invading force. By creating the illusion of a successful invasion, the United States hoped to generate a panic that would provoke and assist in the overthrow of Arbenz.

The plan worked perfectly. On June 18, 1954, the CIA-sponsored "invasion" began. The ragtag, four-hundred-man invasion force advanced six miles into Guatemala, encountered no resistance, and stopped. At the same time, American-piloted planes strafed Guatemalan army barracks and dropped leaflets demanding Arbenz's surrender. Radio broadcasts spoke of major battles and peasants flocking to join the victorious invading forces. Believing that the Guatemalan army would not defend him from the perceived threat, Arbenz ordered the military to distribute arms to people's organizations loyal to him. It was a fatal mistake. The army not only refused Arbenz's request but also demanded that he resign. Without the backing of the army or the active support of the frightened Guatemalan people, Arbenz turned over power to the military and left the country. At the cost of one dead, the United States had successfully overthrown a regime deemed hostile to its interests and replaced it with a pro-American (albeit brutal) leadership.

One of the major escalations of the American involvement in Vietnam came about in the fall of 1963, when Ngo Dinh Diem was overthrown by a military coup.[33] American dissatisfaction with Prime Minister Diem and his brother, Nhu, stemmed from widespread popular protests against their increasingly autocratic and repressive rule. The brothers' violent suppression of large-scale Buddhist demonstrations hurt the American war effort, prompting Washington to try to get Diem to reform. The South Vietnamese leader, however, resisted U.S. pressures, prompting a debate among American policy makers about what to do about the worsening situation.

In general, the military and the CIA favored working with Diem, while the State Department and the White House staff advocated supporting a coup. The interbureaucratic dispute continued while more and more Buddhist demonstrations made clear the absence of a coherent policy on how to deal with the Diem regime. This confusion caused Washington to miss at least one opportunity to rid itself of Diem. At the height of the Buddhist disturbances in August 1963, high-ranking South Vietnamese officers contacted a CIA official to ask if the United States would support a coup. The inability of the United States to provide a clear answer to this request helped account for why the coup was called off.

By early October, the domestic situation had worsened to the point where most high-ranking American officials in Vietnam and Washington now essentially supported launching a coup against Diem, if Washington could be confident of not being publicly implicated. The United States told the potential coup makers that it would not suppress a coup, that it would review the plans of the coup makers to help ensure their success, and that it would support any successor regime. In addition, economic aid was halted to South Vietnam, both in order to destabilize the regime and to demonstrate the lack of American support for Diem. These moves almost failed to reassure the South Vietnamese, because a senior American military advisor (who supported Diem) told a principal coup planner that the United States was against any efforts to overthrow the regime. Only the prompt personal intervention of U.S. Ambassador Henry Cabot Lodge convinced the South Vietnamese officers that Washington did indeed support the removal of Diem and his brother.[34]

With the assurance of U.S. backing, the coup began on the morning of November 1, 1963. The South Vietnamese military quickly took over key points in the capital of Saigon, with only Diem's palace guard offering significant resistance. Trapped in the palace, Diem telephoned Lodge to secure U.S. support, but it was refused. Realizing that he could not remain in power without U.S. backing, Diem and his brother escaped from the palace. They were captured the following morning and killed while in custody. Washington promptly pledged its support for the new regime.

The Diem coup established the United States as the principal power in South Vietnam. For the next few years, Washington became closely involved with determining the composition of a succession of Vietnamese governments. The United States would typically be made aware of impending coups, but usually it did nothing to encourage or discourage them. An exception was made in January 1965, when U.S. Ambassador Henry Cabot Lodge told rivals of South Vietnamese leader Nguyen Khanh that he would support a coup. Largely because of Lodge's encouragement, two of Khanh's colleagues, Nguyen Van Thieu and Nguyen Cao Ky, removed Khanh from power in February 1965. Thereafter a measure of stability came to South Vietnam. This accomplishment was overshadowed, however, by the deepening American sense of responsibility and commitment to South Vietnam, produced by the growing involvement of the United States in determining the Vietnamese leadership.[35]

The American-supported coup against President Joao Goulart of Brazil in April 1964 demonstrated the power of the United States to help topple a regime through behind-the-scenes assistance.[36] Goulart became president of Brazil in 1961, when, as vice-president, he succeeded Janio Quadros, who had resigned after less than a year in office. A wealthy landowner and attorney, Goulart had gained a reputation while labor minister as a populist who supported communist and radical causes. Because of these affiliations, the United States government and the Brazilian military were unhappy with his rise to power, but both were willing to withhold judgment to see how he actually performed in office.

As president, Goulart did not ease the concerns of Washington and the Brazilian military. He developed friendly ties with communist countries, he did little to diminish communist influence in labor and student groups, and he supported legislation hostile to foreign investments. The right attacked Goulart for these and other policies, while the left attacked him for not being radical enough. High rates of inflation and growing political instability further exacerbated Brazil's troubles. The United States and the Brazilian military became increasingly concerned that Goulart would seize dictatorial powers or become a tool of the communists.

The United States had been aware of plots in the Brazilian military to overthrow Goulart ever since he had become president. When the respected chief of staff of the Brazilian military, General Humberto Castelo Branco, joined the conspirators in early 1964, Washington realized that a coup was a realistic possibility. Branco worked closely with the U.S. defense attaché, Vernon Walters, keeping him abreast of developments and sounding out American reactions to a coup.

Convinced that Goulart planned to seize absolute power, the United States agreed to support the coup. Because overt involvement might hurt the coup makers (and American prestige), Washington's offer of assistance focused on covert and contingency aid. This included providing petroleum to the coup makers in the event that Goulart's supporters blew up the oil refineries and preparing to airlift over one hundred tons of small arms and ammunition to the military, should they require it. The United States would also send a carrier task force off the coast of Brazil to help stabilize the situation following the coup and to demonstrate support for the anti-Goulart forces.

The coup began on March 30, 1964, when a local military commander began moving troops and tanks toward Rio de Janiero. This commander apparently was incensed by Goulart's support of rebellious sailors a few days before. Although the coup was begun prematurely, other elements of the Brazilian military, including General Branco, quickly joined in. Working with the United States Ambassador in Brazil, Lincoln Gordon, Washington quickly approved the plans for sending arms, oil, and the carrier fleet to Brazil. The State Department also informed the American embassy to advise the coup makers on how best to establish political legitimacy for the new regime, thus facilitating additional U.S. assistance.

In the end, American assistance was not needed. Goulart's pleas for support from the workers and the military went unheeded and the coup makers quickly seized their objectives. By April 2, the coup was essentially over. The United States halted the task force (covering up its initial movements by saying it was on a training exercise) and canceled the shipments of arms and oil. Washington promptly welcomed the new regime and provided it with record levels of aid.

Although the United States did not directly participate in the coup, American involvement was critical for its success. Because of the importance of U.S. military aid to them, the Brazilian armed forces probably would not have gone ahead with the planning of the coup without explicit approval and encouragement from Washington. Moreover, the contingency support made available by the United States gave confidence to the coup makers that Washington supported them and this support would have played a critical role had it been needed. By remaining in the background and by conditioning the provision of material support on actual need, the United States government was able to play a central role in the overthrow of Goulart without incurring many of the risks and censure that would ordinarily have ensued.

In Cambodia, the United States is alleged to have played a key role in the 1970 overthrow of Prince Norodom Sihanouk.[37] The United States had long been unhappy with the large number of North Vietnamese troops on Cambodian soil. The elimination of this North Vietnamese sanctuary (from which American troops were being attacked) had become a major goal of the American war effort. Sihanouk's toleration of the North Vietnamese, his resistance to an American incursion to drive them out, and his insistence that the United States withdraw from South Vietnam complicated American efforts to deal with the North Vietnamese threat. A more pliable, pro-Western leadership in Cambodia was clearly seen to be in America's interest.

It was in this context that a coup unfolded against Sihanouk, while the prince was taking a two-month vacation in France. Under the leadership of Prime Minister Lon Nol, the Cambodian government first organized demonstrations against the North Vietnamese, including attacks on the embassies of North Vietnam and the Viet Cong. Lon Nol then gave permission for a South Vietnamese task force to cross the Cambodian border to attack the North Vietnamese sanctuaries. At the same time, the Cambodian parliament deposed Sihanouk in a unanimous vote. Although he was not formally named head of state, Lon Nol assumed the leadership of Cambodia. A few weeks later, Lon Nol supported the U.S. incursion into Cambodia to expel the North Vietnamese.

Secretary of State Henry Kissinger argued in his memoirs that the

United States government "neither encouraged Sihanouk's overthrow nor knew about it in advance."[38] Kissinger blamed the coup on Sihanouk's failure to return to Cambodia as soon as the domestic difficulties began. Stating that Sihanouk's rule had met the interests of the United States, Kissinger asserted that Washington only supported the Lon Nol regime when the prince bitterly turned against the United States and toward North Vietnam and the Soviet Union. At that point, the United States had to support the Lon Nol regime because Sihanouk's return to power had become unacceptable.

Despite Kissinger's protestations of U.S. noninvolvement, others saw Washington as the prime force behind the coup. Seymour Hersh argues that the United States used anti-communist Cambodians to launch the coup. Two Cambodian groups, the Khmer Serei based in Thailand and the Khmer Kampuchean Krom based largely in Cambodia, played the key roles. Since they were ethnic Cambodians, the United States was able, Hersh alleges, to infiltrate the Cambodian military and Cambodian society with these groups, where they could serve as the vanguard of the anti-Sihanouk forces.

According to Hersh, planning for the coup began between representatives of Lon Nol and the United States in 1968. The plan (code named "dirty tricks") called for the mercenaries to carry out various actions against the Sihanouk regime and then to support Lon Nol's coup once it was launched. Following the overthrow of the prince, Washington would "reluctantly" support the new regime.

Whether or not the Cambodian mercenaries did in fact carry out this plan cannot be proven. It is clear, however, that Lon Nol was able to mobilize anti-Sihanouk forces in the military and in the streets for his coup. Moreover, the new regime did command "reluctant" U.S. support. In the aftermath of the coup, both Sihanouk and North Vietnam stated both secretly and publicly their conviction that the United States had staged the coup. In any event, once in power, Lon Nol faithfully supported U.S. interests until 1975, when the murderous Pol Pot regime replaced him.

Not all American efforts at backing coups have proved successful. While there are no confirmed cases of Washington actively backing a coup that failed, the United States has reportedly been unable to provoke coups on several specific occasions. Two failures of note occurred, in Chile in 1970 and in Iran in 1979. Both episodes are still mired in controversy over what the United States did or did not do or should have done. Nevertheless, these two cases collectively demonstrate that even when the United States wields considerable influence over a third world military and seeks to provoke it to launch a coup, success is not assured. In a third case, Libya 1981–86, the failure of American efforts to topple Khadaffi reveals the difficulties of Washington's backing of a coup in a country where the United States maintains little influence.

The most prominent example of a failed American attempt to provoke a coup is Washington's involvement in the plot to overthrow Chile's Salvador Allendé in 1970.[39] As the founder of the Socialist Party of Chile, and as an advocate of land reform, of the nationalization of major industries (many of them American), and of close ties with communist countries, Allendé was a source of major concern to United States policy makers. They saw the election of Allendé as having brought about the establishment of an irreversible Marxist-Leninist dictatorship on the continent of South America. Even worse, if Allendé willingly submitted to future elections and demonstrated that communism was not necessarily incompatible with democracy, the capability and willingness of the United States to challenge the emergence of future communist governments in the third world would be dangerously weakened.

American concerns rose dramatically when Allendé won a 36.2 percent plurality of the vote in a three-way race for the presidency in the fall of 1970.[40] As the leading vote gainer, Allendé became the favorite to be selected in a run-off election to be held by the Chilean Congress in October. Suddenly, the Nixon administration confronted the probability that Allendé would democratically assume the leadership of Chile in less than two months.

The Nixon administration responded with a two-track plan, designed to prevent Allendé from becoming president. The more benign Track I provided for continuing the placing of anti-Allendé stories in the press, the bribing of Chilean congressmen to get them to vote against Allendé, exploring the likelihood of the Chilean military launching a coup against Allendé, and attempting to convince the incumbent Chilean president to succeed himself through political machinations. Track II reportedly was a specific plan to encourage and assist the Chilean military to overthrow Allendé. Central to Track II was a plan calling for the Chilean military to kidnap the commander-in-chief of the Chilean armed forces. This would remove a key opponent of any anti-Allendé Chilean coup and create the kind of crisis that would justify military intervention.

Despite Secretary of State Kissinger's protests that Track II was never really implemented, the Chilean commander-in-chief did become the target of several kidnap attempts, the last of which resulted in his murder. Although details remain murky, the kidnappers apparently had been in contact with U.S. officials prior to their actions. Whether they were acting under American direction, or, what is more likely, acting on their own in the killing, is still uncertain. What is clear is that the assassination did not facilitate a coup against Allendé. Instead of creating a climate for a coup, the murder of the Chilean commander made the Chilean people and military more determined than ever to prevent the disruption of the political process. Allendé won the election in the Congress on October 24 and was inaugurated on November 3.

Although the United States failed to prevent Allendé from assuming office and exercising power, Washington's coup-backing effort did not end in 1970. Following Allendé's election, the United States continued to work toward the creation of a political climate conducive to a coup. President Nixon ordered the end of private investment guarantees to American firms doing business in Chile, began pressuring international lending institutions to limit funds for Chile, and ordered the drastic reduction of American aid to Chile. In addition, the United States spent about $6 million in covert funds (mostly for opposition parties and the media) during Allendé's presidency.[41]

Allendé was overthrown by elements of the Chilean military in September 1973. During the course of the coup, either he was killed or he committed suicide. While there is no evidence that the United States was directly involved in the coup or in Allendé's death, Washington bore some responsibility. The continuing anti-Allendé actions promoted by the United States and the knowledge that the United States would support a successor regime could not have helped but contribute to the coup climate that had been worked for but was not achieved until three years later.[42]

A lesser-known but in many respects more significant case of the United States attempting to back a coup came about in Iran in the early days of 1979.[43] It illustrates the temptations of relying on a coup to extricate the United States from a seemingly impossible situation. At the same time, this event demonstrates the difficulties of attempting to back a coup in a revolutionary environment when the policy makers who are in charge are deeply divided about whether the United States should support a coup at all.

By the fall of 1978, it had become clear that the shah of Iran was in deep trouble. Mass protests and public demonstrations supporting the shah's opponent, the Ayatollah Khomeini, were convulsing Iran on an almost daily basis. The shah responded to this threat with weakness and vacillation. He neither ordered an "iron fist" policy of brutal repression nor did he take meaningful steps toward effecting political reforms. If the situation were not changed soon, the shah would be overthrown and America's position vis-à-vis this strategic country would be undermined.

The deteriorating situation in Iran was the subject of a National Security Council meeting on January 3, 1979. Just prior to the meeting, the shah had appointed a pro-Western moderate, Shapour Bakhtiar, as prime minister. With a new regime in power and the shah preparing to leave Iran, Washington's attention was focused on the Iranian military. As the only remaining pro-Western institution capable of restoring order, the military needed to be supported in its unity and cohesion. To that end, it was decided to send a U.S. emissary to Iran. The deputy commander of U.S. forces in Europe, Robert Huyser, was selected. There were problems in Washington, however, as to his exact mission.

Both Secretary of State Cyrus Vance and National Security Advisor Zbigniew Brzezinski agreed that the United States had to support the Iranian military. But they disagreed on how that support should be manifested and on the kind of signals Huyser should give to the Iranian generals. Vance felt that the aim of American support should be to ensure that the Iranian military would support the constitutional process. By ensuring the survival of a pro-Western, civilian regime in Iran, the military could best protect American interests. Although Vance acknowledged the need for "contingency plans" should the Bakhtiar government collapse, he was strongly against our encouraging a military coup. For Vance (and United States Ambassador to Iran, William Sullivan), a coup led by the badly divided Iranian military would simply lead to chaos and to the emergence of an anti-American government.[44]

Brzezinski (supported by Secretary of Defense Harold Brown) did not disagree with the idea that the Iranian military should support Bakhtiar, but he argued that Huyser must prepare the military for a coup in the likely event that the Bakhtiar regime was brought down. Brzezinski recognized the risks of a coup and the difficulties that such gross interference in Iran's internal affairs would bring about, but he believed that the preservation of American interests in Iran was worth the possible costs. With the shah too weak to order a coup on his own behalf, Brzezinski believed that it was up to the United States to act. Bakhtiar should be given a chance ("ten days"), but if he could not restore order, then Washington would have to order a coup while the Iranian military was still capable of launching one. A coup would not necessarily solve the problems of Iran, but (according to Brzezinski's reasoning) it would provide time for Iran to institute political and economic reforms and for the United States to preserve its geopolitical interests.[45]

As was the case throughout the Iranian crisis, President Carter was torn between the views of Vance and Brzezinski. Carter agreed with Brzezinski that if the situation worsened, the best solution might be some form of military takeover. However, the president opposed a coup, both because he was not sure it would succeed and on moral grounds. Carter also agreed with Vance that the prime mission of the military should be to support the Bakhtiar government, but he shared Brzezinski's concerns about what the United States should do if the Bakhtiar government collapsed.

Reflecting these concerns, Carter sent Huyser to Iran on January 5 with a contradictory mission. All agreed that Huyser was to talk to the Iranian generals to assure them of American support, and to work to keep the Iranian military intact.[46] In support of Vance's position, Huyser was to ensure that the Iranian military would not launch a coup against the Bakhtiar regime. At the same time, in support of Brzezinski, Huyser was supposed to help the Iranian generals prepare for a coup in the event that the situation deteriorated.[47]

The Bakhtiar government proved unable to deal with the continuing public riots and protests. The shah's departure for Egypt on January 16 only increased the tide of support for Khomeini. With every passing day, the Iranian military weakened because of defections to the Khomeini forces and because of an overall demoralization. Huyser nevertheless provided Washington with generally optimistic reports about the cohesiveness of the Iranian military and about their ability to launch a coup. Ambassador Sullivan disputed Huyser's observations, arguing that the Iranian military had lost the will to confront the Iranian people and thus could not take over the government.[48] Predictably, Brzezinski pushed for the United States to back a coup immediately, while Vance remained opposed to one.

For the time being, Huyser was instructed to tell the Iranian military to support Bakhtiar. On at least two occasions, the Iranian generals were warned that an attempted coup would result in the United States "cutting them off at the knees."[49] Nevertheless, the threat of a coup was kept alive. It is still not clear whether President Carter would ever have given the go-ahead for a coup or whether he simply wanted to hold out the prospect of a coup in order to force the Bakhtiar government to act more strongly against Khomeini.[50] Huyser was instructed to keep abreast of all coup plans, and an oil tanker was sent to Iran for use by the military in the event of a coup.

The Bakhtiar regime never achieved the support necessary to remain in power. On February 1, Khomeini arrived in Iran to a tumultuous reception. He appointed his own government under the leadership of

Mehdi Barzagan. The Bakhtiar regime still existed, but it was a government in name only. On February 9, air cadets revolted against their officers in support of Khomeini. The revolt spread, as the shah's Imperial Guard proved unable or unwilling to suppress it. On February 11 the Iranian military command ordered their troops to remain in their barracks, and Bakhtiar resigned.

At this late date, when it appeared that the position of the United States was hopeless, Brzezinski turned to the coup option to try to salvage the situation. He asked Huyser, who had left Iran the week before, about the feasibility of having the Iranian military launch a coup. Huyser felt a coup was possible only with massive American military backing, including combat support.[51] He did not recommend that the United States back such a coup. Brzezinski nevertheless felt that if there was any chance for a successful coup, the option should be exercised. On February 12, with violence in the streets of Tehran increasing, Brzezinski had Undersecretary of State David Newsom call Ambassador Sullivan to ask if an immediate coup could be launched. Sullivan cursed and hung up the phone. It is not clear whether Sullivan even relayed the request to the Iranian military.[52]

The United States has also failed to provoke a coup against Libyan leader Muammar Khadaffi. American efforts to topple Khadaffi have proven notable in two respects. First, they offer a rare example of a superpower seeking to back a coup against a regime aligned to another superpower. As already discussed, most of the American coup-backing efforts have been directed against regimes already within the U.S. sphere of influence. Second, in addition to acting covertly, the United States has directly attacked Libya in order to provoke a coup. As such, the American actions constitute the most public example of the United States's seeking to back a coup against an unfriendly regime.

There are several reasons why the United States government has sought to promote the overthrow of the Libyan leader. Khadaffi has sought to subvert pro-Western regimes in Tunisia, Egypt, and the Sudan. He is perhaps the most fervently anti-Israeli leader in the Arab world. He is also one of the major recipients of Soviet arms in the Middle East and has followed policies largely supportive of Moscow's interests. Khadaffi's regime is a highly personalized one. If he is removed from power, there is at least the chance that a successor government would produce major changes in policy. Most important, Khadaffi has been a vocal and substantive supporter of terrorism against the West. Several terrorist groups receive money, arms, and training from Libya. Moreover, Khadaffi has publicly praised several terrorist attacks, while rewarding the perpetrators (e.g., Khadaffi warmly welcomed the terrorists involved in the massacre of Israeli athletes at the 1972 Munich Olympics).

The United States government has also been tempted to overthrow Khadaffi because it believes he is vulnerable to a coup. Despite the fact that Khadaffi has remained in power over fifteen years, he has no shortage of opposition. Economic difficulties stemming from the falling price of oil have produced shortages of basic goods, upsetting large segments of the Libyan public. Religious leaders are opposed to Khadaffi's efforts to eliminate their power, technocrats are upset with his foreign policy adventures and lack of concern for development at home, and supporters of the previous regime have made no secret of their desire to overthrow the existing government.[53] Most critical is the Libyan military. Khadaffi's efforts to place the military under control of the civilian "revolutionary committees" has caused a substantial degree of resentment. This interference with the military's autonomy may have already provoked coup attempts and is likely to serve as a source of future difficulties. The United States also recognizes that Khadaffi lacks the Soviet support and indigenous military capability to challenge seriously American efforts to depose him.

Khadaffi has been a target of American-backed efforts to depose him at least since the Reagan administration assumed power in 1981. Under President Reagan, the CIA and other government agencies contacted and were contacted by several countries concerning joint covert operations against Khadaffi. Egypt was approached while France (which may have backed an abortive 1980 coup in Libya) contacted the United States.[54] On at least two specific occasions, President Reagan authorized covert programs to encourage a coup against Khadaffi. As part of these programs, the United States maintained periodic contacts with opponents of the Libyan leader.[55] Despite American efforts, there is no evidence that any of the many coup attempts launched against Khadaffi from 1981 to 1986 were a result of United States activities.

The strongest action taken by the United States against Khadaffi came in April 1986 when American planes bombed strategic positions in Libya. The air strike followed discovery of evidence that a terrorist bombing in a Berlin discotheque, in which an American serviceman was killed, had Libyan support. Although the main goal of the strike was to deter further support of terrorism by Khadaffi, a clear secondary goal was to provoke a coup against the Libyan leader. In a rare admission by a country of its desire to promote a coup in another state, Secretary of State George Shultz declared that the purpose of the bombing raid was to encourage the "considerable dissidence" in the Libyan military and that a coup would be "all to the good."[56]

In order to encourage the military to launch a coup, elements of Khadaffi's personal guard were attacked while the regular army was left untouched. In addition to weakening the protection around Khadaffi, these strikes signaled that the United States had no quarrel with the Libyan military per se, but only with those units loyal to the existing regime. The bombing raid also tried to communicate to the Libyan military that they and the Soviets would not or could not protect Libya from American retaliation. So long as the Libyan military allowed Khadaffi to remain in power, Libya and its armed forces would have to pay a severe price.

The April bombing raid also tried to provoke a coup by inciting domestic unrest. Fifteen minutes after the raid the Voice of America repeatedly broadcast an editorial urging the Libyan people to overthrow Khadaffi. The Voice of America received the text of the message for translation into Arabic three hours before the attack—an unprecedented action for such a secret mission.[57] In addition, President Reagan, in his speech following the raid, took pains to distinguish America's quarrel with Khadaffi from the sentiment toward the Libyan people "caught in the grip of a tyrant."[58] The obvious message was that the United States could have good relations with Libya if only Khadaffi left the scene. While the Reagan administration probably had few illusions that a popular uprising would topple Khadaffi on its own, it clearly hoped that it would spur the Libyan military to launch a coup.

The American bombing raid, like the covert efforts preceding it, failed to provoke a coup against Khadaffi. Although there were reports of army mutinies in the wake of the American attack, none could be confirmed. Instead, having survived an open American effort to unseat him, Khadaffi, and his hold on power, appeared as strong as ever.

Evaluating U.S.-Backed Coups

As these cases demonstrate, the United States has enjoyed some short-term success by supporting coups against regimes it views as hostile to its interests. Secrecy was essential to every U.S.-backed coup. Although suspicions and allegations of American involvement have surrounded each of these coups, the United States has never been directly linked to any of the operations prior to the actual attempts.

U.S.-backed coups have also been characterized by a dichotomy between the regime and the military in those countries where such coups have taken place. In countries that have become the targets of American-backed coups, the military usually retained a close relationship with the United States, while the regimes in power pursued policies that were considered hostile to American interests. The resulting conflicts provided the motivation and the opportunities for American-supported coups.

American experiences in overthrowing third world regimes have demonstrated the importance of cooperation among the various American agencies involved in backing such coups. The Guatemalan coup proved to be a success largely because the CIA, the State Department, and the business community worked relatively harmoniously with one another. The overthrow of Diem in South Vietnam almost failed because the Pentagon, the CIA, and the White House could not agree on the desirability of the coup, and thus they sent conflicting signals to the coup makers. Conflicting signals and goals also crippled the Huyser mission to Iran.

All of the successful cases have demonstrated the importance of not initiating or assisting a coup against the wishes of the majority of the military and of the people. In each of these successful cases, the armed forces in these countries either actively supported the coup or remained neutral. Similarly, the people in these third world countries either welcomed the new regime or were indifferent to its coming to power. Only in Iran in 1953 did substantial public protest develop, but these groups did not represent a large segment of the population, as evidenced by their quick disappearance once counterdemonstrations were organized.

The failure of the U.S.-backed coup in Chile (1970) illustrates some of the pitfalls of a coup-backing policy. Both Nixon's Track I and Track II involved the United States with unsavory and unreliable elements. However rationalized, that effort placed the United States in the position of attempting to undermine a democratically elected regime. This damaged the reputation of the United States, both domestically and internationally. Moreover, it could not help but harm American efforts to promote democracies and to deter anti-democratic coups elsewhere. On pragmatic grounds, the Chilean attempted coup also failed. The Chilean military leadership was committed to the electoral process. Even if the United States had succeeded in promoting a coup by some elements of the armed forces, a countercoup was always a distinct possibility.

The failure to back a coup in Iran in 1979 provides a clear demonstration of the weaknesses of U.S. policy in relation to backing coups. Despite the growing intensity of the Iranian crisis and the critical American interests involved, top American leaders (including the president and the secretary of state) could not bring themselves to support a coup. Their understandable beliefs that such an action would be immoral, that it might not work, and that it could not be kept secret pushed them to seek other solutions to the Iranian crisis. By the time it became clear that there were no effective alternatives, it was too late. The Iranian military had disintegrated and the Khomeini revolution was in full swing. Even if a military takeover had been engineered, it would have required a major commitment by the U.S. military to protect the regime from large segments of Iranian society. This is not to suggest that the United States should have backed a coup earlier. There is much evidence to suggest that such a policy would not have worked at any time. Nevertheless, after the decision not to back a coup when the situation might conceivably have preserved a pro-Western regime, the decision to try to provoke a coup when it had deteriorated irreparably was doomed to fail.

The inability of the United States to provoke a coup against Khadaffi was due to several factors. First, the failure stemmed from the Libyan opposition. Because it is badly divided and lacks ties to groups within Libya, it proved difficult to mobilize strong forces against Khadaffi. Furthermore, Khadaffi has prevented any single military leader from gaining an independent base of support, making a coup by the armed forces difficult to bring about. The Soviet-East German protective cocoon provided additional protection against any coup not to Moscow's liking.

Most important, the lack of ties between the United States and Libyan groups made a coup-backing effort extremely difficult to bring about. Libya is unlike Guatemala, South Vietnam, or even Iran and Chile, in that the U.S. did not maintain close contacts with the military there, though it sought to back a coup. This explains the almost desperate act of indirectly working to provoke a coup through a military strike (an action that easily could produce the opposite effect). While American efforts may yet bear fruit in Libya, the failure of the United States to undermine Khadaffi after at least five years of attempting to do so illustrates the difficulties of backing a coup against a country outside one's sphere of influence.

Finally, it is significant that the last known successful American-backed coup is alleged to have occurred in 1970. While it is possible that this suggests that the United States is becoming better at concealing its coup-backing efforts, it is more likely that it indicates a declining propensity and capability on the part of the United States to become involved in such activities. This seems to be especially true in light of the failure of Washington to try to overthrow regimes within its sphere of influence, but which showed signs of falling to the communists, like the Somoza regime in Nicaragua. Under what conditions and against which regimes future coup-backing efforts might be undertaken will be considered in my conclusion.

American Allies and Third World Coups

Pro-Western states consciously or not have often supported American interests with regard to coups. France maintains approximately eight thousand troops in Africa deployed to counter external aggression and to protect pro-French governments from internal challenges.[59] French forces overseas include detachments in Djibouti (3700), Central African Republic (1700), Senegal (650), and Gabon (500).[60] Augmenting these African-based troops is the 47,000-man French Rapid Action Force based in France and capable of intervening throughout Francophone Africa. Moreover, since many of the French forces trained for overseas intervention belong to the French Foreign Legion, they are more easily utilized for combat contingencies than troops of the regular French army.[61]

France has played an active role in determining the outcome of several coups. As described in Chapter Four, the prompt intervention of French troops successfully defended the regime of Leon Mba in Gabon from a 1964 coup. The French have also been implicated in the overthrow of several third world leaders. In September 1979, some one thousand French troops from Chad, Gabon, and France entered the Central African Republic, where they overthrew the murderous regime of Emperor Bokassa. Two years later, France supported a successful coup against Bokassa's inept successor, David Dacko, and may have supported a failed coup in the same country in 1982. The French are also suspected of having assisted coups against the leftist regime of Ali Solih in the Comoro Islands in May 1978,[62] and against Libya's Muammar Khadaffi in 1980.

The French role in third world coups has undoubtedly been greater than these few incidents suggest. Many coups have almost certainly been deterred by the large French military presence throughout Africa. Moreover, French security specialists are often discreetly sent to third world countries that are experiencing difficulties that might lead to coups. A French security team sent to Saudi Arabia in 1979 helped that country cope with the seizing of the Grand Mosque. The willingness and ability of the French to send troops rapidly to quell major armed threats also help to protect third world leaders from coups. The French defense of Zaire from Katangese secessionists in 1977 and 1978 and the French defense of Chad from Libyan-backed rebels in 1983 defused threats that could easily have resulted in coups.

Although not nearly as numerous as the French, the British also maintain a presence throughout the third world, which can also have a bearing on the incidence of coups. Small numbers of British military advisors are stationed in Gambia, Ghana, Kenya, Zambia, and Bot-swana.[63] In addition, the British maintain a military presence in several of the Persian Gulf states, including Oman, Qatar, the United Arab Emirates, and Kuwait.[64] Insofar as these advisors can exercise influence over the armed forces in these countries, they might be able to deter, pre-vent, or provoke coups there. British commando units such as the Special Air Services (SAS) are believed to have already played a role in defeating at least one coup, in Gambia in 1981, and they may have been secretly involved in the suppression of several others. Equally important, British military advisors played a key role in backing a coup in Oman in 1970.[65]

Israel has an especially intriguing relationship with third world states, which also often works to the benefit of the United States as far as coups are concerned. Israel's very presence between Syria and Egypt prevented Nasser from intervening with large numbers of troops to pre-vent a 1961 Syrian coup. The failure of Nasser's countercoup meant that Syria was able to secede from the United Arab Republic—a devel-opment welcomed by Washington.[66] Implicit Israeli threats to intervene to prevent control of the West Bank being seized by a government other than that of King Hussein almost certainly have deterred coup attempts backed by other Arab states against the Jordanian monarch.[67] Since Jor-dan is one of the more moderate and pro-Western of the Arab states, Israeli protection of this regime from radical coups is also in America's interest.

In the late 1960s, Israel's intelligence agency, Mossad, reportedly es-tablished secret arrangements with several African governments. Al-though these states broke off relations with Israel following the 1973 Mideast war, many maintained unofficial contacts, particularly in the security sphere. These contacts reportedly have been encouraged and maybe even financed by the United States.[68]

In Ethiopia, Israeli security experts are allegedly replacing East Ger-mans as advisors to the intelligence service. If that is true, the Israelis could be in a position to protect Prime Minister Mengistu from a pro-Soviet coup, should that Ethiopian leader attempt to realign his country with the West.[69] Zaire's President Mobutu revealed in 1982 that he was purchasing $8 million worth of Israeli military equipment to equip his Special Presidential Brigade. This brigade is one of the most important elements protecting Mobutu from a coup and it is virtually certain that Israeli military advisors are part of the arms deal.[70] The kidnapping of a former member of the Nigerian government in Britain by Israeli citi-zens, apparently at the behest of the existing regime, indicates a contin-uing Israeli security role in what was Africa's largest democracy. Israeli countercoup experts are also believed to be working in Kenya (which tacitly cooperated with Israel during the 1976 Entebbe raid), in Liberia, and in the Ivory Coast. Even in places where Israel has no working arrangement with a country's security forces, its intelligence role has proven useful. It is generally acknowledged that one factor in Egypt's President Sadat's decision to visit Jerusalem was a warning given him by Israeli intelligence of a planned Egyptian coup backed by Libya.

Outside of Africa, Israeli expertise in internal security is helping a variety of regimes protect themselves from coups. Israeli experts are reputed to have provided assistance to the governments of Singapore, Thailand, and Indonesia.[71] Israel is also helping the Costa Rican civil guard protect that country's government. Undoubtedly, many more countries have benefited from Israeli assistance, but they have chosen to keep that relationship secret. Because of Israel's desire to break out of its "pariah" status in the international community and because of its exalted reputation in the security field, Israeli countercoup assistance will probably continue to grow.

Other Western countries have indirectly benefited American interests by protecting pro-Western countries from coups. In the aftermath of the second invasion of Zaire's Shaba province in 1978, fifteen hundred Moroccan troops and six hundred Senegalese troops helped ensure that Mobutu's regime would not become the victim of a coup. Senegalese forces proved critical in defending Gambia's pro-Western regime from a leftist coup that threatened to destroy one of Africa's only true democracies.[72] Following the 1979 coup in Equatorial Guinea in which a pro-Soviet regime was overthrown, Moroccan and Spanish military forces helped to ensure the security of the new, more pro-Western government.[73] Finally, Saudi Arabia has provided financial aid to several Middle Eastern and African states (e.g., the Sudan, Egypt, North and South Yemen, and Jordan), which has helped pro-Western regimes in these countries develop countercoup forces and deal with the economic problems that might lead to coups.

Although these examples are impressive, it is important not to overestimate the role of pro-Western countries in furthering U.S. interests with regard to third world coups. The United States maintains a much looser and less hierarchical relationship with its allies than does the USSR. The relative independence of America's allies usually makes it difficult for the United States to control or even to influence their behavior. While occasionally the United States is able to coordinate its efforts with friendly countries, U.S. gains are far more likely to come about through a fortuitous coincidence of its interests with those of its allies, rather than from Washington's control of the situation.

Conclusions

The United States has pursued a variety of policies in the third world that affect the outcome of coups. Many have not been designed specifically to deal with coups, but they have had an impact on them nevertheless. Washington's promotion of democracy, its giving of aid for economic development, and its tendering of security assistance all fall into this category. These policies have at times advanced American interests because of their effects on coups, but their effectiveness has been limited, in part because they do not deal with the implications of coups directly.

Policies designed to influence the initiation and outcome of coups have also been pursued by Washington. Warnings to potential coup makers not to launch coups have been especially common in cases where the United States maintains an influence (and especially troops) in the country that is threatened by a coup. On rare occasions the United States has actually suppressed coup attempts. American personnel at the scene of the coup, often at their own initiative, have either assisted indigenous forces to defeat the coup, as happened in Ethiopia, or have provoked them to act against the coup makers, as happened in Laos and in Bolivia.

The United States has also backed coups more or less directly in several third world countries. The degree of American involvement in these efforts has varied greatly. In South Vietnam, the American role was limited to indicating to the coup makers that the United States would not interfere with their efforts and would support a successor regime. American encouragement, plus the offer of material support for the coup makers should they need it, helped bring about a coup in Brazil in 1964. In Iran in 1953 the United States helped to plan the coup and assisted directly in its execution. American efforts to encourage coups in Guatemala and Chile in 1970 included helping to create a climate of instability to provoke otherwise reluctant military officers to topple these existing regimes. The plan worked in Guatemala, perhaps because of direct American involvement, but it failed, at least initially, in Chile. The alleged introduction of coup makers into the Cambodian military reportedly enabled Washington to back a coup against Prince Sihanouk. However, even the direct order of the U.S. national security advisor to the American ambassador in Iran could not prompt the Iranian military to launch a coup in the wake of the Khomeini revolution. Finally, as seen in Libya, a direct attack by American forces can fail to provoke a coup when the United States lacks ties with powerful indigenous groups.

The great majority of coups drawing upon U.S. involvement have been veto coups.[74] The United States has acted both to topple governments and to protect governments that have been challenged by a military seeking to "veto" the inclusion of new groups in the power structure. In Iran in 1953, in Guatemala, in Brazil, and in Chile, the United States encouraged military forces to launch coups against regimes that sought to broaden their power bases to include the lower classes. In Cambodia, the United States is reported to have encouraged a coup to prevent communist forces from gaining greater government influence. In Libya, the United States has tried to provoke a coup by playing upon the dissatisfaction of the armed forces with Khadaffi's increasing reliance upon ideologically motivated civilians to oversee the military. Since the ascension of these groups to power threatened both American interests and the interests of these indigenous militaries, the United States was usually able to work together with the armed forces to launch coups in these places.

The United States has also blocked veto coups against several regimes. In Laos, Bolivia, the Dominican Republic, and El Salvador, Washington acted to deter or to suppress veto coups. In each of these cases, rightist coup makers sought to topple a leftist or moderate regime they believed to be appealing to groups they wished to see excluded. American threats, conveyed through U.S. diplomats, prevented these plots and attempted coups from succeeding. Instead of working with the military, this defense of regimes from veto coups required Washington to work against the indigenous armed forces, who generally backed the coups.

Guardian coups (i.e., those designed to preserve the existing order) have played a lesser but still important role in American strategy. U.S. coup-backing efforts in South Vietnam in 1963 and 1965 attempted to preserve a stable pro-Western government in that country in an atmosphere of chaos. The coups succeeded in the short term largely because they were supported by a cohesive military and were not opposed by important elements of the society. Washington's efforts to precipitate a coup in Iran in 1979 were a last desperate gesture to bring order and moderation to a revolutionary situation. Its failure stemmed from the disintegration of the military in the face of mass opposition.

Despite the fact that breakthrough coups replace traditional leaders with more radical ones, they have not provoked American involvements to the extent that one might expect. Breakthrough coups have occurred in such important countries as Egypt (1952), Libya (1969), and Ethiopia (1974) without bringing about an American or any foreign response. The only true examples of the United States acting to defeat breakthrough coups occurred in Iraq in 1958 and in the Dominican Republic in 1965. As shown in Chapter Four, even in these cases the United States did not act directly to defeat the coups. The United States never intervened in Iraq and only sent troops to the Dominican Republic when the coup had transformed itself into a full-scale rebellion. The lack of American responses to breakthrough coups has stemmed largely from U.S. ignorance about the political orientations of the coup makers. As long as Washington does not know or cannot accurately project the nature of the regime that will emerge from a coup, it will be reluctant to act to defeat it. In the aftermath of the Ethiopian coup in 1974, for example, Washington felt it could work with the new government and even welcomed a change from the leadership of the elderly Haile Selassie. That the coup eventually produced such a bitterly anti-American regime came as a surprise to U.S. policy makers. For the United States to react to a breakthrough coup, therefore, requires that it recognize the coup's implications before it has had a chance to take hold.

The United States has enjoyed considerable success in protecting friendly regimes from coups and in overthrowing unfriendly regimes by supporting coups. Its failed efforts have been far fewer than its successes. Because of American actions, friends have been maintained in power—Haile Selassie in Ethiopia—countries have been kept free from communist or leftist influences—Guatemala, Brazil—and democracies have been protected—Bolivia, the Dominican Republic. Moreover, the regimes Washington has protected from coups and the regimes placed into power by American-backed coups have proved to be no less stable or enduring than their predecessors.

What is common to successful American coup policies has been their focus on coup-prone states governed by a narrow domestic elite. Defensive policies have worked best when the threat has come from a small group, while offensive policies have been most effective in cases where the removal of the leadership elite would not produce greater societal repercussions. Successful countercoup policies and coup-backing efforts did not go against the wishes of the people or against the purposes of large elements of the armed forces. Significantly, when National Security Advisor Brzezinski attempted to institute a coup to quell a revolutionary situation, he failed.

American efforts to protect third world regimes against coups have supported U.S. long-term interests far more effectively than have efforts to back coups. There have been few costs and many substantial gains for U.S. policies defending pro-Western regimes from coups. The record of U.S.-backed coups against third world regimes is much less impressive. In Iran in 1953, the CIA's success in restoring the shah was a factor in the anti-American feeling that supported the Ayatollah Khomeini twenty-five years later. The United States succeeded in helping to topple a leftist regime in Guatemala, but it left a legacy of brutal governments that ended the democratic experiment there. In South Vietnam, the American-supported coup against Diem plunged Washington ever more deeply into the Vietnam morass because the United States assumed a greater and greater responsibility for the composition of Vietnamese governments. American support for the coup in Brazil may have ended a leftist threat, but only at the cost of its democracy and the tarnishing of America's reputation. The alleged U.S.-backed coup against Sihanouk in Cambodia gave Washington the opportunity to attack the North Vietnamese sanctuaries there, but it brought about the end of Cambodia's neutrality and led to the country's subsequent fall to the barbarous Khmer Rouge. American participation in the failed coup against Allendé weakened the U.S. stand in favor of self-determination and paved the way for the repressive Pinochet regime. America's effort to promote coups in Iran in 1979 and in Libya in 1986 may have had no major costs, but it did expose the fact that when the United States wished to promote a coup in another country, it lacked the ability to do so.

In sum, the history of American-backed coups shows that even where they are successful, the long-term cost of supporting groups overthrowing their governing regimes has often worked to the detriment of U.S. interests. By hindering the attainment of democracy, by exposing the United States to domestic and international censure, and by closely identifying Washington with a regime it might prefer to distance itself from, coups encouraged by the United States have solved immediate problems while creating future difficulties.

3

The Soviet Experience with Third World Coups

Few developments have affected the Soviets' position in the third world as much as coups d'état have. A great number of countries in the third world have turned toward the USSR or have realigned themselves to the West as a result of coups. This should not be surprising, given the frequency of coups in the third world and the propensity of the Soviets to exploit instability when it arises. What is surprising is the lack of analysis devoted to the implications and consequences of Soviet policies toward third world coups.

That the Soviet Union has gained and lost much in the third world as a result of coups is beyond dispute. In terms of gains, the USSR has recognized that virtually the only way pro-Soviet governments come to power in the third world is through violence and that the coup is the most frequent form of violent regime-change among the developing states. Third world states that have turned toward the Soviet Union following a coup include Egypt (1952), Iraq (1958), Syria (1966), Peru (1968), Somalia (1969), Libya (1969), Sudan (1969), Benin (1972), Ethiopia (1974, 1977), South Yemen (1978), Afghanistan (1978), Grenada (1979), and Suriname (1980). The degree and significance of the pro-Soviet alignment differed markedly among these cases. But in each case, a coup placed a regime in power that (immediately or over time) proved more supportive of Soviet interests than its predecessor had.

The Soviets have also lost influence in the third world as a result of coups. Formerly pro-Soviet states that have left or moved away from Moscow's sphere of influence following successful or abortive coups include Guatemala (1954), Iran (1953), Iraq (1963), Indonesia (1965), Algeria (1965), Ghana (1966), Mali (1968), Sudan (1971), Chile (1973), and Equatorial Guinea (1979). In the Indonesian and Sudanese cases, the Soviets lost their influence because of successful countercoups launched by the indigenous militaries. In the remaining countries, coups resulted in the establishment of governments less sympathetic to the Soviet Union.

Aside from specific gains and losses, the Soviet Union is interested in third world coups because it is interested in the third world. Like the United States, the Soviet Union maintains a wide range of strategic, political, and economic interests in the third world. These include the establishment of military bases to assist in the projection of their power (especially the Soviet navy), control over critical raw materials, the containment of the West and of the People's Republic of China, diverting American resources away from the defense of Western Europe, and the traditional desire of a great power to extend its influence beyond its borders.

Equally important, as the historian and political scientist Adam Ulam has suggested, the Soviet leadership seeks to gain influence in the third world to perpetuate its own rule. The emergence of new third world regimes proclaiming their loyalty to Marxism-Leninism and to Moscow demonstrates the continuing relevance of communist ideology and presages the ultimate decline of the West. Despite the repression practiced by the Soviet state and its inability to meet the economic needs of its people, third world successes show that the Soviet regime is on the correct side of history and that it is therefore legitimate.[1] What is critical is not so much which countries turn to the USSR, although, of course, certain countries are considered more valuable than others, but that new regimes continually come to power professing pro-Soviet allegiances. Because coups are the most likely way for such new regimes to come into being, the USSR has an understandable interest in controlling their initiations and outcomes.

However one evaluates the USSR's experience with coups, they have had a significant effect on Soviet interests in the third world. By examining the historical background of Soviet policies towards third world coups, their present policies towards coups, Soviet successes and failures, the importance of coups to the Soviet Union, and lessons that might be gleaned from Moscow's experience with coups, we can learn a great deal about the strengths of the Soviets' position among the developing states.

Background

Under Stalin and Khrushchev, third world coups were not considered an important concern of Soviet policy. The Kremlin believed that in time decolonization would bring pro-Soviet regimes to power automatically, with little or no assistance from Moscow. This belief in the inevitability of Soviet gains at first appeared to be borne out, as independent leaders emerged in the third world who were sympathetic to the USSR. During the mid-1950s and early 1960s, the Kremlin welcomed several third world leaders who had adopted hostile policies toward the West and had turned to Moscow for support. These leaders included Sekou Touré of Guinea, Kwame N'krumah of Ghana, Mobido Keita of Mali, Gamal Abdel Nasser of Egypt, Ben Bella of Algeria, Ne Win of Burma, Adhmed Sukarno of Indonesia, and Fidel Castro of Cuba.[2]

In the mid-1960s, Soviet optimism concerning the third world faded as the leaders friendly to Moscow became the victims of coups. The first setback occurred in Iraq. The Soviets had initially welcomed the Iraqi revolution of July 1958. Under the leadership of Abdel Karim Kassem, one of the most pro-Western Arab countries was transformed into a radical pro-Soviet state. Kassem's policies, however, soon produced problems for the Soviets. Kassem's claim on Kuwait, his hostility toward Egypt's Nasser, his brutal repression of the Kurds, and his eventual purge of the Iraqi Communist Party were either supported or ignored by Moscow. This placed the Soviet Union at odds with most of the other Arab countries. No doubt the Soviets believed that in time their support of Kassem would pay them dividends by providing a strong influence in a key Arab country. Instead, however, their painful investment produced nothing because a 1963 coup led the Ba'ath Party to power and the new leaders angrily withdrew Iraq from the Soviet camp.

A second Soviet setback occurred in Algeria in June 1965. Since Algeria had won its independence from France, President Ben Bella of Algeria had been engaged in a power struggle with Army Chief of Staff Colonel Boumedienne. Ben Bella's support came largely from local political leaders and from their guerrilla forces, while Boumedienne's strength grew out of the regular army. When Ben Bella attempted to supplant the role of the army by creating a "people's militia," composed of guerrilla troops loyal to him, Boumedienne struck. The coup was successful and Boumedienne replaced Ben Bella as the head of state.[3] The Soviets played no role in the coup, but they were affected by its consequences. While the removal of Ben Bella did not result in Algeria adopting a pro-Western stance, the strength of Algeria's Soviet alignment was diminished and Moscow had lost one of its earliest and closest friends in the third world.

Several months after the Soviet setback in Algeria, Moscow suffered another loss in Indonesia. President Sukarno had been moving Indonesia closer to the left since that country had achieved independence from the Netherlands in 1949. By 1965, Sukarno was openly embracing and receiving support from the Soviet Union and the People's Republic of China. At the same time, he adopted a hostile policy toward the United States and the West in general. It is believed that Sukarno knew in advance of and supported a communist coup against the army in September 1965. When the coup was swiftly and ruthlessly defeated by army forces under General Suharto, Sukarno's position was undermined. General Suharto gradually gained power, until in 1967 Sukarno was formally removed from office. Under Suharto, Indonesia moved away from the Soviet Union and adopted a truly nonaligned posture.[4]

An especially disappointing reversal for the Soviet Union came with the overthrow of Kwame N'krumah of Ghana. As the leader of Ghana since its independence from Britain in 1957, N'krumah pleased Moscow with his increasingly anticolonial, anti-Western, and Pan-African policies. While N'krumah's stature as an African and an international political figure grew, he committed the fatal error of antagonizing his own armed forces. The Ghanian military resented the growing corruption of N'krumah's regime and an economic downturn caused by a drop in cacao prices and incompetent planning. Most important, the British-trained army resented the challenge to their autonomy stemming from N'krumah's establishment of the "President's Own Guard Regiment." This private force was detached from the army's chain of command, was made responsible directly only to N'krumah, and it received better equipment and pay than the regular army.[5] Reacting to this situation, the military and police staged a coup and overthrew N'krumah in February 1966. A "national liberation council" replaced N'krumah and realigned Ghana away from the Soviet Union.

The Soviet Union suffered a fifth setback in the West African state of Mali. Under the leadership of Mobido Keita, Mali had gradually been transformed into the kind of "progressive" country the Kremlin likes to see in the third world. Keita severed traditional ties with France, from which Mali had received its independence in 1960, and established a one-party state. He proclaimed his commitment to socialist policies and made no secret of his pro-Soviet sentiments.

Ironically, the downfall of Keita began when he attempted to move Mali back toward the West. In 1967, Keita sought French assistance to cope with economic difficulties that were engulfing Mali. This move toward France angered various elements in Mali, prompting Keita to form a "people's militia." As in Algeria, Ghana, and Indonesia, the regular army of Mali came to resent this militia, especially as it grew to be three times its original size. When several army officers were arrested by the militia in 1968, the army reacted by launching a successful coup. The new leadership reversed many of Keita's domestic and foreign policies, moving Mali away from being a pro-Soviet state.

The loss of these countries upset and confused the leaders in the Kremlin. Military coups were supposed to be agents of change on behalf of socialism. It is true that the Soviets had suffered losses from coups in Iran and Guatemala, but these they thought were due to American involvement. The idea that truly indigenous coups could also reverse Soviet gains had not previously been considered by the Kremlin hierarchy. Following Khrushchev's ouster in 1964 and the various setbacks suffered by the USSR in the third world, a debate emerged between the Soviet military and the Communist Party regarding how best to deal with coups that threatened Soviet gains.

The Soviet military argued that more had to be done to ensure the loyalty of third world armies. They asserted that the low level of development of most third world states, combined with the fragility of their political institutions, made their militaries the most powerful elements in third world societies. The importance of the military in the third world was further heightened by their tendency to seize power. As a Soviet authority on the third world, G. I. Mirskiy, stated following the coups of the 1960s, the "transfer of power to the military is no longer an exception but almost the rule."[6]

The way to preserve Soviet gains in the third world, according to Soviet military analysts, was to ensure that the armies of the developing countries maintained the "correct" (i.e., pro-Soviet) orientation. The reverses of the 1960s had demonstrated that "progressive" regimes could fall victim to "reactionary" armies. Only by ensuring that third world armies do not follow a "reactionary" path could Moscow's gains be secured.[7]

The Soviet military's insistence on the central importance of third world armies was reinforced by events in the late 1960s and early 1970s when several rightist regimes were overthrown by leftist military coups. These occurred in Iraq, in the Congo (Brazzaville), and in Peru in 1968, in Somalia in 1969, in Dahomey (now Benin) in 1972, and in Ethiopia in 1974. These coups again demonstrated that the prime determinant of a third world country's political orientation was its military. It seemed to prove that, if handled correctly, these militaries could act to improve significantly the position of the Soviet Union in the third world. To protect Soviet gains against pro-Western coups d'état and to increase the Kremlin's influence through pro-Soviet coups d'état, the military was the crucial factor.[8]

Soviet civilian analysts disagreed with this point of view. While they accepted the importance of third world armies in determining third world political alignments, they tended to deny that this had central significance. For the civilians, the lessons of the anti-Soviet coups of the 1960s had less to do with the military and more to do with the lack of political development within these third world countries. They doubted whether existing third world leaders could ever achieve true socialism or develop revolutionary regimes, given the inherent conservatism of most third world societies.[9] The civilian strategists were also much less optimistic than the military about the likelihood of third world armies safeguarding those "progressive" regimes that did manage to move toward socialism. They argued that all third world armies, no matter how radical they might appear, were essentially bourgeois and would act in their class interests should a socialist regime challenge their privileged position.[10]

The civilian analysts concluded that the third world states needed a vanguard party to protect the integrity of "scientific socialism" and to preserve Soviet influence. Such a party would be a tightly controlled, hierarchical organization characterized by the domination of a narrow elite and guided by a coherent ideology, preferably Marxism-Leninism. It would be composed of "representatives of the proletariat, the peasantry, the progressive intelligentsia, and the radical portion of the military."[11] Power in these states would be concentrated in the vanguard party, which would suppress political dissent and oversee the transformation of the society in a Leninist fashion. With a vanguard party in place, the masses would be mobilized and indoctrinated to support a pro-Soviet, socialist way of life. Moscow's position in the third world would not then be at the mercy of a few individuals who might be overthrown or who might undergo an ideological change of heart.[12] As examples of what a vanguard party would accomplish, the Soviets could point to Vietnam, North Korea, Cuba, and Mongolia. In none of these states is the Soviet position or the socialist way of life under any threat. By spreading vanguard parties to other third world countries, anti-Soviet coups and reverses would become vestiges of the past. Thus the establishment of vanguard parties was to be encouraged throughout the third world.

This Soviet military-civilian dispute about whether to encourage third world armies or vanguard parties continued until 1976/1977, when events gave the civilian position the upper hand. During this time both Egypt and Somalia had abrogated their treaties of friendship and cooperation with the Soviet Union, and Peru's leadership had begun to turn toward the West. At least in print, the Soviet military concurred with their civilian counterparts that the major reason for these setbacks lay with the absence of deep-seated internal support for Moscow in these societies. Without such support, individual third world leaders were free to turn their backs on the Soviet Union, bringing their states into the Western camp. At this point, the military agreed that the presence of a vanguard party was important for preserving Soviet gains in the third world.[13]

The apparent resolution of this dispute did not mean that the Soviet Union would now ignore the role of the military in the third world. The power of third world armies to undo Soviet-supported regimes could not be overlooked. The Kremlin also had few illusions about the difficulties of establishing vanguard parties in the third world. Moscow knew that third world armies would perceive the influence of vanguard parties as a challenge to their autonomy. Third world leaders would similarly resist the creation of vanguard parties, seeing them as threats to their personal rule. Many third world societies lacked the infrastructure in terms of which vanguard parties could be effective. Moreover, even the establishment of vanguard parties would not ensure the Kremlin's success. Soviet civilian analysts were forced to concede that third world countries with vanguard parties still faced the "possibility of aberration and reversals."[14] This concession was reinforced when Somalia, despite the presence of a leftist vanguard party, realigned itself with the West in 1978. While vanguard parties might offer the best hope for preserving Soviet influence in the third world, they could not accomplish the task alone.

Soviet Policies toward Coups

The reverses of the 1960s, combined with general instability in the third world, convinced the Soviet Union to pursue a multifaceted approach to coups d'état. For the long term, Soviet policies emphasized establishing Marxist-Leninist vanguard parties in the third world and gaining influence with third world armies. Recognizing that these steps would take time to become effective, the USSR also took steps to protect and expand its interests in the interim. These steps included the use of proxies for maintaining Soviet interests and direct Soviet involvement to protect friendly regimes from anti-Soviet coups. They also resolved to assist pro-Soviet groups in the overthrow of "reactionary" regimes.

Soviet results from the establishment of vanguard parties in the third world in the 1970s and 1980s have been mixed. They continue to believe in the potential of such parties to transform some third world societies into true Marxist-Leninist states that would be virtually coup-proof. They recognize, however, that the vast majority of third world states have not developed vanguard parties along Moscow's lines, and that they are not likely to do so.

The result of this realization has been a policy emphasizing the establishment and assistance of vanguard parties where conditions permit. The Kremlin focuses on countries that already have influential vanguard parties, like Angola, or on countries in which the creation of a vanguard party stands a good chance of transforming the society along Marxist-Leninist lines, like Ethiopia. In both of these conditions, the Soviets have demonstrated great flexibility in approving the type of vanguard party established. In contrast to their policy in the early 1960s, when such parties had to be virtual copies of the Soviet Communist Party, the Kremlin is now much less strict about the kind of vanguard parties it will support. In the late 1970s, the Soviets cited several characteristics as necessary for earning Moscow's recognition as a vanguard party. Such a party must first be made up of a "revolutionary democratic" alliance of workers, peasants, and others. This alliance must work toward influencing the masses to adopt the correct (i.e., pro-Soviet) attitude concerning the transformation of society. Moreover, a vanguard party, while not necessarily a Marxist-Leninist party, must at least move toward adopting Marxist-Leninist thought. Finally, a vanguard party must cooperate with Communist Parties elsewhere.[15]

Due partially to Moscow's support, Soviet-approved vanguard parties have proliferated throughout the third world. In the 1960s only North Vietnam, North Korea, Cuba, and Mongolia were led by vanguard parties recognized by the USSR. By the early 1980s, the Soviets had recognized seven additional ruling vanguard parties. These were the Popular Movement for the Liberation of Angola Labor Party (MPLA-PT), the Mozambique Liberation Front (FRELIMO), the Congolese Labor Party (PLT), the Benin People's Revolutionary Party (PRPB), the (South) Yemen Socialist Party (YSP), the People's Democratic Party of Afghanistan (PDPA), and the Commission for Organizing the Party of the Workers of Ethiopia (COPWE). The New Jewel Movement of Grenada (prior to the American intervention) and the Sandinista National Liberation Front of Nicaragua have come close to earning Soviet recognition as vanguard parties.[16] In addition, Cape Verde and Guinea-Bissau are countries led by self-proclaimed Marxist-Leninist regimes, although neither has been formally recognized by the USSR as maintaining a "true" vanguard party.

The relationship of vanguard parties to coups is complex and difficult to ascertain. Nevertheless, certain observations warrant attention. There have been no anti-Soviet coups d'état in any of those states where Soviet-approved vanguard parties exist or are close to being formed.

The only Soviet reversal among states with recognized (or nearly recognized) vanguard parties occurred in Grenada, and that required an American invasion. Coups have also proved important in the establishment of ruling vanguard parties. Truly indigenous coups, ones without substantial foreign involvement, have led to the creation of vanguard party regimes in Benin and in Ethiopia. In Afghanistan, South Yemen, and Ethiopia, coups have replaced existing pro-Soviet regimes with successor regimes even more aligned to the Kremlin.

Vanguard parties have proven effective in allowing the USSR to control the outcome of coups, both because of the way they strengthen and the way they weaken third world regimes. Vanguard parties strengthen regimes against coups by means of their centralization of power, politicization of the military, and efficient suppression of dissidents. As the Soviet regime knows from its own historical experience, a vanguard party organized on Leninist lines holds out the promise of guaranteeing power for a small elite. This model is understandably attractive to many existing and potential third world leaders.

Vanguard parties also weaken third world regimes in ways that increase Soviet control. Because Soviet-approved vanguard parties adopt the internationalist ideology of Marxism-Leninism, they are likely to arouse nationalist opposition. To deal with such opposition, which could come in the form of coups, Soviet or proxy assistance is often required. Along with Soviet assistance comes Soviet influence. Moreover, the multiple contacts that party-to-party relationships create allow the Soviets many more opportunities for control than would be possible if they were dealing with a single individual. Party-to-party contacts permit the Kremlin to establish bases of influence independent of the existing leader. These pro-Soviet bastions can then be used to threaten coups against wavering third world leaders or actually to remove regimes from power.[17] It is noteworthy that third world states with vanguard parties have become especially attractive targets for Soviet-assisted coups. As we will see, Moscow is suspected of having backed coups in several third world states with vanguard parties, including Afghanistan, South Yemen, Angola, Ethiopia, and Grenada. In each of these cases, Moscow's ties with the vanguard party helped to place it in a position to encourage a coup.

Complementing Soviet efforts to establish vanguard parties is a continuing Soviet emphasis on military assistance policies designed to gain influence with third world armies. An emphasis on conventional arms transfers has been central to these policies. Beginning in the mid-1950s, the USSR concluded arms deals with Egypt, Syria, Indonesia, Iraq, and Afghanistan.[18] By the 1960s, the USSR had expanded its list of major customers to include Somalia, South Yemen, India, Iraq, Algeria, Iran, and the Sudan.[19] The rise of Colonel Khadaffi and of regional conflicts in Africa made Libya, Angola, and Ethiopia principal recipients of Soviet weaponry in the 1970s. In the early 1980s, Libya, Iraq, Syria, and Algeria became the major third world purchasers of Soviet arms.[20]

More impressive than the number of third world countries receiving large amounts of Soviet weapons is the magnitude of the arms transfers themselves. From 1955 to 1980, Soviet bloc countries supplied over $51 billion of military aid to the third world (excluding Cuba, North Korea, and Vietnam), of which $9.8 billion was provided by Eastern European countries. This compares with only $28 billion worth of economic aid furnished to the third world during the same time period.[21] By the late 1970s, the Soviet Union (in some years) had replaced the United States as the principal arms supplier for the third world.[22] To supplement these arms transfers, the Kremlin has trained some fifty-two thousand third world military personnel (up to 1980) in the Soviet Union and other communist countries, while placing approximately the same number of Soviet bloc military advisors in the third world.[23]

The appeal of Soviet military assistance to third world armies is great. Because of its position as the world's leading producer of conventional arms and its tendency to stockpile even old weapons, the USSR is able to transfer large amounts of arms to other countries without drawing on its own forces. Combined with a relatively streamlined arms control process, this production capacity enables it to send arms to third world states on the average twice as quickly as the United States.[24] The cost of these weapons is generally much less than that of their Western counterparts, especially when the USSR includes (as it often does) a substantial discount. While the quality of Soviet arms, particularly its jet fighters, is not always up to Western standards, this is often irrelevant to third world forces because they lack the training and expertise to fully exploit sophisticated weaponry. What is critical to most third world conflicts is which side has enough relatively simple and usable weapons, such as small arms, artillery, surface-to-air missiles, and even tanks, to overpower its adversary. The Soviets excel in supplying large amounts of these and other weapons to third world clients. Soviet military assistance is also sought by third world military leaders because along with the weapons often come skilled proxies to use them. As was demonstrated in Angola and Ethiopia, the introduction of several thousand well-trained Cubans can make the difference between victory and defeat for third world forces.

This is not to suggest that the Soviet Union would always be preferred over the United States as an arms supplier. American support and services are generally far superior to those of the USSR, because Moscow attempts to keep its clients dependent on it for spare parts. Furthermore, American advisors are usually better liked and more effective than are their Soviet counterparts, and this usually makes the United States better for the long-term structural development of third world forces. Nevertheless, for a third world army needing a quick infusion of weaponry, or for an army in a country with a poor human rights record, the USSR might well be the supplier of choice.

Whether Soviet military assistance policies have affected the likelihood of coups in the third world is impossible to determine conclusively. On an impressionistic level, it is noteworthy that of the fifteen major recipients of Soviet bloc military aid (those countries that have received over $400 million of military assistance from the USSR and its allies), only in Indonesia has a pro-Soviet regime been replaced by a pro-Western military government.[25] This does not mean that the Soviets have had unqualified successes in influencing third world armies. The pro-Western realignments of Egypt's Sadat, Sudan's Numeiry, and Somalia's Siad Barre could not have taken place in the face of determined opposition by their Soviet-trained and Soviet-equipped armed forces. In fact, some of the most anti-Soviet elements in these countries were those military officers with the closest contacts with the Soviets. The absence of anti-Soviet coups among states receiving substantial Soviet military assistance, however, may indicate that in the absence of a change of political orientation on the part of the existing leader, a Soviet-backed army will be inhibited from overthrowing a regime friendly to Moscow.

One of the most important elements in Soviet policy toward the short-term threats and opportunities presented by coups is its use of proxies. To protect friendly third world leaders from coups, the Soviet Union utilizes foreign forces both to protect and to threaten third world leaders. This kind of arrangement did not originate with the USSR. As Aristotle wrote, "the guards of kings are composed of his citizens but those of a tyrant are foreign mercenaries. The one according to law rules over willing subjects; the other arbitrarily rules over those who consent not. The one therefore is guarded by the citizens, the other against them."[26] The use of outsiders to guard foreign regimes also occurred during the Roman Empire. Just as the praetorian guard of the Roman Empire began as a special military unit designed to protect the emperor and became a source of control over the regime it defended, so the praetorian guards of the Soviet Union have sought to become a significant extension of Moscow's power. While the Soviet use of proxies has not always succeeded in controlling third world leaders, they often have proved effective. By surrounding third world leaders with a "cocoon" of Cuban and East German "advisors," the Soviets have made the prospect of a successful coup against a friendly regime highly unlikely.

The "cocoon" strategy is effective for two reasons. First, the nature of most third world states is such that the political orientation of a country is determined by a single individual or a small group. It is relatively easy to defend this political elite with a small force, that is, with no more than a few hundred soldiers, if it is well-trained. Furthermore, a coup d'état by definition involves an attempt to seize power by a small group. Since the nature of this principal threat to third world governments—and to their pro-Soviet positions—involves a narrowly based thrust, defenses against coups do not require a major military effort.

It is not difficult to understand why the Soviets turned to the Cubans to assist them in protecting friendly third world leaders from coups. The Cuban presence in third world countries does not arouse the regional or American opposition that a direct Soviet involvement would engender. As a small third world country itself, Cuba does not threaten the sovereignty of other developing states the same way the superpowers do. Cuba is also free from the imperialist stigma that afflicts both the United States and, increasingly, the USSR. Furthermore, since most of the Cubans sent to Africa are black, they do not incur the racial animosity that so often accompanies a direct Soviet or American involvement. The Cubans are also good at what they do. While the Soviets are almost universally disliked for their boorish and clannish ways, Cuban advisors are generally praised for their easy-going manners and their good relations with the host population. The Spanish-speaking Cubans also have a language advantage over the Soviets in countries like Angola. Finally, Cuba's own revolutionary goals, its desire to achieve great power status, and its dependence on the USSR for economic and military support usually make it a willing accomplice to Moscow's designs.

The Cubans are especially effective for training bodyguards and security personnel for the protection of third world leaders. The Cubans began setting up special security formations for third world leaders in the mid-1960s. Then military coups in Algeria and Ghana deprived the Cubans of their only guerrilla bases in Africa and convinced them that more had to be done to protect existing "progressive" regimes. They began by training presidential guards for the governments of Guinea and Congo-Brazzaville.[27] They subsequently became involved in the protection (either directly or indirectly) of third world leaders in Libya, South Yemen, Angola, Ethiopia, Benin, Sierra Leone, Grenada, and Nicaragua. In addition, the Cubans have trained the security forces of two of Africa's most murderous regimes: Idi Amin's Uganda and Macias Nguema's Equatorial Guinea.[28] The Cubans' presence guarantees high-quality protection for the regime by personnel who are not likely to participate in any anti-Soviet plots. Moreover, by playing such a sensitive role so vital to these heads of government, the Cubans are in a position to threaten (tacitly or otherwise) leaders who might wish to stray from Moscow's path. Whether they are protecting or threatening the regime, or doing both simultaneously, the Cubans are well-placed to ensure that a pro-Soviet regime or its successor will remain friendly to the USSR.

The Cubans have also been active in establishing third world militias. These militias are trained, equipped, and sometimes led by Cuban personnel. The creation of these Cuban-dominated armies has given the Cubans and their Soviet patrons enormous influence over coup-prone states. Because these militias are often stronger than the regular armies they are ostensibly supplementing, the Cubans control the most powerful institution in the state. They are well-placed to initiate or to defend against coups, without fear of significant internal opposition. The Cubans have trained or established militias in the Congo-Brazzaville, Guinea, Equatorial Guinea, South Yemen, Iraq, and Angola.[29]

The Soviets must be particularly pleased with the progress of these Cuban-established militias. The Kremlin is well aware that its setbacks in the 1960s in Algeria, Ghana, Mali, and Indonesia were all largely due to the regular army intervening to prevent militias or other rival military forces from being established. If the Cubans succeed in developing ideologically "correct" militias without provoking the existing military establishment to action, the USSR will have succeeded in overcoming one of its major early problems in attempting to prevent reverses in the third world.

The Soviet use of East Germans in the third world has also been significant. East Germany is one of the most competent and loyal of the Soviet satellite states. East Germany's strength in the third world lies in its establishment and domination of the internal security apparatuses of many developing countries. Much more active than the West Germans, the East Germans have taken the lead in penetrating and controlling the upper echelons of several third world governments. Beginning with a military agreement in 1973 with the government of the Congo, the East Germans have expanded their presence in Africa to include nearly three thousand military and security advisors by the end of the 1970s.[30] The East German State Security Service (SSD) has been especially active in Angola, Ethiopia, Mozambique, Zambia, South Yemen, and Libya. Its responsibilities have included the training of bodyguards, advising military and civilian agencies, and establishing secret police networks.[31]

These activities have placed the East Germans in an ideal position to deter, prevent, and initiate coups.

The Soviet Union's policies toward third world coups also entail more direct uses of Soviet personnel. Soviet military advisors deter coups in much the same ways as Cuban and East German forces. Several thousand Soviet advisors or troops are based in Afghanistan, Algeria, Ethiopia, Libya, Syria, South Yemen, Madagascar, and Mongolia.[32] Their presence establishes a *de facto* countercoup force that must be considered by any potential coup makers. The most intriguing example of this kind of presence is the Soviet "combat brigade" in Cuba, whose existence caused so much consternation in Washington and helped to derail the SALT II treaty. Instead of presenting a direct threat to the United States or any other country in Latin America, the purpose of these three thousand troops is more likely the protection of Castro's regime (or a successor) from a coup d'état.[33]

Another element of Soviet policy toward coups is the rapid dispatch of personnel and equipment to protect newly established pro-Soviet regimes from countercoups. The Soviets recognize that new regimes—especially if they came to power through a coup—are especially vulnerable. To safeguard their gains, the Soviets arrange for the quick arrival of Cuban and East German forces to protect the new leadership, for rapid arms transfers to the military to placate their demands, and for immediate recognition of the new regime to help legitimize its rule. In addition, treaties of friendship and cooperation may be concluded to raise the prospect of Soviet intervention in the event of a "reactionary" coup.

The Soviets have also encouraged, assisted, and sometimes initiated coups against third world regimes. Although conclusive evidence is lacking, there are several cases in which Moscow is believed to have played a significant role in supporting coups against existing governments. These include the attempt to overthrow President Numeiry of the Sudan in 1971, Colonel Mengistu's consolidation of power in Ethiopia in 1977, coups in 1978 against President Rubayi Ali of South Yemen and Prime Minister Mohammed Daoud of Afghanistan, the attempt of Afghan President Nur Mohammed Taraki to overthrow Prime Minister Hafizullah Amin in 1979, and Bernard Coard's coup against Maurice Bishop in Grenada in 1983.

Evaluating Soviet Policies toward Coups

As was the case with the United States, assessing the effectiveness of the USSR in deterring coups is no easy task. The absence of successful coups against pro-Soviet regimes is an indication of the Kremlin's success, but, as is always the case with deterrence, this absence is hardly proof that a specific policy is responsible. The suppression of actual coups is a more tangible demonstration of the effectiveness of Soviet policy, but it too has limitations. The Soviets might conceal successful countercoup actions so as not to give the impression that they are keeping a regime in power. Furthermore, even if it is successful, the suppression of an actual coup reveals the failure of the Kremlin to deter this coup in the first place.

Evaluating Soviet policies concerned with initiating coups against pro-Western regimes is no easier. For obvious reasons, the Kremlin will seek to conceal its role in supporting or encouraging coups. While it is often suspected of having provided assistance to coup makers or even for having been responsible for a coup itself, it is almost always impossible actually to prove Soviet involvement. The ability of the USSR to keep many of its activities secret makes it all the more difficult to prove Soviet complicity. In addition, the simple fact that a regime adopts a pro-Soviet orientation following a coup is not enough to demonstrate Moscow's involvement. Several coups that produced pro-Soviet governments were carried out with no Soviet involvement (e.g., in Ethiopia and in Benin). Third world leaders may also falsely claim a Soviet involvement in a coup attempt to conceal their own domestic problems or to gain U.S. support. President Numeiry of the Sudan had been accused of doing this on several occasions before his overthrow in 1985.

The failure of the USSR to prevent coups against regimes in Moscow's orbit represents a more tangible measure of the effectiveness or lack of it of Soviet policies. The Soviet Union cannot conceal the overthrow of its clients, especially when they are replaced by regimes adopting a pro-Western alignment. The Kremlin's reaction to a new government often serves as a good indicator of whether it sees a coup as a setback. Nevertheless, caution is required even in this area. The Soviet commitment to protecting friendly regimes from coups can be very weak, making the Soviet failure to defend certain regimes less significant than might otherwise be concluded.

Despite these qualifications, it is possible to make some judgments about the successes and failures of Soviet attempts to affect the outcome of coups. In reviewing the pertinent cases of Soviet involvement, two points should be kept in mind. First, they collectively demonstrate an extensive and continuing Soviet involvement in coups throughout the third world. It is an involvement that is both effective and central to understanding Moscow's position in the third world.

In addition, the cases of Soviet involvement in coups demonstrate the way the USSR, like the United States, focuses its coup policies on countries already within its sphere of influence. Although active in supporting subversive elements throughout the third world, more or less direct Soviet efforts to protect regimes from coups or to use coups to topple regimes have focused on governments that have been at some time within the Soviet camp. Egypt's Sadat, Sudan's Numeiry, Somalia's Siad Barre, South Yemen's Rubayi Ali, and the People's Republic of China's Mao all had cordial relationships with the Soviet Union at some time while they were in power. When they rejected their pro-Soviet alignments and to a certain extent turned toward the West, the Kremlin allegedly acted to remove them. The Soviets have also tried to remove leaders who have retained their alliances with the USSR but have showed signs of independence. This was the case with suspected Soviet attempts to assist coups against Ethiopia's Mengistu, Angola's Neto, Afghanistan's Amin, and Grenada's Bishop.

Soviet Successes

The USSR has been very successful in protecting friendly regimes from coups. Since its reverses in the mid-1960s, the Kremlin has lost only two friendly regimes to coups d'état. During the same time, the USSR increased its third world influence due to pro-Soviet coups in Benin (1972), Ethiopia (1974 and 1977), Afghanistan (1978), South Yemen (1978), Grenada (1979), and Suriname (1980).

The Soviet record is all the more impressive because both of its "losses" cannot be construed as failures of Soviet countercoup policies. The first setback occurred in Chile in 1973 when the regime of Salvador Allende was overthrown by a rightist military coup. Although the Soviets may have regretted the demise of this elected Marxist president, ties between Chile and the USSR were not close and the Kremlin never took steps to deter or to prevent the coup that resulted in Allende's downfall.

The second Soviet loss, the 1979 coup in Equatorial Guinea, also cannot be labeled a failure of Moscow's policies. It is true that the pro-Soviet regime of President Francisco Macias Nguema was overthrown by a coup d'état in August 1979 by elements of the military, who then reoriented Equatorial Guinea more toward the West. In addition, the new regime ended Soviet fishing rights off the coast of Equatorial Guinea, expelled some two hundred Cuban advisors, and denied the Soviets access to a small military base on the Gulf of Biafra, which had been used as a communications intelligence post and as a staging area for Soviet-Cuban interventions in Africa.[34] Closer investigation, however, reveals that the Soviets and the Cubans in Equatorial Guinea were not committed to the regime's survival.

Macias Nguema's regime was one of the most brutal in Africa. Although the Kremlin often overlooks human rights abuses, even it could not ignore a regime that murdered over thirty thousand of its own citizens and forced an additional one hundred thousand into exile. On strictly pragmatic grounds, backing such a government was bound to have costs elsewhere in Africa. In addition, there is no evidence that Soviet personnel or the two hundred Cuban advisors stationed in Equatorial Guinea assisted Macias Nguema in his attempt to defend himself against the coup. This despite the fact that the coup only succeeded after several weeks of fighting in which foreign involvement on the side of the existing regime might have proven decisive. Most significant, a key element in the success of the coup against Macias was the transportation to the mainland of rebel troops from the island of Malabo. This critical redeployment of forces was carried out by Soviet pilots (after a brief protest), using Macias's personal Antanov aircraft.[35] It is inconceivable that the Soviets would have agreed to this plan if they had been truly interested in defending Macias's regime.

Although the coup resulted in the downfall of a pro-Soviet government, Moscow's position was not irrevocably undermined. Soviet diplomats and advisors remained in the country, as did a small group of Soviet pilots and mechanics who operated aircraft for the new government. In 1981 the USSR signed agreements with Equatorial Guinea on cultural and scientific cooperation and Moscow has provided much needed relief aid to the African state. While Moscow's influence is not at the same level that it was with Macias, neither does the Kremlin have to justify to a skeptical world why it acted to defend such a pariah regime. The USSR did not so much "lose" Equatorial Guinea to a pro-Western coup as it allowed an increasingly embarrassing liability to fall by the wayside.

There are no public examples of Soviet forces playing a principal role in the suppression of actual coups. Nevertheless, Soviet proxies have defended several third world regimes from coups. In June 1966, Cuban military advisors prevented a coup against the government of President Massamba-Debat in Congo-Brazzaville.[36] East German advisors reportedly played a role in defending Libya's President Khadaffi from a 1980 coup attempt. The effort to topple Khadaffi was suppressed at the cost of four hundred lives and apparently the suppression involved the direct participation of East German personnel working with the Libyan air force and army.[37] In addition to this 1980 attempt, Khadaffi has also survived other major challenges to his rule, in 1975, 1978, 1981, 1984, and 1985. Evidence of East German assistance in defending Khadaffi against these attempts remains sketchy. Still, the presence of nearly two thousand East Germans in Libya administering the secret police and making up Khadaffi's personal security guard suggests they have played a major role in keeping the Libyan leader in power.[38]

The Soviet navy has played a small role in protecting friendly third world regimes from coups by helping them maintain their hold immediately after taking power. At this early stage, new regimes are often vulnerable to either internal or external countercoups, making the Soviets' tangible and symbolic assistance all the more valuable. Following Siad Barre's coup in Somalia in October 1969, the USSR sent warships to visit Somali ports as a sign of support. These ships helped keep Siad Barre in power during a time of great instability. Soviet ships also came to Somalia in 1970, perhaps in response to a coup attempt against Siad Barre that had just been defeated.[39] The Soviet navy also assisted Prime Minister Siaka Stevens of Sierra Leone stay in power after a major coup was barely suppressed by Stevens's forces. By sending a destroyer to Sierra Leone, the Soviets helped to legitimize Stevens's shaky rule.[40] The Soviet navy may also have helped to maintain Khadaffi in power. Tripoli radio announced that the presence of Soviet warships had prevented a British countercoup soon after Khadaffi's seizure of power in 1969. While there is no evidence that the British ever contemplated such a move, Soviet warships were present and they may have strengthened the position of Khadaffi's new regime.[41]

In Grenada, Cuban support helped to protect the new pro-Soviet regime of Maurice Bishop from a countercoup. A small Caribbean island with a population of about 100,000, Grenada attracted little attention until a coup overthrew Prime Minister Eric Gairy. The coup occurred after the erratic and increasingly repressive Gairy ordered the arrest of the leaders of a leftist group called the New Jewel Movement. Before the arrests could be carried out, a small group of New Jewel members seized the airport and radio station, overwhelming Gairy's two-hundred-man army in March 1979. Under the leadership of Maurice Bishop, Grenada moved sharply to the left, intensified its ties to Cuba, and became a major irritant to the United States. It remained one until October 1983 when an even more radical Marxist-Leninist group overthrew the government and executed Bishop. This prompted an invasion by the United States, which returned Grenada to the Western camp.

Cuba's importance in the Grenada affair lies in its protection of Bishop's regime, especially during the critical period immediately following the coup. With Gairy still alive in the United States and with only a handful of supporters, Bishop's hold on power was very tenuous. Castro's decision to send arms and advisors quickly to the Grenadian army and to set up anti-aircraft guns at the island's airport may very well have prevented a countercoup.[42] The time gained by the Cuban intervention allowed Bishop to consolidate his position and to maintain himself in power until the 1983 leftist coup.

The USSR has also had some success in encouraging, assisting, and consolidating the coups of groups sympathetic to its aims, even though it did not directly engineer the coups themselves. Grenada's 1983 coup may be a case in point. After Bishop seized power, a major struggle ensued between him and his deputy, Bernard Coard. The dispute stemmed from a struggle for leadership and from differences concerning the future course that Grenada should follow. Although friendly with Fidel Castro, Bishop talked seriously of moving his country closer to democracy and (in the spring of 1983) to the United States. Coard, on the other hand, was known for his strong adherence to Leninist principles and had established close ties with the USSR. Not surprisingly, Soviet involvement was suspected when Coard launched the coup that overthrew Bishop. Suspicions of a Soviet role in the coup increased when Moscow praised the new regime that seized power despite its brutal murder of Bishop and some of his followers. The Soviet reaction was in sharp contrast to that of Cuba, which bitterly condemned the coup and may even have planned a countercoup.[43]

The rise to power of Colonel Mengistu in Ethiopia is another instance of suspected Soviet encouragement of a coup. Mengistu first came to prominence as one of the members of the military council, called the Dergue, that overthrew Haile Selassie in 1974. Mengistu quickly came to be known as one of the most anti-American and ambitious of the Ethiopian leaders. The Soviets, however, held back, not fully supporting Mengistu for fear that his position was not secure. Mengistu allayed their doubts on February 3, 1977, when, in a bloody shoot-out in the Grand Palace, eight senior officials of the Dergue were killed, including the chairman. Mengistu then became the leader of the Dergue and furthered Ethiopia's realignment away from the United States and toward the Soviet Union.

The Soviet connection with these events came about just before and just after Mengistu's seizure of power. Prior to the 1977 coup, the Soviets had concluded a secret arms agreement with Mengistu in December 1976. The agreement strengthened Mengistu's influence and allowed him to reorganize the Dergue along Marxist-Leninist lines. Furthermore, perhaps as an incentive for Mengistu to act, the agreement reportedly contained conditions delaying the shipment of weapons to Ethiopia until Mengistu had seized power.[44]

Less than twenty-four hours after Mengistu's coup, he met with the Soviet Ambassador to Ethiopia, Anatoli Ratanov, and received a personal message of congratulations from Fidel Castro. Shortly thereafter, the Soviet Union and all the Eastern bloc countries sent messages of support to Mengistu. A major arms agreement and the dispatch of Cuban troops to Ethiopia followed in May. The speed of the Soviet and Eastern bloc's reaction to Mengistu's coup gave credence to reports that Mengistu had had secret contacts in the Ethiopian capital of Addis Ababa with Soviet and Cuban diplomats to provide for the immediate recognition of his regime and support once he became the undisputed leader of Ethiopia.[45]

The Soviet Union played a more important role in the coup that toppled the Afghan regime of Mohammed Daoud in April 1978. Although Daoud initially had adopted a pro-Soviet line when he seized power in 1973, he gradually edged away from Moscow's influence toward a posture of authentic nonalignment. Opposing Daoud were two rival Marxist-Leninist factions, the Khalq and the Parcham. Following the assassination of a Parcham leader and a large communist demonstration at his funeral, Daoud initiated an anti-communist purge to protect his rule. His efforts, however, were inadequate to cope with the mounting communist threat. Under the leadership of Hafizullah Amin, and with the support of the military, a coup was carried out against Daoud. The new regime consisted of Nur Mohammed Taraki, a Khalq leader who became prime minister; Hafizullah Amin, the most radical of the group, who became deputy premier and foreign minister; and Babrak Karmal, the leader of Parcham, who also assumed the post of deputy premier. They rapidly aligned Afghanistan with the USSR and concluded a treaty of friendship and cooperation with the Soviet Union in December 1978.[46]

Although it is believed that there was no direct Soviet participation in the coup, the Soviets were important to its success.[47] Former American Ambassador to Afghanistan Theodore Eliot argues that the Soviets convinced the Khalq and Parcham factions to join in a coalition in 1977 so as to be in a better position to launch a coup against Daoud.[48] The Kremlin may also have provided secret assistance to the Afghan armed forces to prepare them for the coup. It is noteworthy that many of the key army and air force officers who supported Amin's coup were trained in the USSR. Following the overthrow of Daoud, the Soviets immediately recognized the Democratic Republic of Afghanistan, indicating that they knew about and supported the political orientation of the new leadership. To make certain the Khalq-Parcham coalition would hold on to power, the Soviets sent hundreds of civilian advisors to the Afghan government and doubled the number of its military advisors in Afghanistan to seven hundred. A communications link between Moscow and the Soviet military advisory group in the Afghan capital of Kabul was also established.[49]

The Soviet role in the 1978 overthrow of the Rubayi Ali regime in South Yemen marked perhaps the strongest involvement of Moscow in a third world coup. South Yemen (officially called the People's Democratic Republic of Yemen) achieved independence from Great Britain in 1967. It is a desperately poor country, with virtually no natural resources and a population in 1978 of approximately 1.6 million people. Despite its lack of wealth, South Yemen has proved to be of concern because of its strategic location bordering on Saudi Arabia and overlooking the Bab el Mandeb straits through which pass much of Western Europe's oil.

In the summer of 1978, following a bizzare series of events, the newly installed leader of South Yemen, Hafez Ismail, successfully defended his government against the man he had just deposed, Rubayi Ali. The roots of this coup and countercoup can be found in the involvement of the Soviet Union and its proxies in an internal political dispute in South Yemen.

In late 1977 the President of South Yemen, Rubayi Ali, was challenged for the leadership of the country by Hafez Ismail, the head of South Yemen's sole political party, the National Front. Part of their conflict stemmed from disagreements over foreign policy. Rubayi sought to move South Yemen toward a more neutralist posture, while Ismail worked to intensify the existing pro-Soviet alignment. Ismail became especially incensed at Rubayi's planned meeting with American representatives in June 1978. The two also clashed over a Soviet request to use Aden as a transit point for the passage of Soviet supplies and a request for South Yemeni troops to assist the Ethiopians in their war with Eritrea.[50] Rubayi wished to remain neutral in that war, in which most of the Arab states supported the Eritreans, while Ismail readily agreed to the Soviet requests.

More fundamentally, the dispute revolved around who would lead South Yemen. Although Rubayi was the nominal head of state and retained the support of much of the army, Ismail had the backing of the Soviets and their proxies, who dealt only with him. With their support, Ismail pushed for the establishment of a new "vanguard" party to be led by himself. Rubayi resisted such a move, recognizing that the new party would effectively deprive him of power. The conflict reached a new level in May 1978 when Ismail arrested 150 army officers who were loyal to Rubayi and formally opposed Ismail's plan for a new party.[51]

Rubayi responded by sending an envoy to North Yemen to enlist the support of its leader, Ahmad al-Ghashmi, against Ismail.

On June 24, 1978, the envoy was supposed to leave South Yemen carrying a briefcase filled with sensitive papers. Before leaving, however, the envoy was reportedly arrested by Ismail's men, under the orders of the East Germans. A new messenger with a new briefcase was substituted.[52] Ismail's envoy then took a private aircraft to the North Yemeni capital of Sana, arriving on June 24. Once in Sana, the envoy went directly to the North Yemeni president's office. He shook hands with the president, took a seat in his private office, and then opened his briefcase, triggering an explosion that killed them both.[53]

The murder of the president of North Yemen had immediate and drastic repercussions. Blaming South Yemen for the assassination, the new North Yemeni leaders broke off relations between the two countries. Apparently, Ismail had anticipated this reaction, because he used it to put into motion a plan to frame Rubayi for the assassination. Using the break in relations with the North as an excuse, Ismail called an emergency meeting of the South Yemeni Central Committee, which operated under his direction. Realizing the meeting was stacked against him, Rubayi refused to attend and instead submitted a letter of resignation. The Central Committee voted 120 to 4 to adopt a resolution "dismissing him (Rubayi) from the presidency of the state and all his other functions." In addition, the Central Committee formally accused Rubayi of plotting the murder of the North Yemeni president and ordered him to leave for Ethiopia.[54]

At this point it appeared that Ismail had launched a successful coup. Rubayi had been formally deposed and the leadership of South Yemen had passed to his opponent. Not surprisingly, Ismail emerged as the real power, although titular authority rested with his associate, Nasser Muhammad. Aside from supporting Ismail, the new leaders were all known for their pro-Soviet views.

Before the new government could entrench itself, however, Rubayi acted. On June 26, Rubayi launched a countercoup to regain power. He mobilized loyal units in the armed forces and the Palace Guard in an attempt to have Ismail and his colleagues arrested. In most third world states, this support of the army and the Palace Guard would have been enough to guarantee success. But in South Yemen, the situation was different. For months preceding the coup, Cubans had been building up a "people's militia" under the control of Ismail. With twenty thousand men, it was equal in size and superior in training and equipment to South Yemen's regular army.[55] Augmenting the militia was an internal security force called Tanzim established and led by the East Germans.

In addition, Cuban and Soviet advisors had been busily training and teaching the South Yemeni air force and navy.

On June 26, 1978, Ismail's militia and air force destroyed Rubayi's hopes for a successful countercoup by attacking the Presidential Palace. Although Rubayi's guards put up a heroic fight, they were overcome by Ismail's superior forces. While South Yemeni supporters of Ismail bore the brunt of the fighting, significant Soviet proxy involvement apparently took place in the critical battle for the Presidential Palace. Reportedly, Soviet warships shelled the palace, while Soviet or Cuban pilots flew air strikes against it. Cuban troops were said to have taken part in the final assault against the Palace that sealed Rubayi's fate.[56]

The fact that Rubayi was scheduled to meet with some representatives of the United States government to discuss the resumption of relations between their two countries just a few days later than the day he was overthrown indirectly supports the view that the Soviets participated in Ismail's defense. The Kremlin was also unhappy over Rubayi's desire to expel some Soviet advisors and his concluding an economic agreement with the People's Republic of China.[57] Although tangible proof of the exact nature of the Soviet involvement is lacking, there is no denying that the USSR played a major role in enabling Ismail's coup to succeed.[58]

Although sporadic fighting continued outside the capital for a few days, the battle for Aden ended quickly. With his forces defeated, Rubayi and some of his closest supporters were tried and executed on the day of their attempted coup. When they heard of the executions, additional units of the South Yemeni army began to revolt, once again threatening Ismail's position. Their cause was lost, however, because of Cuban and Soviet actions. Additional Cuban troops from Ethiopia flew into Aden on Soviet transport aircraft within hours of Rubayi's attempt to regain power.[59] At the same time, the Soviet Union announced it would assist the new government against any outside intervention. With outside support and the backing of the party and the militia, Ismail remained firmly in power.[60]

Most observers did not appreciate the significance of the South Yemeni coup and countercoup. Because South Yemen was already in the Soviet orbit, the intensification of that alignment did not appear to be cause for much concern. What many overlooked was the manner in which Ismail seized and retained power. Without having to incur the political and military costs of a direct outside intervention, the Kremlin overthrew a leader it did not approve of, placed in power someone more to its liking, and protected its choice from significant internal opposition. The prospects for a successful pro-Western coup in South Yemen or for the realignment of any existing South Yemeni leader are virtually nonexistent.[61]

Soviet Failures

The greatest failure of Soviet policy has been its general inability to initiate coups. With the exception of South Yemen, it is believed that the USSR has not played a central role in any of the coups that brought pro-Soviet regimes to power.[62] This weakness is all the more striking because of suspicions that the Soviets have attempted to overthrow several unfriendly leaders but have not been able to do so.

During the course of his stormy relationship with the Soviet Union, Egypt's Anwar Sadat suspected Kremlin involvement in the planning of several coups against him. The plotting of coups apparently began soon after Sadat assumed power in September 1970, following the death of President Nasser. Egyptian Vice-President Ali Sabrri and several other high officials of the Egyptian government allegedly planned to use public disturbances as pretexts for launching a coup against the Egyptian leader. According to Sadat, the Soviets, who had close ties with Sabri, supported the potential coup makers. The plot was uncovered, however, before any coup could be launched. The Soviets then quickly signed a treaty of friendship and cooperation with Sadat to shore up their position.[63]

From the time of the Sabri affair up until Sadat's assassination, the Soviets were suspected of having assisted several other failed plots against the Egyptian leader. Working at different times with the Egyptian Communist Party, Libyan intelligence, a secret political organization called the Egyptian Worker's Party, and student groups and leftists, the Soviets allegedly tried to encourage coups in 1972, 1973, and 1974. None got so far as to produce an actual coup attempt, and there is no credible evidence that the Soviets were involved in Sadat's assassination.[64]

The failures of these alleged plots drove Sadat further into the American sphere of influence. Following the October 1973 war, Sadat turned to the United States for Egypt's military supplies, abrogated the Egyptian-Soviet treaty of friendship and cooperation, signed the American-sponsored Camp David accords, and generally became the most pro-Western Arab leader. While many factors led to Sadat's realignment, the perception that the Soviets had continually backed coups against him undoubtedly contributed to the Egyptian leader's reevaluation of his position.

The Soviet Union has also been implicated in several coups attempted against President Gaafar al-Numeiry of the Sudan. The most serious occurred in 1971, when only the prompt action of both Egypt and Libya succeeded in preserving Numeiry's rule.[65] Numeiry also accused the Soviets of having been involved in a July 1976 coup attempt that saw the capital of Khartoum attacked by some two thousand Sudanese rebels, and of a further attempted coup on February 2, 1977, in the southern city of Juba. Aside from Numeiry's allegations, there is little evidence to substantiate Soviet support for these two abortive coups, both of which stemmed from domestic grievances. Nevertheless, all three coup attempts were cited by Numeiry as a justification for his realignment away from the Soviet Union and toward the West.[66]

The Soviets were implicated in two additional plots in the Horn of Africa in the spring of 1978. In Somalia, President Siad Barre suppressed a coup that he claimed was backed by the Soviets. Although the coup was launched by Soviet-trained Somali army officers, and although the Kremlin had reason to want to topple the increasingly hostile Siad Barre, domestic strife among Somali clans could just as well have been the cause of the coup. In Ethiopia, at roughly the same time, the South Yemenis, Cubans, and perhaps the Soviets were involved in an attempt to challenge the rule of Prime Minister Mengistu. An Ethiopian Marxist, Negede Gobeze, was smuggled into Ethiopia against the wishes of Mengistu, with the assistance of at least the Cubans and Yemenis and possibly the Soviets. At that time, the Soviets were unhappy with Mengistu's reluctance to establish a Marxist-Leninist vanguard party in Ethiopia. Whether an actual coup was really planned is not known because Negede Gobeze's presence was discovered before any action could be taken.

In the wake of these incidents, Siad Barre intensified his pro-Western alignment, eventually providing the United States with military facilities in Somalia. Prime Minister Mengistu at first ordered the diplomatic expulsions of the Cuban ambassador and the South Yemeni chargé d'affaires. The Soviet ambassador left on his own. Shortly afterward, the Soviets solidified their shaky relationship with Ethiopia by concluding a treaty of friendship and cooperation with Mengistu in November.[67]

Three additional examples of alleged Soviet involvements in backing coups warrant special attention. In Angola, a possible Soviet-backed coup was suppressed with the assistance of Cuban forces. Understanding this event could be profoundly helpful for our understanding of the Soviet-Cuban relationship. There is also some evidence linking the USSR with Lin Piao's 1971 plot to launch a coup against Mao Tsetung in the People's Republic of China. The details of this case remain especially murky, but they at least raise the possibility that Moscow sought to engage in actions that, had they proved successful, could have resulted in a major shift in the world distribution of power. Finally, the USSR is acknowledged to have tried to support a coup in Afghanistan against President Amin. Its failure there led to the Soviet invasion of that country a few months later.

The first case is one of the most intriguing of a failed coup with possible Soviet support. It occurred in Angola against President Agostinho Neto. The coup began on May 27, 1977, when armored cars of the Angolan army crashed through the gates of the main prison in the capital city of Luanda. This assault on the prison freed many inmates, including (it is believed) Nito Alves, who had served as minister of internal administration and as a member of the MPLA (the ruling party) Central Committee until his arrest six days earlier. Along with the attack on the prison, Angolan army units also took control of the Luanda radio station and tried to take over the Presidential Palace. Although the coup had the support of high officials throughout the government and army, it lacked the momentum to achieve a quick victory. Several hours after it began, loyal MPLA troops recaptured the radio station and soon suppressed the coup.[68]

The first extraordinary facet of this affair is that it appears that Cuban troops played a major role in defeating the coup. Four Cuban tanks reportedly assisted government forces in retaking the city.[69] Suspicions of Cuban involvement were also aroused when the monitoring of radio broadcasts from Luanda on the day of the coup revealed the presence of Spanish-speaking individuals at the station when the loyalist forces evicted the coup makers.[70] One report declared that when the radio station was captured, the end of the coup was accidentally announced in Spanish instead of Portuguese.[71] The apparent presence of Cubans at the station has never been explained. Other factors linking the Cubans with the coup's suppression include Castro's assertion a month prior to the coup attempt that Cuba "will aid Angola to every possible extent," and the arrival of Cuban Vice-President Raul Castro for talks with Neto a week after the abortive coup. While conclusive evidence for the Cuban role is absent, there is substantial current agreement that the Cubans did indeed play an important role in protecting Neto from the Alves coup attempt.[72]

What makes the Cuban role even more extraordinary is the possibility that the defeated coup was either actively backed by the Soviet Union or the Soviets had advance knowledge of the attempt and failed to warn Neto.[73] The key to this relation lies in the leader of the coup, Nito Alves. At first, Alves strongly supported Neto and played a critical role in the Angolan president's bid for power. Neto rewarded Alves for his efforts by naming him minister of internal administration, thus placing Alves in charge of the development of mass organizations and in control of the appointment of many senior officials. In time, however, Alves became disenchanted with Neto's refusal to appoint more blacks, as opposed to mesticos—people of mixed race—to government positions. Alves was also critical of the overall performance of Neto's regime, particularly in the light of widespread food shortages. Neto responded to Alves's increasing attacks by publicly condemning "factionalism" and having him arrested on May 21. Alves's supporters launched their coup only six days later.

Several facts support the proposition that the Soviets supported Alves's coup. Moscow had never been entirely comfortable with Neto's nationalistic leadership. In 1973 it tried to block Neto's rise to power by backing a more ideologically reliable rival. In the years since then, the Kremlin has reportedly been upset that the MPLA could not reach some agreement with opposition forces that would end Angola's costly and protracted civil war. The problems between Neto and the Soviets became open when, a week before the attempted coup, the Angolan leader was forced to declare publicly that he was not anti-Soviet.

Nito Alves and his colleagues, on the other hand, were closely linked with the Soviet Union. The Kremlin admired Alves's popularity with the masses, his dynamic black nationalist image, and his dedication to Marxism-Leninism. The Soviets' fondness for Alves was not lost on Neto, who expelled a Soviet diplomat with close ties to Alves in October 1976. Neto may have feared that the Soviets saw in Alves the opportunity to place a less nationalistic and more pro-Soviet leader in power in Angola.[74] Soviet involvement is also suspected because one of the coup's leaders expected the Soviet embassy to rescue him after the coup failed.[75]

The Cuban suppression of the coup remains a puzzle. The Cubans may have acted reflexively and in ignorance of Soviet intentions when the coup began. Especially if Soviet support for the Alves group was hidden and indirect, neither the Cubans nor the Soviets may have been aware that a coup was being planned. In the context of the short timeframe of the coup attempt, Cuban protection of the Neto regime from an attack of unknown origin is understandable. Alternatively, the Cubans may have known of the Soviets' involvement with Alves, but, in a display of independence, they may have chosen to follow their assigned mission of defending the Neto regime. If the Cubans had acted against Soviet wishes, their behavior in Angola in connection with their opposition to the Soviet-supported Coard regime in Grenada indicates that they are sometimes prepared to challenge the USSR over major issues when their interests conflict.

Following the abortive coup, both the USSR and the MPLA denied any Soviet involvement. In a move similar to what took place in the aftermath of the Ali Sabri affair in Egypt and the Negede Gobeze affair in Ethiopia, the USSR and the Angolan regime moved to cement their ties. A treaty of friendship and cooperation signed in October 1976 was ratified by both countries just a few months after the attempted coup. After Neto's death (following an operation in Moscow), the Soviet position in Angola remained secure.

A major setback to Soviet interests in terms of the benefits a success would have brought about occurred in September 1971 when a coup was supposedly planned against Chinese leader Mao Tse-tung. The alleged abortive plot originated in a power struggle between Mao and his designated heir, Lin Piao.[76] The dispute between the two ranged over a variety of issues, including Lin's concern that Mao's "continuing revolution" was hurting the Chinese economy, Mao's emphasis on preparing the People's Liberation Army for war with the Soviet Union, and the highly personalized leadership style of Mao. Mostly, however, the dispute stemmed from Lin's desire to create an independent source of support in order to prevent Mao from changing his mind about the succession and to enable Lin to rule effectively once Mao had passed from the scene.[77]

The struggle between the two leaders surfaced in a meeting held at Lushan in late August 1970. At the meeting, military leaders loyal to Lin directly challenged Mao's authority by attempting to establish the position of state chairman. Although Mao succeeded in having the military's demands rejected, he realized that he would have to act decisively to deal with Lin. Following the Lushan meeting, Mao criticized Lin's supporters, reorganized the military's leadership (a major source of Lin's power), and transferred units loyal to Lin out of the Peking area.[78]

By February 1971, Lin may have concluded that he would have to act against Mao if he hoped to survive. He reportedly informed his son, the deputy director of operations of the air force, to begin planning a coup that would replace Mao with himself. Several senior military officials apparently supported the plot. The coup plan, labeled "Project 571," the numbers of which are a homonym for "armed uprising," called for mobile air force units to gain control of the Shanghai-Nanking area and then extend their control to other military units. The plan also called for assassinating Mao by bombing his train when he was in the Shanghai area. The plan failed when Lin's daughter revealed the plot to Premier

Chou En-lai, who warned Mao in time to save his life.

Upon hearing of the plot's discovery, Lin, his wife, and his son attempted to escape China by jet. They died when their aircraft crashed in Mongolia on September 13, 1971, while en route to the USSR. Following the crash, Lin's accomplices were quickly arrested.

Evidence of Soviet involvement in this planned coup is necessarily circumstantial, but it is intriguing nevertheless. According to the plans of "Project 571," the coup makers had declared that they would have the support of the USSR in their attempt to overthrow Mao. This support included the use of Soviet military forces in the coup and included the initiation of hostilities on the Sino-Soviet border to provide a pretext for the movement of Chinese troops needed to carry out the coup. The coup makers also reportedly planned "a pincer attack from north and south in alliance with the Soviet Union."[79] Lin's lack of hostility toward the USSR compared to Mao and his attempt to fly to the USSR once the coup plot failed are further indications of Soviet involvement.[80] Whether the Soviets were involved or not, the demise of Lin Piao meant a continuation of the Sino-Soviet conflict, with all its attendant risks and costs.

Suspected Soviet involvement in the failed plot against Mao illustrates the potentially tremendous gains the USSR could produce by encouraging coups in key countries. If the Soviets had successfully helped the Lin Piao group to overthrow Mao, Moscow would have achieved its greatest triumph in the third world. In one action, the USSR would have drastically lessened the threat posed to it by its most bitter antagonist. The threat of nuclear war between the two communist giants that loomed so large during their 1969 border clashes would have been virtually eliminated. The nearly one million Soviet troops on the border with China could have been demobilized or, what is more likely, redeployed on the European front. That the coup did not succeed no doubt disappointed the Kremlin. Nevertheless, the Lin Piao scheme showed the way major gains might be achieved at virtually no risk, even should the attempt fail.

The most costly Soviet failure in backing a coup occurred in Afghanistan in the fall of 1979. Prior to the Soviet invasion, events in Afghanistan were rapidly getting out of control. Under the direction of Deputy Premier Amin, radical policies of land redistribution and antireligious educational programs were being carried out, which had eroded support for the Afghan government. By March 1979, tribal revolts were occurring throughout the country. At this time, Amin replaced the more moderate and Soviet-favored Taraki as prime minister and later he took control of the armed forces himself.

Under Amin, the situation in Afghanistan deteriorated further. His programs continued to provoke tribal revolts, at the same time further narrowing the bases of his support, even in the Afghan army. Despite the precariousness of his position, he rejected the Soviets' advice to moderate his actions. If he were to continue in power, the Soviets would face the prospect of a countrywide revolt, which would place a hostile Muslim state on its border. It was even possible that Amin would re-align with the United States, as had Egypt's Sadat, Sudan's Numeiry, and Somalia's Siad Barre.[81] On the other hand, if Taraki, who still held the post of president, could seize power, the Afghan rebellion might be quelled through the implementation of more conciliatory policies.

Sources in the United States believe strongly that Soviet Prime Minister Brezhnev personally approved of and encouraged Taraki to launch a coup against Amin when Taraki visited Moscow on September 10, 1979.[82] But Taraki's coup did not succeed. Perhaps because he was tipped off by one of Taraki's bodyguards or by a senior Afghan official, Amin learned of the plan and he struck first.[83] In a violent confrontation, Taraki was deposed on September 16 and executed on October 8.[84] Some of his remaining supporters were protected by the Soviet ambassador, which lent credence to the supposition that the Kremlin had been involved in the Taraki plot. Amin then assumed sole leadership of the country.[85]

The failure of the Soviets to successfully carry out the coup against Amin placed Moscow in its worst position yet. Following the abortive plot, Amin became increasingly suspicious of Soviet intentions, making a similar Kremlin overture to another rival leader impossible to implement. Moreover, Amin retained control over most of the military in Kabul and over the internal security apparatus. This eliminated the coup as an option for removing him. Instead, the Kremlin was forced to remove Amin by means of a massive invasion by Soviet forces. During the course of the invasion, for which Amin refused to provide an invitation, the Afghan leader and his family were apparently murdered by Soviet troops.[86]

A successful Soviet-sponsored coup against Amin in September 1979 could have had a major impact on the Soviets' position in the third world. At the very least, if the Soviets had succeeded in placing Taraki in power, they could have intervened in Afghanistan at the genuine request of the existing leader. No doubt, if that had happened, many in the West would have argued that the USSR was fully justified in responding to a plea for assistance from a legitimate government. Instead, the Soviets had to endure the stigma of having murdered a third world leader and his family, at the same time having invented a *post facto* request for intervention that all but the most pro-Moscow groups have rejected as illegitimate. More important, a successful Taraki coup would have raised the possibility of containing the Afghan revolt short of a direct massive Soviet involvement. Under the more moderate and pliable rule of Taraki, an indigenous Afghan solution to the country's turmoil might have been developed, eliminating the need for an overt Soviet invasion. The thousands of casualties, the huge expenditures, and the political costs engendered by the Soviet invasion and occupation might have been avoided.

The Importance of Coups and Coup Policies to the Soviet Union

Just how important have coups and coup policies been to the Soviet Union? Even in cases in which there is no evidence of Soviet involvement, coups have greatly affected the Kremlin's position in the third world. While it is true that most coups affecting the Soviet Union have occurred in countries of little strategic significance, this has not always been the case. Coups in Egypt (1952), Iraq (1958), Syria (1966), Libya (1969), and Ethiopia (1974) have all led to important increases in Soviet influence in the third world. The Kremlin has also lost substantial ground due to coups in such key third world countries as Indonesia (1965) and Ghana (1966).

Soviet-assisted coups have provided a clear demonstration of how the USSR advances its interests in the third world. Because even Soviet-backed coups are seen as internal events in third world countries, Moscow has been able dramatically to expand its influence in the world without provoking a reaction from the West. When the Soviets supported the 1978 coup in Afghanistan to increase its control of that country, the United States and its allies were able to do virtually nothing. When the Soviets invaded Afghanistan in 1979 to accomplish the same end, the United States and its allies treated the invasion as a major escalation of the cold war. Similarly, there was virtually no Western protest against the 1978 Soviet-sponsored overthrow of the South Yemeni leader, Rubayi Ali. Clearly, one of the least risky ways for the Kremlin to extend its interests throughout the third world comes by means of the installation of friendly regimes through coups.

Soviet protection of its friends from coups is one of the most significant achievements of Soviet policy toward the third world. The USSR has largely succeeded in eliminating threats of pro-Western coups against its third world friends. This is a major accomplishment, because the fear of a coup often dominates the leadership elites of many third world leaders. By diminishing or removing this fear, the USSR has increased its appeal to third world leaders.

Protecting third world leaders is especially important because, while the USSR might be able to help keep third world elites in power, it has little else to offer. The Soviet Union is not a major economic power and thus cannot provide the aid and trade necessary to most developing states. As a net food importer, the Soviet Union also cannot meet the food needs of its third world clients—as was so graphically demonstrated by the pitiful response of the USSR to the 1984 famine in Ethiopia. Even Soviet ideology has lost much of its appeal. With the virtual end of decolonization, many third world leaders are looking for a more pragmatic approach to governing than can be found in Marxist tracts. Furthermore, the grey, plodding bureaucrats of the Kremlin are hardly models of revolutionary inspiration for either third world elites or masses.

The inability of the Soviet Union to meet the long-term needs of its clients means that the Kremlin's position in third world countries is not secure. Although third world groups will turn to the USSR for quick infusions of arms and for proxies to help them deal with short-term threats, as happened in Angola and Ethiopia, once the threat is past, a strong tendency asserts itself to turn to the West for economic assistance. This temptation to adopt a long-term pro-Western or neutralist stance sometimes results in an existing leader changing his pro-Soviet alignment, as did Sadat, Numeiry, and Siad Barre, or in disaffected groups launching a coup to free their country from the constraints brought about by close ties with Moscow. Either way the Soviet Union loses.

An effective coup policy can help the Soviet Union compensate for these weaknesses. By defending regimes from coups, the USSR can attract leaders to a pro-Soviet alignment and prevent "reactionary" groups from reversing Soviet gains. In this purpose the Kremlin has largely succeeded. An effective coup policy also includes a credible coup-making capability to threaten governments and keep them from realigning themselves. The Soviets have not achieved this goal, but they are clearly attempting to do so.

On balance, the Soviet Union's coup policies have been a central, if largely unnoticed, part of its foreign policy. This does not mean that they have not or will not continue to suffer setbacks. Rather, the crucial point about Soviet coup policies is that they enable the USSR to play a major role in the third world. By preventing third world countries from realizing their national interests through policies of true nonalignment or by a pro-Western orientation, Soviet policies toward coups ensure that the USSR will continue to be a major influence among the developing countries.

Lessons and Conclusions

Several lessons emerge from this survey of Soviet policies toward third world coups. First, Soviet policies have been designed to meet both long- and short-term interests. For the long term, the Kremlin seeks to change the nature of friendly third world societies so that they are less likely to experience coups. This is best accomplished through the establishment of Marxist-Leninist vanguard parties, which seek to institutionalize a pro-Soviet ethos throughout the society and especially in the military. In addition, military aid programs attempt to gradually transform third world armies into reliable instruments of Soviet influence.

Until this stage of influence has been consolidated, Soviet policies rely on a foreign (i.e., Soviet or proxy) presence to ensure the loyalty of third world regimes. By placing protective and threatening "cocoons" around third world leaders, Moscow puts itself in a position to inhibit realignments to the West. The USSR also protects regimes from coups by establishing ideologically reliable militias to serve as counterweights to the regular army and by signing treaties of friendship and cooperation to raise the specter of Soviet intervention in the event of a pro-Western challenge to the government.

The Soviets appear to have accepted the fact that coups are a central feature of life in the third world and that they are likely to remain so for the foreseeable future. Their extensive involvement in protecting regimes from coups indicates that they no longer believe that change in the third world must necessarily move in a socialist direction or that the only solution to the prospect of further coups is Marxist political development. Rather, they recognize the inherent fragility of third world regimes and seek to use that fragility to their advantage by deterring anti-Soviet coups and holding out the prospect of their support for coups against leaders seeking to get out from under Soviet influence.

The Soviet Union has directed most of its coup efforts at countries in Africa and the Middle East. Many of the states in these regions suffer from chronic instability. They are coup-prone regimes, which facilitates Soviet involvement. Moreover, the absence of clearly defined spheres of influence in these regions allows Moscow to meddle there without fear of an overt American response. The relative stability of countries in East Asia and America's disproportionate interest in Latin America inhibit (but do not eliminate) Soviet manipulations in those regions. Soviet coup policies have also tended to focus on relatively undeveloped countries with weak military forces. Third world states that encompass complex societies and have modern armies are less likely to be the subjects of the Kremlin's putative control, and consequently they are less likely to be targets of Soviet coup efforts. (The People's Republic of China and Egypt are notable exceptions to this generalization.)

More important, the Soviet Union's overall strategy in relation to third world coups is designed to preserve Soviet gains rather than to expand Soviet influence. As all of the cases we have discussed show, the Soviet Union attempts to affect the outcomes of coups among states that are within its sphere of influence or that have just left the Soviet sphere of influence. It is not difficult to see why these kinds of states are the targets of Soviet-sponsored coups. Regimes friendly to the USSR understandably provoke Soviet efforts to defend them from coups. Regimes seeking to leave the Soviet orbit provoke Moscow's hostility, and the Soviets often retain ties with elements of the power structure in such cases. These elements provide the means for a coup. Regimes firmly in the Western camp do not provide either the motivation of defense or the means for a successful coup. Consequently, the focus of Soviet strategies regarding coups lies less in eroding the gains of the West than in preventing Soviet reverses.

The Soviets have been much more successful protecting friendly third world regimes from coups than they have been in initiating coups against hostile regimes. The Soviet record of deterring or preventing "reactionary" coups in countries in which they wish to maintain their influence is nothing short of remarkable. The Soviets have not, historically, been able to intimidate existing leaders into keeping a pro-Moscow alignment when they have chosen to turn to the West. The failures of the USSR to overthrow China's Mao, Egypt's Sadat, Sudan's Numeiry, Somalia's Siad Barre, and Afghanistan's Amin send a message to other third world leaders that it is possible to discard Soviet influence when it is no longer needed. And as was made plain by the cases of Sadat, Numeiry, and Siad Barre, Soviet attempts to overthrow third world leaders can result in them drawing even closer to the Western camp.

Nevertheless, one should not depend overmuch on this Soviet weakness. As the Kremlin has demonstrated in South Yemen and may be demonstrating presently in Angola and Ethiopia, for a third world country, pursuing a course of action independent of the Kremlin's desires is no easy task. The Soviets recognize that many third world leaders will over time be attracted to the greater economic benefits offered by the West. They are also keenly aware that their past setbacks came not from coups but from ruling leaders realigning their countries. By surrounding third world leaders with a "cocoon" of Cuban and East German "advisors," the Kremlin hopes to make it much more difficult for these leaders to realign themselves. The "cocoon" accomplishes this not only by protecting third world leaders from coups, but (implicitly or explicitly) by threatening to overthrow leaders who would otherwise turn away from the USSR. This "cocoon" policy may well be responsible for the lack of such realignments to the West since Siad Barre's 1978 decision in that direction.

The Soviet Union has become involved in a wide variety of coups whose only common feature is that they have consequences for Soviet interests. In some cases the USSR has encouraged radicalizing coups to place more pro-Soviet elements in power. This occurred in South Yemen, the Sudan, and Afghanistan (1978), and the same pattern probably accounts for what took place in Egypt, Angola, and Grenada. Not all coups backed by the Soviet Union have been designed to place more radical elements in power. In Afghanistan in 1979 the USSR attempted to replace a radical local leadership with a more moderate one. The Soviets were thus backing a variant of the guardian coup. This Soviet coup departed from the traditional conception of a guardian coup because it did not involve a case of the military temporarily taking power in order to remedy a deteriorating situation, after which it was ready to return to the barracks. In Afghanistan, the Soviets clearly were attempting to install a civilian regime that would rule indefinitely. Nevertheless, the Soviet attempt had certain elements in common with a guardian coup because it was an attempt to preserve the existing order by replacing an incompetent government with one the Kremlin felt would be more effective. In doing this, the Kremlin became involved with the kind of coup effort usually associated with conservative Latin American armies.

The success of the USSR's coup-deterrent policies, however, provides us with little material for analyzing and assessing Soviet coup-suppression efforts. Nevertheless, the USSR is prepared to defend pro-Soviet governments from coups. The major setbacks that were suffered by the Soviet Union in Iraq, Ghana, Mali, Indonesia, and Chile have convinced the Kremlin that it must be concerned about veto coups. As discussed in Chapter One, veto coups are coups carried out by conservative elements trying to prevent regimes from broadening their appeal by seeking the support of radical (often communist) groups. Successful veto coups threaten to realign pro-Soviet states away from the USSR and toward the West. Although veto coups have been the major threat to the USSR in the third world, they have not been the only threat. Any coup that threatens to replace a pro-Soviet leadership with one less friendly to the Kremlin is bound to be resisted by the USSR. As the case of Afghanistan in 1979 illustrates, the Soviets might suppress a breakthrough coup, if they thought that the radicalization of the regime was not to their benefit. As with coups backed by Moscow, the key determinant of whether the Soviets will become involved in suppressing a coup comes not from the type of coup but from its likely impact on Soviet interests.

The Soviet Union maintains several advantages over the United States with regard to coup-related policies. Soviet proxies have been far superior to American proxies in defending third world regimes from coups. The willingness of the Cubans and East Germans to deploy troops and advisors throughout the third world, combined with the high quality of the protection they provide, gives the USSR a unilateral edge over the United States in this regard. This is all the more true because the Cubans and East Germans usually expand their activities to include the establishment of militias and secret police organizations. As is demonstrated by the case of South Yemen, a third world country can be brought under the influence of Moscow without the USSR incurring the costs that a large overt Soviet presence would generate. The looser alliance structure in the West makes it very unlikely that the United States would be able to utilize proxies worldwide with the effectiveness and general obedience displayed by the Cubans and East Germans.

The USSR also maintains an advantage over the United States in terms of the long-term transformation of friendly third world countries to make them less susceptible to coups. Third world states can become less coup-prone either through totalitarianism (administered through a Soviet-approved vanguard party) or by means of democracy. The appeal of totalitarianism lies in its ability to mobilize the population in support of the regime and to make the armed forces subservient to the wishes of the government or the party. The realization of these aims helps ensure that the government in power will remain in power.

The democratic model advocated by the United States, however, does not guarantee the preservation of the existing leadership. Democracy, with its emphasis on popular participation and human rights, often threatens the leaders who might embrace it. Although a democratic form of government might be in the long-term interests of the country, this is of scant interest to a third world leader who fears for his short-term loss of power. Consequently, when faced with the prospect of continued coups d'état, some third world leaders will be tempted to choose the totalitarian approach, which ensures their hold on power, over the democratic approach, which threatens it. If third world leaders reject democracy, the long-term transformation of their countries along democratic lines is precluded.

Furthermore, the unwillingness of many in the United States to become involved with coups, and the inability of the government to keep such involvements secret, provides Moscow with important advantages. The Soviet Union does not have to justify its involvement to a skeptical public concerned about unwarranted interference in the internal affairs of another country. Because the details of Soviet involvements can often be kept secret, Moscow can credibly deny involvement in coups, thus preventing international condemnation. American involvements in coups, on the other hand, have often been revealed, resulting in major domestic and international criticism, as in relation to Iran in 1953, Guatemala in 1954, and Chile in 1970. Whether or not such criticism was justified, its existence demonstrates that the Soviets face fewer constraints when becoming involved in coups than does the United States.

The Soviets have already made some significant progress in protecting friendly third world regimes from coups and they are developing more effective ways of initiating coups against uncooperative leaders. Their apparent goal is the promotion of a third world in which all coups advance the Kremlin's interests—or they do not succeed. Because of the central role played by coups d'état in the East-West competition in the third world, the coming to being of such a world would dramatically enhance the Soviets' position.

Whether or not they could succeed in bringing about such a world depends on many factors, including the degree to which third world regimes continue to remain narrowly based and thus remain vulnerable to coups and to Soviet domination and the extent to which the United States is prepared to intervene to prevent the Soviets from establishing a strong influence among third world regimes. If the United States fails to prevent pro-Soviet alignments, it remains to be seen how far the United States is prepared to entice third world leaders away from the Soviet "cocoon." The determination of the Kremlin to protect its gains from indigenous threats is also a factor in its success. What specific policies the United States can and should pursue to meet the Soviet challenge is beyond the scope of this study. What has been made clear is that it is impossible either to understand or to cope with Soviet policies in the third world without analyzing and evaluating Soviet efforts to determine the outcomes of third world coups.

4

Defending Third World Regimes
from Coups d'État

Efforts to generalize about ways of defeating coups have been discouraged by the quickness with which they occur, the wide range of motivations that precipitate them, their seeming uniqueness, and their ease of success in many third world states. This neglect has been a critical oversight, however, because the suppression of coups is far from an impossible task. Too often we forget that the narrow scope of a coup, which helps to account for its success, can also bring about its failure. There are several ways in which the protection of third world regimes against coups can be accomplished.

The preferred method and long-term way for states to become less coup-prone is for them to develop the institutions and the sense of community necessary to eliminate the coup as an accepted means of resolving political disputes. This kind of development is not impossible. The creation of a strong central party, embodying the legitimizing symbols of the revolution, has enabled Mexico to reach a point where the prospect of a coup d'état there has become extremely remote. In Venezuela, a skillful president, Betancourt, dedicated to democratic principles, a successful counterinsurgency campaign, and a cooperative military have all combined to bring stability and the rule of law to a government that had been much plagued in its history by coups. During the early 1980s, several other Latin American countries, including Ecuador, Peru, Bolivia, Argentina, Guatemala, and Uruguay, have attempted to change their coup-prone histories by taking the first steps toward developing democratic institutions.

While these efforts bring hope, these examples are not a cause for optimism. The vast majority of third world states (especially those in the Middle East and Africa) are not heading in the direction of democracy. Levels of political participation in these countries remain low, political institutions cannot keep up with the demands they must confront, and political legitimacy remains an elusive goal. Moreover, as is evident in the Persian Gulf, the problems these states are confronting are growing fast. Even where a movement toward a greater sense of political community and democracy is in its beginnings, decades more of development will be needed before these countries lose their vulnerability to coups.

Another way by which regimes can lessen the threat of coups d'état is for them to develop into totalitarian states on the Soviet model. It is noteworthy that Cuba, North Korea, Outer Mongolia, and Vietnam have not experienced any coups since they have adopted a Marxist-Leninist form of government. By maintaining total control of political life by means of an extensive network of secret police, by subordinating the military to party control, and by keeping alive the potential threat of Soviet involvement should the regime be threatened, the likelihood of a coup is dramatically lessened.

Despite its anti-coup benefits, however, most third world regimes are not likely to follow the Marxist-Leninist model. Because decolonization is largely over, the appeal of communist ideology has lessened. The West has much more to offer most third world states in the increasingly important area of economic development than do the Eastern bloc states. Moreover, the military, which still plays the dominant role in most third world countries, fears the advent of communist control as a threat to its own autonomy. Although direct Soviet involvements, Soviet proxy interventions, and the desire to suppress domestic opponents effectively will continue to draw desperate leaders into the USSR's sphere of influence, the Soviet model is unlikely to be willingly emulated by the vast majority of the governments in the third world.

Third world regimes can take steps to guard themselves against coups. These steps—many of which we will discuss shortly—are helpful, but, as the high number of continuing successful coups d'état demonstrates, these kinds of steps often prove inadequate for coping with the actual threat. Furthermore, actions taken by leaders to curb their military's ability to launch a successful coup often also impede its effectiveness in defending the state from external aggression. For example, during the Arab-Israeli war of 1967, the leader of Syria, Salah Jadid, kept his best troops in Damascus, away from the fighting, not for defensive purposes in relation to the Israelis, but in order to guard against a possible coup in Syria.[1] Similarly, President Mobutu of Zaire refused to send paratroopers to halt an invasion of his country by Katangese exiles in 1977, because he preferred to keep his soldiers in the capital.[2]

Kenyan President Daniel Moi dismissed virtually the entire Kenyan air force for its alleged involvement in a coup in 1982.

Finally, and most important for understanding the role of the United States, direct foreign intervention can play a decisive role in defending regimes against attempted coups. Although they are not common occurrences, countercoups have succeeded in protecting regimes in the past, and there have been very few examples of such overt foreign assistance having failed to defeat a coup. This does not mean that the United States or any country can approach lightly the task of launching an anticoup. Clearly, countercoup interventions on the part of the United States should be undertaken only under extraordinary circumstances. At the very least, the threatened regime would have to be very important to American interests, and convincing evidence would have to exist that the people behind the coup would threaten those interests if they gained power. The application of these criteria to most cases would lead the United States to overlook the vast majority of coups that take place in the third world. Nevertheless, the possibility of a situation arising that would require direct action is not remote. The United States could do a great deal to assist the countercoup interventions of other countries to defend third world regimes important to American interests but not vital enough to justify direct U.S. involvement.

Understanding how the United States and other outside powers can protect friendly regimes from coups requires studying past foreign involvements in countercoup actions. This is not to deny the uniqueness of each coup or to imply that the means used to suppress a coup in one situation would necessarily succeed in another. Rather, it is to say that the lessons that can be learned from the suppression of coups in the past can generate insights into the ways coups have been suppressed by outside actors and can demonstrate what conditions are most likely to facilitate future coup-suppression efforts.

Defending Third World Regimes from Internal Threats

The purpose of this section is to determine the ways in which coups taking place in third world states have been defeated by foreign involvement in defense of the existing regime. The criteria for distinguishing the cases we will be considering are that they be third world states, that they be states that have attempted to defeat an actual coup, and that they have required direct foreign assistance for their countercoup efforts. These criteria are particularly well-suited to developing generalizations about defenses against coups, because they allow us to concentrate on the actual suppression of coups, minimizing the impact of the different contexts in which such coups have taken place. States that have put down coups without overt, direct foreign assistance will not be considered.

Before turning to these case studies, it would be useful to consider briefly some cases that provide specific insights into countercoup intervention, but that do not meet the criteria for this study. These include the British intervention in East Africa in 1964, the American and British interventions in the Middle East in 1958, the U.S. intervention and subsequent military involvement in the Dominican Republic in 1965–1966, the Guinean intervention in Sierra Leone in 1971, the U.S. involvement in Iran in 1953, and the U.S. invasion of Grenada in 1983.

East African Mutinies

A series of mutinies broke out among East African troops in January 1964. These actions can be used to demonstrate the importance of outside intervention in defending third world regimes from internal threats that are not, strictly speaking, coups d'état.[3] The mutinies began in the East African country of Tanganyika, now called Tanzania. Two battalions of Tanganyikan troops arrested some members of the Tanganyikan cabinet, took hostage some fifty British officers attached to the army, seized strategic points throughout the capital city of Dar es Salaam, and participated actively in the rioting that followed. The President of Tanganyika, Julius Nyerere, escaped arrest because his location was not known to the mutineers.

The leaders of the mutiny took pains to declare that they were not attempting to overthrow the government and, in fact, they did not try to establish a rival regime. Rather, their motivation for the action appeared to be grievances concerning promotions, pay, and especially the privileged positions of British officers in the Tanganyikan army (Tanganyika received its independence from Great Britain in 1961). Within days of the mutiny, similar actions took place in Kenya and Uganda, apparently motivated by the same grievances.

These mutinies in Tanganyika, Uganda, and Kenya were suppressed by means of the prompt intervention of British troops. Acting in response to the requests of the three East African governments, all former colonies of Great Britain, and drawing on the sizeable British garrison maintained in Kenya, the British were able to transport forces to the areas of conflict within hours of having been asked to do so. Adding to the effectiveness of the British troops were an aircraft carrier and a destroyer, which fired blank charges at the mutineers. The British actions, and conciliatory political statements made by the beleaguered governments to their armies, succeeded in breaking up the mutinies and restoring order. Following these interventions, steps were taken by the governments to meet the demands of the soldiers, especially the demand that British officers be replaced by Africans.

Although the suppression of these mutinies serves as a powerful example of the efficacy of prompt foreign action in protecting friendly third world regimes, the East African mutinies were not cases of countercoup intervention. The statements made by both the insurgents and by President Nyerere that no coup was intended are supported by the almost apolitical course of the rebellions. This is not to suggest that widespread disorders did not threaten these East African governments. If the mutinies had persisted and if the rumors of communist penetration of the troops had had any validity, the fall of one or more of these regimes may well have occurred. The swift British intervention did not defeat an actual coup, but it did quiet internal disturbances that could have developed into a coup.

Middle East, 1958

American and British policies toward Lebanon, Jordan, and Iraq in the period of the tumultuous summer of 1958 provide another example of the importance of foreign (but not strictly countercoup) intervention for the survival of third world regimes. The central event in the series of American and British interventions and noninterventions that took place at that time was the Iraqi coup of July 14, 1958. The coup ruthlessly removed the pro-Western government of Nuri al Said, replacing it with a radical regime headed by Abdel Karim Kassem. Because it occurred so soon after the merger of Syria and Egypt in February 1958, the new regime's seizure of power caused alarm in its neighbors, in the United States, and in Great Britain, who all feared that a Nasser-backed, pro-communist tide would soon engulf the Middle East.

Lebanon was particularly vulnerable to the effects of the Iraqi coup.[4] Prior to the takeover, Lebanon's delicate political structure had already been disrupted by Nasser's successes in the Middle East. By May 1958, a virtual civil war there threatened the pro-Western government of President Camille Chamoun. In response to a request by President Chamoun, the United States, which had pledged in terms of the Eisenhower Doctrine to defend the Middle East from communist and other threats, agreed to send arms to Lebanon and to move the Sixth Fleet closer to its shores. These efforts to bolster the Lebanese government and end the fighting proved ineffective and Lebanon slipped further into chaos. It became increasingly apparent that some more forceful action by the United States would be needed to protect the Chamoun regime.

At this point the Iraqi coup occurred, and this removed any remaining inhibitions the United States might have held about instituting a direct intervention in Lebanon. Incorrectly viewing the demise of the Iraqi government as part of a pro-Nasser, communist plot, the United States quickly landed some fourteen thousand troops in Lebanon. The purpose of the troops was to calm the Lebanese situation and, should the opportunity present itself, to assist or precipitate a coup in Iraq to restore the old regime. Equally important, the American intervention was designed to demonstrate that the United States could and would act decisively to stem the tide of communism and Nasserism in the area. By intervening in the Middle East, Washington hoped to deter Soviet expansionism there and demonstrate to the nonaligned countries that the United States was a more reliable patron than the USSR.[5]

The first of these goals was achieved. The presence of American troops enabled a compromise president to be elected, which restored peace and stability to Lebanon for a time. The Iraqi countercoup was never attempted, however, because no elements of the old order were left in Baghdad to request outside assistance or to serve as leaders of a new regime. The broader goal of stemming the tide of Nasserism and communism in the area was not met. The Arab regimes in Egypt, Syria, and Iraq were not intimidated by the American intervention into changing their political orientations. With the Lebanese problem solved and the Iraqi problem beyond help, American troops departed Lebanon in November.

The situation that obtained in Jordan at that same time presented many parallels with the situation in Lebanon. Before the Iraqi coup, Jordan's King Hussein, like Lebanon's President Chamoun, had faced an internal challenge that was a result of Nasser's growing influence in the whole region. This internal threat in Jordan worsened in the wake of the Iraqi coup, prompting King Hussein to request troops from Great Britain. Acting in concert with the American intervention in Lebanon, the British rapidly transported paratroopers to Jordan. The British acted for much the same reasons as the United States had in Lebanon— to preserve a pro-Western government, to keep alive the option of intervening in Iraq, and to halt the spread of radicalism in the Arab world. Their action also produced similar results. They succeeded in helping to keep King Hussein in power, but they were also unable to reverse the course of events in Iraq. Having accomplished what they could, the British left Jordan at the same time the United States withdrew from Lebanon.

The American and British interventions in Jordan and Lebanon, and the failure of both of these great powers to reverse the Iraqi coup, should not be considerd as countercoup exercises. The American and British interventions were designed to stabilize a general situation of unrest. Neither in Jordan nor in Lebanon was there a clear, concrete attempted coup. And the decisions of the United States and Great Britain not to intervene in Iraq to reverse the Kassem coup cannot be considered a failure to initiate a countercoup intervention. This was simply not feasible. The purpose of this study, however, is to focus on what happens to countercoup interventions that actually occur.

Dominican Republic, 1965

American intervention in and subsequent military and political involvement in the Dominican Republic represents a third example of a type of foreign action assisting the survival of a third world regime but not an action against a coup d'état.[6] Since the early 1960s, American policy toward the Dominican Republic has sought to prevent the emergence of a pro-Castro regime in that country. Toward that end, the United States first supported the right-wing dictator, Trujillo, and then, when it appeared that Trujillo's rule might generate another Cuba, the United States worked to get rid of him. In May 1961, perhaps with American assistance, Trujillo was assassinated. A little more than a year later, in December 1962, Juan Bosch was freely elected as the president of the Dominican Republic. Although Bosch was not a communist or a disciple of Castro, Bosch's leftist policies of land reform and his toleration of radicals caused him to lose favor with the United States. A military coup overthrew Bosch in September 1963 and he was exiled to Puerto Rico.

A new government under the command of Donald Reid Cabral emerged and quickly won the approval of the United States. The regime was challenged, however, in April 1965, when two army barracks sympathetic to Bosch seized the army's chief of staff and declared their intention to overthrow the government. What started out as a coup soon became a full-fledged rebellion. The insurgents distributed arms to as many as ten thousand sympathizers, mostly lower-class civilians. The armed populace and the rebellious troops together demanded the return of Bosch. The military resisted their call out of the fear that Bosch would undercut their authority by setting up a leftist militia. A major clash between the military and the insurgents began. The latter quickly gained the upper hand.

It was at this point, on April 28, 1965, that the United States intervened. The purpose of the intervention was to deny the rebels a military victory that could lead to the creation of a pro-Cuban government in the Dominican Republic. In addition, the United States sought to establish a hemispheric precedent by means of which collective action could be sought and legitimized for use against Latin American dictatorships. This precedent might then be used to justify a similar action against Castro's Cuba.[7] By May 9 over twenty thousand American troops had arrived in the Dominican Republic. They succeeded in imposing a cease-fire and they assisted in the establishment of a provisional government. Acting under the authority of the Inter-American Peace Force, which was made up overwhelmingly of American troops, the United States stabilized the situation. For the next several months, the United States directly prevented a series of military rebellions and plots from developing into coups by making it clear that Washington would act forcefully against any "illegal" seizures of power.[8] After having satisfied themselves that the Dominican Republic would not lapse into either anarchy or communism, the American forces withdrew.

The American intervention in the Dominican Republic was not a countercoup action as that is defined in this study, because its purpose and effect were not to defeat a coup d'état against an existing regime. By the time the United States decided to intervene, the initial coup had long since been transformed into a full-scale rebellion, involving elements of a real civil war. The American troops were sent not to protect the Dominican Republic from a coup but to quiet an increasingly violent situation. In this purpose, they succeeded admirably. Because of the American intervention, leftist forces were not able to exploit the Dominican Republic's instability to establish a communist regime there and democracy was subsequently restored to a major Caribbean state. The intervention did not, however, lay the basis for an action against Castro.

Sierra Leone, 1971

Another kind of foreign involvement that does not constitute a countercoup intervention occurs when an outside state sends troops to bolster a regime after indigenous forces have already suppressed a coup. This kind of foreign involvement occurred in Sierra Leone in 1971.[9] The Prime Minister of Sierra Leone, Siaka Stevens, had proposed a defense pact with Sekou Touré of Guinea to protect his small, weak country from a wide range of threats. Elements of the Sierra Leonean army, however, saw the proposed treaty as a threat to their own autonomy. Tribal and political grievances had also turned much of the military against Stevens. Because of these resentments, it was not a surprise when, following a trip Stevens made to Guinea to discuss the pact, soldiers of the Sierra Leonean military launched a coup.

The coup began on March 23 when a dissident army major sent a detachment of troops to attack Stevens's home. Stevens managed to flee to his office, which was also being attacked. Fighting quickly spread throughout the capital between the coup makers and the armed forces loyal to Stevens. After a day of violent conflict, Stevens's forces finally managed to suppress the coup. Nevertheless, anti-Stevens feeling among some Sierra Leonean soldiers remained high, and there was doubt as to whether the army would hold together to defeat the next challenge to his regime.

Three days after the abortive coup, Stevens traveled to Guinea, where he hastily concluded a mutual defense treaty, calling on both states to act against "aggression from any quarter." On March 28, some two hundred Guinean soldiers were sent to Sierra Leone, where they formed the guard for Stevens's residence and generally maintained order. As the Cubans and East Germans have done several times,[10] the Guinean soldiers helped to consolidate the defense of a regime that had defeated a coup on its own.

Grenada, 1983

The intervention by the United States in Grenada is a highly visible example of the way a coup can provoke a major public reaction.[11] Following his 1979 coup, Maurice Bishop moved Grenada sharply to the left, intensified its ties with Cuba, and became a major irritant to the United States, as we discussed in Chapter Three. It remained in that condition until October 1983, when an even more radical Marxist-Leninist group overthrew and executed Bishop.

The United States decided to intervene militarily for several reasons. The chaos and bloodshed following the coup presented a potential threat to the over five hundred American medical students who were studying in Grenada. The radicalism of the new regime threatened its neighbors and caused the Organization of East Caribbean States, together with Jamaica and Barbados, to request American assistance to ensure stability in the area. The situation in Grenada also presented an opportunity for the United States to reverse a perceived Cuban gain in the Caribbean—and to do so at an acceptable cost. Moreover, by invading Grenada the Reagan administration would be able to back up its "hard line" rhetoric with concrete action. Finally, the invasion could serve to frighten leftist regimes in Latin America (e.g., Nicaragua and Suriname) into adopting less pro-Cuban/Soviet positions.

The American invasion of Grenada began on October 25, 1983. A force of 1,800 Marines, 700 Army rangers, 1,600 Army paratroopers from the 82nd Airborne, and some 50 Navy SEAL commandos quickly subdued the mostly Cuban opposition and took over the island. Grenada's Governor-General Sir Paul Scoon was placed in charge and he promptly expelled all Libyan and Soviet diplomats from the country, as well as most of the Cubans. After an initial increase in forces, the United States began withdrawing most of its troops from the island, leaving a multinational Caribbean force to perform basic policing duties.[12]

It is possible to characterize the American involvement in Grenada as a defensive action. Once Bishop was overthrown by Deputy Prime Minister Bernard Coard, it could be argued that legal authority had reverted to Governor-General Scoon. By responding to Scoon's request for assistance, the United States was merely protecting the legitimate government of Grenada from Coard's coup.

Grenada, however, is not an appropriate case study for the understanding of the defense of third world regimes from coups. While Scoon may have been technically the legal authority in Grenada following Bishop's ouster, at no time did he wield any power. The American intervention cannot therefore be interpreted as a defense of an existing regime from a coup. Insofar as there was an existing regime at the time of the U.S. invasion, it was the regime backed by Bernard Coard—which Washington overthrew. Moreover, since the Coard government was toppled by forces all of which came from outside Grenada, its overthrow lacks the internal involvement definitionally required of a coup. Grenada is an illustration of an outside invasion forcibly replacing an unfriendly regime with one that meets its interests.

Cases of Countercoup Intervention

There have been at least fourteen cases in the past twenty-five years of outside states acting to defeat actual coups. They include the United States in Ethiopia (1960), in South Korea (1961), in the Dominican Republic (1962), in Laos (1973), and in Bolivia (1984); the Egyptians in Syria (1961); the French in Gabon (1964); the Cubans in Congo-Brazzaville (1966) and Angola (1977); the Egyptians and Libyans in the Sudan (1971); the Syrians in Lebanon (1976); the Soviets, Cubans, East Germans, and Ethiopians in South Yemen (1978); the East Germans in Libya (1980); and the Senegalese in Gambia (1981). In each of these cases, reliable objective evidence demonstrates that an outside state played a critical role in attempting to defend a regime from a coup.

The list in table 1 is not meant to be definitive. Different ways of defining coups (and thus of determining when such coups have been suppressed) result in different cases being included or excluded. The criteria used to constitute evidence of a coup-suppression effort also ac-

Table 1. Foreign Suppression of Third World Coups d'Etat, 1945–1985

Use of Foreign Forces	Material Assistance
Egypt in Syria (1961) (failed)	United States in Ethiopia (1960)
France in Gabon (1964)	United States in the Dominican
Cuba in Congo-Brazzaville (1966)	Republic (1962)
Egypt and Libya in Sudan (1971)	
Syria in Lebanon (1976)	*Advice and Encouragement*
Cuba in Angola (1977)	United States in South Korea (1961)
USSR, East Germany, Cuba, and	(failed)
Ethiopia in South Yemen (1978)	United States in Laos (1973)
East Germany in Libya (1980)	United States in Bolivia (1984)
Senegal in Gambia (1981)	

Note: Included here are only those cases for which there is public and convincing evidence of significant foreign involvement to suppress a coup. Where several policies were employed to defeat a coup, the principal means was used to categorize the coup-suppression effort.

count for a particular compilation of illustrative cases. In addition, some cases may have been overlooked. Coups also of course are carried out covertly, and some have never been confirmed by public sources. Obtaining reliable information about Soviet and Soviet bloc coups is particularly difficult because of the secrecy that surrounds such events. Conversely, the relative openness that surrounds American efforts in that direction probably exaggerates the role the United States plays in defeating coups as compared to other countries. Nevertheless, while this list may not be all-inclusive, the cases I present here represent a reasonably comprehensive collection of foreign countercoup efforts.

In order to gain an understanding of why and how actions to suppress coups are launched, and what accounts for their success or failure, several of these cases will be examined in detail. The cases selected for detailed study are Ethiopia in 1960, Gabon in 1964, Congo-Brazzaville in 1966, the Sudan in 1971, Gambia in 1981, and a failed attempt of foreign coup suppression, Syria in 1961.

These cases were selected for several reasons. First, these cases were not dealt with in other chapters. The Cuban suppression of the 1977 coup in Angola and the Soviet suppression of the coup in South Yemen were examined in Chapter Three. Second, the major details of the coup-suppression efforts in each of these cases have been made public. Instead of having to rely on rumors or conjecture, enough reliable information is available for us to be able to reconstruct what actually occurred. A lack of reliable, detailed information precluded the inclusion in this study of the East German suppression of a coup in Libya (1980) and of the Syrian defeat of a coup in Lebanon (1976). In the East German case, the Ninth Army Brigade in Libya apparently launched a coup in August 1980. The coup attempt was led by the Libyan head of intelligence for the eastern section of the country. East German advisors reportedly helped to suppress the coup, which resulted in four hundred people being killed. Although it cannot be confirmed, French intelligence may have supported the coup because of Libyan attacks on the French embassy in Tripoli and its support of an armed incursion into Tunisia several months before. A senior official of the French intelligence service resigned in the autumn, supposedly because of the failed Libyan coup.[13]

In the other case, Syrian forces reportedly defeated a coup against Lebanese President Franjiyya in January 1976. The coup was launched by Muslim soldiers who seceded from the Lebanese army and were led by Lieutenant Ahmad al-Khatib. Khatib sought to depose President Franjiyya, a Christian, and replace him with a radical Muslim leadership. The Syrians, who have had forces in Lebanon since 1975, protected Franjiyya because they feared a radical Muslim state would be difficult to control and might provoke an Israeli attack. Due to these Syrian efforts, Franjiyya remained in office until the end of his term in September 1976.[14]

Finally, these specific or particular cases were selected because they illustrate the broad range of methods used by outside states to protect foreign regimes from coups. The American protection of the regime in Ethiopia demonstrated that enabling a leader traveling abroad to communicate with his military forces and providing advice to loyalist forces can help to suppress a major coup. The French in Gabon demonstrated the value of a prompt intervention using troops from outside the country for defeating a coup. The successful action of the Cubans in Congo-Brazzaville illustrated the importance of maintaining military advisors in a country that could be the target of a coup. The Sudanese case of 1971 showed how two countries (Libya and Egypt) can cooperate in defeating a coup by preventing its leaders from reaching the country and by transporting foreign and indigenous troops to the capital. The Senegalese effort in Gambia showed the way neighboring third world countries with treaties providing for mutual internal as well as external defense can protect each other from coups. Finally, the events in Syria showed some of the ways a foreign countercoup effort may fail.

These cases collectively demonstrate the effectiveness of rapid foreign assistance in defending third world regimes from coups. They also illustrate the ability of these regimes to survive long after the foreign presence has departed. Most important, these cases demonstrate that the outcome of coups is at times determined not by the state in which it takes place, but by the actions of foreign parties.

This examination and analysis of the cases of foreign countercoup intervention is divided into two broad parts. First, the facts of each case are summarized. A brief background of the country will be given, including the political environment preceding the coup attempt, why the coup was initiated, who was behind it, the details of the actual coup, the reaction of the existing government to it, and the role of foreign forces in trying to defeat the coup. Although not all of these details in each case study are directly related to the coup-suppression effort, they are essential in understanding the context in which it took place.

The second part of the analysis considers the lessons that can be learned from these cases. This evaluation includes the various forms that countercoup interventions can take, when direct military intervention is required, what accounted for the successes and failures of these countercoup interventions, the importance of the mistakes made by the coup makers to the outcomes, and how third world states can better defend themselves against coups.

Ethiopia, 1960

Ethiopia in 1960 appeared to be one of the most stable African states. Founded on a fertile plateau surrounded by desert and wasteland, Ethiopia's origins can be traced back thousands of years before Christ, making it the oldest black African state. Its leader, the Emperor Haile Selassie, had been in power since 1930 and enjoyed the continuing support of the aristocrats, the Ethiopian Orthodox Church, and the military. Virtually untouched by the colonial powers and enjoying a close relationship with the United States, Ethiopia showed itself apparently an exception to the fragility of its newly emerging neighbors.

Underneath its facade of stability, however, Ethiopia faced enormous difficulties. Its 20 million people (in 1960) were desperately poor and divided among a multiplicity of hostile religious and ethnic groups. Even more significant was the growing resentment felt by a group of young, foreign-educated Ethiopians at the near-total control of the country exercised by the Emperor. Led by two brothers, one a provincial governor and the other the commander of the Imperial Bodyguard, this group decided to overthrow Haile Selassie and the anachronistic system they believed he perpetuated.

The coup was launched on December 13, 1960, while the Emperor was on a state visit to West Africa and South America. It met with immediate success. Most of the Ethiopian leadership were lured to the Imperial Palace and subsequently placed in custody. Soon afterwards, Imperial Guard units fanned out to strategic points in Addis Ababa, putting much of the capital under the control of the rebels by the morning of December 14. On that day, the crown prince and presumed successor to Haile Selassie was forced to announce the proclamation of a new government.

The announcement proved to be premature. As the coup unfolded, several high officials loyal to the Emperor who had escaped the initial sweep were planning to defeat the insurgents. The personal intervention of the Emperor and the prompt organization of an effective loyalist counterattack were both crucial for the success of their countercoup. In both of these areas, American assistance would prove to be very important.

Haile Selassie learned of the coup on December 14, while he was traveling in Brazil. Just how he learned about it so quickly, despite a telecommunications cut-off from Ethiopia by the rebels, is still not clear. Different reports attribute the responsibility for this intelligence to Israel, to the United States, and to Britain.[15] Whatever the source of his information, the Emperor immediately left for home, stopping en route in Liberia on December 15. In Liberia, the United States placed an elaborate communications network at the Emperor's disposal, enabling him to speak directly to his generals in Ethiopia. This communications link proved invaluable because it enabled Haile Selassie personally to speak with the military in his country and provided him with the latest information on the progress of the countercoup.[16]

At the time when the Emperor was being appraised of the situation, pro–Haile Selassie forces were already acting to blunt the impact of the coup. The air force distributed leaflets promising a salary increase to all members of the military and reminding them of their duty to support the Emperor. The air force also set up a clandestine broadcasting facility, which announced (prematurely) that the Emperor had returned and that he sought the support of the Ethiopian people.

The leaflets and the broadcast had an immediate effect. Many of the Imperial Guardsmen realized for the first time that they were not fighting to defend the Emperor, as they had been told, but against him. Some of the coup leaders now began to recognize that the struggle to replace the Emperor could no longer be kept peaceful and that it might not succeed. Many guardsmen and some of their leaders abandoned their posts. The largely dormant Ethiopian population, sensing the changing tide of events, began to side actively with the loyalists.[17]

The success of the countercoup was, however, far from assured. Key loyalist forces (especially in the air force) held off from active support of Haile Selassie until they had determined which side would emerge triumphant. At this critical point, the involvement of foreign agents again proved critical to the loyalists' cause. While the air force pilots wasted precious time deciding whether to act, General von Lindhal, a Swedish advisor to the Ethiopian air force, ordered the pilots in no uncertain terms to back the Emperor.[18] His action paved the way for a massive transport operation, which flew nearly one thousand Ethiopian troops to a base near the capital where they reinforced existing loyalist forces.

In the final attack on the rebel positions in the capital, foreign assistance again proved critical. As the coup unfolded, the U.S. ambassador tried in vain to get a clear indication from Washington as to what American personnel should do. Following a request by the loyalist Ethiopian chief of staff to an American military advisor for military assistance, the U.S. ambassador decided to act on his own authority. Since Haile Selassie's regime represented the last American-recognized government in Ethiopia, the U.S. ambassador agreed to allow American military advisors to assist in the planning of the countercoup.[19] Aerial photographs of the rebel positions and telecommunications equipment were provided. In addition, an American advisor to the Ethiopian air force established a communications network between the loyalist army and air force, permitting the coordination of their assault. When Ethiopian pilots again balked at flying combat missions against the rebels, another American advisor taunted them into attacking, going so far as to threaten to have Americans fly the planes. These and other actions prompted the speculation that American pilots flew missions against the coup makers.[20] At the very least, American efforts did persuade the Ethiopian air force to attack the rebels with such effectiveness that the Ethiopian chief of staff subsequently noted, "At least 75 percent of the battle against the abortive coup d'état was won by the air force."[21]

The combined air and ground assault routed the rebel forces. Before being defeated, however, they murdered fifteen Ethiopian dignitaries. Those rebels who were not killed or captured fled into the countryside. Haile Selassie returned to Addis Ababa, where he received an enthusiastic welcome as he rode from the airport to the Imperial Palace. Riding ahead of the Emperor, sitting in an open jeep with the commander of the Ethiopian air force, was an American military advisor.[22]

Gabon, 1964

Located in western Africa, with a population of 440,000 (in 1964) and an area of 102,240 square miles, Gabon is the smallest country in French equatorial Africa. Colonized by the French in the latter part of the nineteenth century, Gabon became internally self-governing in 1958 and achieved full independence within the French community in

1960. Never a major power in Africa, Gabon's chief points of distinction have been its major deposits of strategic minerals, including manganese and uranium and the fame it achieved as the site of Dr. Albert Schweitzer's hospital.

The first president of Gabon was Leon Mba, who headed the Democratic Bloc Party. Mba's main opposition came from Jean-Hilaire Aubame, the leader of the rival Democratic and Social Union Party. One of the chief points of contention between the two parties involved the amount of influence France would continue to wield in Gabon. Generally, Mba accepted a high number of important French officials in the Gabonese government, while Aubame pushed for more "Africanization" of the regime and for less economic dependence on France.[23]

The two parties, which were of nearly equal strength, ruled Gabon as a coalition. That arrangement broke down in February 1963, forcing Aubame into the opposition. Mba then consolidated his control by establishing a one-party state, led by himself, with only his followers allowed to stand for election.

The prospect of a meaningless election perpetuating the increasingly autocratic rule of Mba galvanized his opponents into action. On the night of February 17, 1964, just six days before the proposed election, a group of army and police officers with at least the tacit support of Aubame took over the capital of Libreville without casualties. President Mba was arrested and imprisoned at a nearby army barracks. Aubame assumed the leadership of a hastily formed government.[24]

At this point, the coup appeared to be a success. Without any bloodshed, Mba's regime had been overthrown and all potential Gabonese opposition neutralized. Life in Libreville carried on as usual, with only the presence of armed guards at public buildings serving as an indication of the coup. For Gabon and much of the rest of the world, the change in leadership quickly became an accepted fact.

This was not the case, however, as regards the French. They did not look kindly on the prospect of a new regime taking power in Gabon. In part this was because the French government had signed a secret treaty with Gabon in May 1961, obliging it to act if the president was in any way threatened. The French also saw the Gabonese coup as narrowly based and thus as easy to suppress. Finally, President de Gaulle did not want an anti-French government emerging in a country that possessed needed strategic minerals.

The French decided to act immediately upon learning of the coup. On February 18, 1964, the first French troops, accompanied by African mercenaries, flew to the unguarded Libreville airport from bases in the Congo and Senegal. In Gabon, they reinforced the existing French garrison of 150 troops. Although the French later claimed they had intervened only at the request of the Gabonese vice-president, this appears to be untrue, because at the time of the French action, the vice-president was off campaigning in a remote part of Gabon.[25]

Once in Gabon the French quickly entered the capital, which fell to them without resistance. The next morning they launched a combined air (mostly for psychological effect) and ground attack on the army barracks, bringing about their prompt surrender. Casualties on both sides were minimal, with one French soldier and eighteen Gabonese reported killed. Realizing that they were defeated, the Gabonese turned President Mba over to the French unharmed. He was restored to the presidency, where he remained until his death from natural causes in 1967.[26]

Congo-Brazzaville, 1966

Situated on the equator in west central Africa, Congo-Brazzaville has a population of some 900,000 people (in 1966), spread out over an area of 135,000 square miles. It is a poor country that lacks major resources and derives its principal wealth from agriculture. Aside from its strategic location bordering several states, including Zaire and Angola, Congo-Brazzaville is mostly noteworthy for its revolutionary zeal and its close friendship with major communist nations.

Following the granting of full independence from the French in 1960, Congo-Brazzaville, then called the Republic of the Congo, adopted a moderate foreign policy, aligning itself with the West. This changed in 1963 when a new government under Alphonse Massamba-Debat came to power. Although he himself was a moderate, President Massamba-Debat was forced by radical elements in his government to pursue leftist policies. Massamba-Debat responded by proclaiming the advent of "scientific socialism" and by establishing a militant youth wing of the country's ruling party called the Youth of the National Revolutionary Movement (JMNR). Driven by ideological fervor, the JMNR attempted to extend government control over all aspects of Congolese life, including the Catholic Church. The power of this militant faction increased markedly in early 1964, when President Massamba-Debat formed a people's militia, called the Civilian Defense Corps, consisting mostly of militant members of the JMNR.[27]

President Massamba-Debat's plans for a militia meshed well with Cuban leader Fidel Castro's strategies for Africa. Castro had been unhappy when two of Cuba's closest allies in Africa—Algeria's Ben Bella and Ghana's Kwame N'krumah—were overthrown by military coups. Not only did Castro lose two important friends, he also lost the only guerrilla training bases Cuba maintained in Africa to assist revolutionary movements. Castro acted quickly to reestablish such a base in Congo-Brazzaville. This time Castro wanted to make certain that a coup would not again reverse Cuba's gains. Since "reactionary" armed forces had caused the previous reverses, Castro decided that the solution to safeguarding the government of President Massamba-Debat lay in creating a military power stronger than the existing armed forces. The development of a militia made up of the young "true believers" of the JMNR appeared to meet this need.[28]

By mid-1965, approximately 250 Cuban military advisors were in Congo-Brazzaville, training the new militia. This was the first time that Cuban forces had been sent abroad for this purpose. Cuban advisors also served directly as bodyguards to President Massamba-Debat and helped to develop for him a special presidential guard detachment.[29]

With Cuban training and Soviet weaponry, the militia soon rivaled the strength of the regular armed forces. Instead of being a ragtag voluntary group, militia members began drawing a salary and they were then housed in barracks. They proudly proclaimed themselves to be the sole protector of the revolution and openly scorned the "colonialist" army and police.[30]

The resentment of the regular armed forces over the militia's increasing power and political attacks came to a head in June 1966. President Massamba-Debat issued a decree setting up a "collective" command of the military and establishing a political department to indoctrinate all of the troops in Marxist-Leninist thought.[31] These actions threatened to further diminish the influence of several Congolese army officers, among them the popular Captain Marien Ngoubi. When Captain Ngoubi was transferred to a remote post, in anticipation of his opposition, several hundred of his supporters marched to protest. They demanded his reinstatement and sacked the building housing the governmental headquarters. On June 27, 1966, three days after the demonstration, the army launched its coup.

Under the apparent command of Captain Ngoubi, the Congolese army quickly took control of Brazzaville. Encountering little resistance, they took up strategic points throughout the city, set up regular patrols, and established a curfew. With President Massamba-Debat in Madagascar attending a conference, all that remained for the coup makers to do was to neutralize the remaining senior officials of the government. This appeared to be a relatively easy task, because the regime's leadership had all taken refuge in the Brazzaville sports stadium.

The coup makers, however, failed to consider the role of Cubans. While the coup unfolded in Brazzaville, the Cuban-trained presidential guard and militia and several black Cuban advisors themselves protected the gathered government officials. For three days, while the Congolese army had total control of the area surrounding the stadium, the Cubans and their Congolese supporters prevented the army from entering the stadium. Although the Congolese army probably could have overpowered the Cuban guard, they chose not to. No doubt, the presence of Cuban advisors elsewhere in Africa, as well as the prospect of confronting a major third world military power, deterred the army from making an attack.

With the leadership protected and the Cubans holding firm, the coup collapsed. President Massamba-Debat returned to power, publicly praising the Cubans for their role. In the next few months, the Cuban presence was increased to one thousand men. Two years later, however, Massamba-Debat lost the presidency in a power struggle unrelated to the Cuban presence. The number of Cuban forces was subsequently reduced, although a small contingent of advisors remained to train Angolan troops. Despite the Cuban withdrawal, the presidential guard and militia remained as counterpoints to the army and as guarantors of the country's leftist orientation.

The Sudan, 1971

Comprising an area of nearly a million square miles, the Sudan is the largest country in Africa. Its population of nearly 15 million (in 1971) is approximately two-thirds Arab, living mostly in the north, and one-third negroid, living mostly in the south. The Sudan achieved full independence in 1956 following a half-century of joint British and Egyptian rule. After independence, the Sudan faced enormous problems, including an ongoing civil war, a deteriorating economy, and continuing political instability.

Responding to these mounting difficulties, a Sudanese colonel, Gaafar al-Numeiry, seized power in a bloodless coup in 1969. Lacking education and politically inexperienced, Numeiry turned to the large, well-organized Sudanese Communist Party for assistance. The Communists had long sought to rule the Sudan, and they were delighted to have the opportunity to join the government. At first, Numeiry and the Communists were able to cooperate, but gradually it became clear that the Communists aimed to supplant the Sudanese leader. Numeiry responded with a massive purge of the Communists, including many high officials in his government.

Numeiry's actions hastened the Communists' plans for a coup d'état.[32] Realizing that they were running out of time, the Communists struck on July 19, 1971. Sudanese troops made up of elements of the Presidential Guard and the regular army entered Khartoum behind a column of tanks and rapidly seized control of the Sudanese capital. Numeiry and his supporters were placed under armed guard. In a few hours, without resistance or casualties, the two-year-old government of Numeiry had seemingly come to an end.

The good fortune of the insurgents began to change, however, when it became clear to the people because of statements the new leaders made on domestic and foreign policy that the new government would follow a Communist line.[33] In the Sudan itself, latent anti-Communist sentiment became aroused, particularly among the traditionally conservative officer corps. This anti-Communist feeling was shared by the leaders of Sudan's two largest neighbors—Libya's Muammar Khadaffi and Egypt's Anwar Sadat. Despite the apparently successful conclusion of the coup, these anti-Communist forces united in a *de facto* alliance to suppress the new government of the insurgents and to reinstate Numeiry.

The Libyans acted first. After the apparent overthrow of the Numeiry government, two of the leaders of the coup based in Britain boarded a BOAC jetliner to return to the Sudan. When the jet entered Libyan air space, it was ordered to land in Libya or be shot down. After the British pilot complied with the demand, Libyan security officials removed the two Sudanese plotters from the aircraft, thus depriving the coup of some of its most needed leaders at a most critical time.[34]

Egypt played an even more important role in defeating the coup. As soon as Numeiry was placed in custody, Sadat sent an Egyptian delegation to the Sudan to ensure his safety. This gesture may very well have saved the president's life. Sadat then turned his attention to a Sudanese brigade stationed at the Suez Canal. Correctly concluding that the Egyptian-based Sudanese brigade would not have been included in the coup machinations, Sadat allowed the Sudanese defense minister (who was outside of the Sudan at the time of the coup) to assume command of the Sudanese troops in Egypt. On July 22, just three days after the coup began, the Egyptians airlifted portions of the loyal Sudanese brigade to a base near Khartoum.

The arrival of the Sudanese canal brigade coincided with a counterattack mounted by loyalist troops and tanks manned by Egyptian personnel stationed in the Sudan.[35] Encountering little resistance, the troops overcame the rebel forces in the capital. In the ensuing confusion, Numeiry escaped his guards and joined the loyalist forces. He then went on television and radio, where he declared the coup defeated. Under Numeiry's personal command, the last remnants of the rebel forces either surrendered or were killed.

Once firmly back in power, Numeiry accused the Soviet bloc countries of complicity in the coup. It is clear that the Soviets—with over one thousand military advisors in the Sudan—could scarcely have overlooked the military preparations for the coup. Reports of the Soviets delaying the Sudanese troops trying to suppress the coup, the Soviets' immediate recognition of the new government, and the known Soviet sympathy for the Sudanese Communist Party all lend credibility to Numeiry's charges.[36] Following the abortive coup, Numeiry ordered the recall of the Sudanese ambassador from the USSR, expelled several Soviet diplomats, and turned the Sudan away from the pro-Moscow drift that had existed since he had assumed the presidency. Numeiry remained in power for fourteen more years. In 1985 he was deposed by a coup that apparently involved no foreign or communist elements.

Gambia, 1981

With an area of 4,000 square miles and a population of about 500,000 people (in 1981), Gambia is one of the smallest and least populous states in Africa.[37] Surrounded by its much larger neighbor, Senegal, Gambia has not played a major political or economic role in Africa since achieving independence from Great Britain in 1965. Gambia is distinctive among African countries, however, by virtue of its relatively stable political existence, its lack of a standing army, and its democratic form of government.

During the early 1980s, Gambia's reputation for democracy and stability began to erode. The government of President Dawda Jawara faced mounting charges of corruption and nepotism. The already poor Gambian people were forced to endure greater hardships as a prolonged drought caused food shortages. Reacting perhaps to the worsening economic situation, members of a leftist Gambian political party, with suspected Libyan backing, attempted to overthrow the president in October 1981. With the assistance of 150 paratroopers from Senegal, the attempt was defeated. Nevertheless, many of the insurgents and even more important the conditions that had spurred them into action remained as constant threats to the government.

These threats erupted on July 30, 1981, while President Jawara was in England attending the wedding of Prince Charles. Several hundred insurgents stormed the capital city, closed off the border, shut off telecommunications links, and distributed weapons from a captured armory to hundreds of criminals they released from prison. Many hostages were taken, including foreigners and the president's wife and children.

The rebel forces included members of Gambia's paramilitary field force, which made up approximately one-third of Gambia's nine-hundred-man police force. Their apparent leader was an avowed Marxist, a supporter of Libya, and a member of the Gambian Revolutionary Socialist Party that had been banned in the wake of the failed October uprising against the government. According to its leader, the purpose of the coup was to establish "a dictatorship of the proletariat."

At first it appeared that the coup might succeed. The Gambian people enthusiastically welcomed the prospect of a new government as a possible solution for their economic plight. The Gambian police force was in disarray and it lacked the strength to resist a determined effort. With the president out of the country, there was no legitimate authority around which the disparate anti-coup forces could rally. The replacement of a pro-Western, democratic African government with a regime backed by Libya appeared to be a real possibility.

It was in this context that Senegal intervened to quash the coup d'état. Senegal justified its intervention by citing a request for assistance it had received from President Jawara, who flew to Senegal upon hearing of the coup. The Senegalese also cited as justification the mutual defense treaty between the two countries and the Senegalese president's belief that the rebels were "foreign-trained and equipped." Whatever the justifications, Senegal reacted quickly, sending troops to Gambia the very afternoon of the coup. While the Senegalese could not wrest control of the capital from the rebels immediately, their prompt intervention prevented the quick victory sought by the insurgents. The delay they caused provided time for the Gambian people—who were angered by the looting and violence of the released prisoners—to turn against the rebels they had initially supported.

After three days of fierce fighting, the Senegalese troops, who now numbered over one thousand, forced the coup makers out of the capital city of Banjul. The president immediately returned to the capital from Senegal. The Senegalese forces continued to drive back the rebels, although their progress was slowed by strong resistance and by their concern for the hostages. Finally, on August 5, 1981, the rebels were expelled from their last stronghold and fled into the bush. The hostages, perhaps with the help of British commandos, were rescued unharmed.

The cost of suppressing this coup was high. Estimates of the civilian dead range from 500 to 2,000. The Senegalese reported casualties of 236 wounded and ten dead. Despite the costs, the success of the Senegalese action can hardly be questioned. President Jawara was restored to power and close ties between Gambia and Senegal were resumed. In fact, in the wake of the coup attempt, the Gambian leader opened negotiations with Senegal with the goal of eventually uniting the two countries. Of equal importance was the positive reaction to Senegal's action by its neighboring African states. Rejecting the view that Senegal's intervention was interference in another country's internal affairs, expressions of support were forthcoming from most of the African countries. Of special note were the approvals of Tanzania's Julius Nyerere; the chairman of the Organization of African Unity, Kenyan President Daniel arap Moi; and the leader of Guinea-Bissau—the country the rebels had turned to for assistance.

Syria, 1961: The Countercoup Intervention That Failed

Located in the heart of the Middle East, with a population of some six million people (in 1961) and an area of 71,647 square miles, Syria has long been a pivotal country in the Arab world. In the decades following its achievement of independence from the French in 1941, other Arab states and the great powers have all vied for Syrian approval for their various plans and strategies regarding the conflict with Israel, pan-Arabism, and the cold war. In part, this competition has been due to Syrian strength. As a major Arab state with a relatively strong army and a dynamic ideology emphasizing Arab nationalism, Syria giving its support is an essential part of any state or power seeking influence in the Middle East. The competition for Syrian approval also reflects its weakness. Because of chronic political instability, Syria has been particularly vulnerable to the pressures and passing political currents of the Middle East.

It was this political instability that led the Syrian leadership in the latter part of 1957 and the beginning of 1958 to seek a union with Egypt. At this time, the leading party in Syria, the Nationalist Ba'ath Party, feared that growing communist influence in their country would result either in a pro-Soviet coup or in a closer political alignment with the hated West.[38] By placing Syria under the charismatic leadership of Egypt's Gamal Abdel Nasser, the Ba'ath leadership believed that the communist threat could be neutralized and that Syria at the same time would be placed in the vanguard of the Arab nationalist movement. To Nasser, the union of the two very different and noncontiguous states seemed to be premature at best, but as the leading advocate of pan-Arabism, he could not deny Syria's request. Consequently, after ordering the Syrians to dissolve their political parties and to keep their army out of politics, Nasser agreed to the union of the two countries in February 1958.

Nasser's concern over the viability of the union between the two countries was not ill-founded. The Syrians proved more difficult to govern than the Egyptians. The middle and upper classes in Syria were especially resentful of the currency controls, increased taxes, and nationalizations of major businesses that came with Egyptian rule. Equally important, the Syrian military did not like taking orders from Egyptians and opposed having their pay reduced to Egyptian levels. In sum, the Syrians were different from the Egyptians, and they did not like being relegated to second-class status in their own country.[39]

In response to these concerns and to increasing Egyptian repression, Syrian military officers began planning a coup in January 1961. At that time, a small group of officers with the ranks of major up to brigadier general began to initiate contacts with disgruntled business interests in Damascus. The businessmen were all too happy to declare their support for any action that would end Nasser's economic policies. The Syrian officers also received a promise of asylum in Jordan should the coup fail.

The coup began in the early hours of September 28, 1961. From the Kataneh barracks just north of Damascus, twenty rebel tanks supported by two battalions of infantry seized the capital at dawn. Almost immediately and with virtually no resistance the Damascus radio, telegraph, post office, and Ministry of Defense fell to the rebels. Most important, the Syrian forces were able to overpower the Egyptian guards at the residence of Abdel Amer, the Nasser-appointed head of Syria, and they took him into their custody. The coup makers then demanded that Amer reverse some of Nasser's key policies. Amer asked for and received permission to telephone Nasser for instructions.

During the telephone conversation, Nasser reportedly asked what opposition existed to the Syrian action. When he was told that there were pro-Egyptian elements, many of them Egyptian military officers, in the Syrian cities of Aleppo and Latakia, Nasser decided that the coup could be defeated. He told Amer to stall the coup makers but not to give in to their demands. Since Damascus appeared to be firmly in rebel hands, Nasser, on the very day the coup was launched, decided to send troops to the Syrian port of Latakia. The Egyptian merchant fleet was commandeered to serve as troop transports and the air force was ordered to fly two thousand paratroopers to Latakia. Once there, this force was to join with the five thousand Egyptian troops already stationed in Syria and with pro-Egyptian Syrian troops in order to end the coup.[40]

This countercoup launched by Nasser turned out to be a complete failure. Syrian military units refused to obey orders issued by Nasser to suppress the coup. More important, Nasser's attempts to send his own forces into Syria proved to be a fiasco. Some 100–150 Egyptian troops were airlifted to Latakia, where they briefly engaged Syrian forces. The outnumbered Egyptian troops were quickly surrounded and captured.

With few options left to him, Nasser suspended the remainder of the countercoup operation and, in effect, allowed Syria to secede from the United Arab Republic. Approximately fifty deaths were reported for both sides.[41]

Following his cancellation of the countercoup, Nasser gave up all claims to Syria as part of the United Arab Republic. A new government took power in Syria and promptly reversed many of Nasser's policies. Egypt and Syria exchanged bitter radio messages but no military actions developed between them. The United States, happy with any development that hurt Nasser, promptly recognized the new government.

Lessons and Conclusions

As these case studies demonstrate, direct foreign involvements to defend friendly regimes from coups d'état can take several forms. First there is the direct intervention of foreign troops in response to a coup. The French intervention in Gabon, the Senegalese intervention in Gambia, the Egyptian intervention in the Sudan, and the abortive Egyptian intervention in Syria are all examples of this kind of intervention. Although they were not precisely countercoup operations, the British intervention in East Africa and the American interventions in the Dominican Republic and in Grenada also demonstrate the effectiveness of direct foreign intervention in response to coups.

The use of foreign troops already deployed in a third world country can also be used to put down coups arising in that country. Cuban troops based in Congo-Brazzaville played a key role in defeating the coup against the regime of President Massamba-Debat, and these kinds of foreign forces also helped suppress coups in Angola and South Yemen. Egyptian forces stationed in the Sudan proved essential for defending President Numeiry from a leftist coup. In addition, Syrian forces in Lebanon defeated a coup by radical Muslim forces against President Franjiyya in January 1976 and East German advisors helped suppress a coup in Libya in 1980. Third, military advisors in a third world country can bring a great influence to bear on the armed forces they are assisting. American advisors did a great deal to provoke the Ethiopian military to defeat a coup launched by the Imperial Guard. The Cuban-trained militia and presidential guard played a critical role in safeguarding the Marxist-Leninist regime in Congo-Brazzaville. Finally, American diplomats played key roles in defeating coups in the Dominican Republic (1962), in Laos (1973), and in Bolivia (1984). This type of countercoup involvement is especially attractive because it is the least costly politically.[42]

These case studies also illustrate indirect ways by which foreign involvements have defended third world regimes from coups. In the Ethiopian case, communication facilities provided by the United States allowed senior officials of the threatened regime to rally the military on their behalf. Because many coups occur when a country's leader is out of the country, this type of assistance is important in enabling the head of state or his representative to communicate with his supporters. The leadership can then reassert its authority and assist in the planning of the countercoup. Providing transport for foreign troops is another indirect way outside forces have helped to defeat coups. Many third world states lack the logistical means for sending troops rapidly to the site of an attempted coup. As demonstrated by the Egyptian airlift of Sudanese troops of Khartoum, such assistance can be critical for successfully defending a regime against one.

Because there are many ways by which states can assist other states in the suppression of coups, it is reasonable to ask why the drastic action of taking direct military intervention is ever the correct choice of policy. After all, the consequences of the failure of a direct military intervention are visible, serious, and not easily forgotten by the new regime that takes power. Not surprisingly, direct intervention was in fact only undertaken in three of the cases we studied, one of which failed; the other countercoups relied on less risky actions.

When direct intervention was undertaken, it proved to be the only choice available for saving a threatened regime. The use of diplomats, military advisors, or other indirect forms of assistance to help a regime defeat a coup are acceptable, so long as any or all of these policies are capable of accomplishing their purposes. In those cases where such policies are precluded, because no military advisors are present in the threatened country, or they are not sufficient, and foreign diplomatic pressures might not influence the coup makers, direct military intervention is required. In those cases in which direct military intervention was employed—Gabon, Syria, and Gambia—it is difficult to conceive of any alternative policy that had a reasonable chance of succeeding in defending the regime against the coup.

The cases we studied illustrate also the way foreign efforts at coup suppression can be directed at several types of coups. The Senegalese intervention in Gambia was provoked by a breakthrough coup that threatened to place a radical, anti-Western government on the border of the intervening state. Fear of a breakthrough coup also helped to account for the U.S. direct involvement in defense of Haile Selassie in Ethiopia. In the Sudan, the attempt by communists to carry out a radicalizing coup to replace Numeiry with a Marxist-Leninist regime brought about the Libyan and Egyptian coup-suppression operations. Syrian forces successfully carried out a veto coup to stem the rising tide of Egyptian influence in their country, despite Nasser's attempts to suppress their efforts. In the Congo, the regular army attempted a veto coup in order to diminish the control of Marxist-Leninist elements, but they failed, largely due to the actions of Cuban advisors. In each of these cases, the critical determinant of the nature and extent of foreign involvement was not the type of coup, but the recognition that its success would threaten the interests of some outside power.

The success of five out of six of these cases of foreign countercoups was due to several factors. In all of the cases we have discussed, the leader of the existing regime survived the coup attempt. Even in the most coup-prone states, the actual leader retains a certain measure of legitimacy and commands some degree of loyalty among both the people and the military. If that leader, or an accepted or designated successor, is not entirely removed from the scene, doubts will linger as to whether the old order has indeed been destroyed. These doubts inhibit mass defections to the coup makers, depriving them of the "bandwagon" effect they so desperately need. In this atmosphere of confusion and indecision, a strong sign from the head of state or his representative that the regime is still in power (e.g., a radio broadcast) can effectively mobilize latent popular and military support, which could spell the difference between success and failure for the coup. The roles played by Ethiopia's Haile Selassie and Sudan's Gaafar al-Numeiry are clear examples of the importance for defeating coups of keeping the existing leadership alive.

Successful countercoup interventions were also marked by the speed of their responses. As all of these case studies have shown, the first few days—or even the first few hours—of a coup are crucial to its success or failure. It is during this time that supporters, opponents, and those who have not committed themselves try to determine which side has the balance of power in its favor. It is necessary for defendants of the existing regime to make clear at the earliest possible time that the backers of the coup have not achieved a *de facto* victory and that organized resistance in defense of the existing regime still remains alive. In all of the cases of successful countercoups we studied, the actions of the defenders of the regime were taken immediately, as soon as the coup became known. Responsive actions were taken often within hours of the threatened overthrow. In the face of such actions, the coups were unable to develop the crucial momentum necessary for their success.

There were other factors that contributed to the success of these foreign countercoups. In several of the cases—Sudan, Gabon, and Gambia—tacit or formal agreements existed calling formally for foreign assistance in the event of a coup. These understandings facilitated and legitimized the interventions that followed the coups in those countries. Moreover, such agreements can assist a regime in consolidating its gains, once a coup has been suppressed. The quick conclusion of a mutual defense treaty with the more powerful state of Guinea enabled the leader of Sierra Leone to hold on to power in the wake of a major coup attempt there. In addition, many of the actions taken to defeat these coups were operations launched from states that had a detailed knowledge of the conditions of the country they were assisting. This knowledge had been gained through previous colonial rule in some instances, like France and Gabon, perhaps Britain and Gambia, or by means of a military presence in the country, like the United States in Ethiopia, or Cuba in Congo-Brazzaville.

Geographical proximity also played a role in successful efforts to counter coups. Most third world states lack the logistical capability to project force over long distances. Only when they share a border with a country undergoing a coup can direct intervention by an interested third world country become a fully viable and effective policy choice, as happened with Egypt and the Sudan, and Senegal and Gambia. The leaders of the outside state assisting the regime faced with a coup must be aware of the political loyalties of the coup makers and backers. This knowledge changes what might have been paralysis and indecision into rapid, effective reactions.

The lone failure among the countercoups we considered in detail also provides valuable lessons for future involvements.[43] Tactically, Egypt's actions proved incapable of reversing the Syrian coup because the coup makers controlled most of the country's airports and the port of Latakia. Because Egypt and Syria share no common border, it was very difficult for Nasser to undertake any large-scale intervention. Nor were the Egyptian forces stationed in Syria much help to Nasser. Because they were largely intermingled with the much more numerous Syrian troops, independent action by the Egyptians as cohesive fighting units proved to be impossible. Moreover, inasmuch as the Syrian army controlled most of the United Arab Republic's armor in Syria, actions taken by the Egyptian troops probably would not have succeeded in reversing the coup, even if they could have been undertaken.

Most important, although Nasser initiated his countercoup operations at a time when the Syrian action could still be considered a coup, by the time his troops arrived, the coup had become a full-scale rebellion. The transformation of the coup into a rebellion had its roots in the fact that the United Arab Republic was a single state in name only. After years of second-class treatment and of buckling under to laws designed for Egyptians, most of the Syrian army and people were ready to withdraw from the union and to resist foreign (i.e., Egyptian) efforts to prevent them from doing so. Whether they formed an actual majority of the Syrian population or not is impossible to tell and is not very significant anyway. What is important is that the central element that defines a coup and allows for its suppression—the lack of participation in its action by a significant number of the people or the military—was quickly lost in this case. It was Nasser's recognition of the widespread support that the Syrian action produced and, consequently, the massive and protracted effort he would have had to undertake to defeat it that lay at the heart of the intervention's failure. As Nasser later said, "Unity is a popular will. It cannot be a military operation."[44]

The lessons to be derived from this example are clear-cut. In order to intervene successfully with military force to defeat a coup, it is first necessary to ensure access for your troops in the country where the coup is taking place. Where forces are already deployed in the threatened state, they must be able to operate as separate cohesive units and with sufficient strength to overcome the troops backing the coup. When a coup succeeds in generating widespread support, especially among the military, it ceases to be a coup and the means necessary to defend the existing government become much more demanding and operations on its behalf become much less likely to succeed.

The cases in this study demonstrate an extraordinarily high rate of success for foreign involvements in defeating attempted coups. Overall, only two out of these fourteen cases of foreign involvement failed in their attempt to suppress a coup. While this success rate suggests that a great deal can be done to defeat coups in third world states, it does not mean that foreign involvement guarantees that regimes can be confidently protected from coups. In each of the successful cases, mistakes were committed by the coup makers that made foreign actions to combat them potentially effective and therefore attractive. These mistakes included the failure of the coup makers to eliminate completely the existing leadership, their inability to neutralize opposition elements, their inadvertent leaving open of points of access for an interventionary force, and their too quickly proclaiming their political intentions and inclinations upon assuming power.

Where critical mistakes are not made, contemplated foreign interventions might not be carried out. This kind of hesitation can be seen in the failure of the United States and Britain to intervene in Iraq in 1958. The absence of important mistakes on the part of the coup makers can also result in the foreign intervention failing to defend the regime from the coup, as was the case with the aborted Egyptian effort in Syria. This is not to suggest that a coup that fails to make mistakes cannot be defeated. Rather, I mean to argue that suppressing a flawless coup would be much more difficult for foreign interests and, consequently, that it would be less likely to provoke a foreign intervention.

Foreign efforts to defeat coups have on the whole been remarkably successful. However, they have been used only against a tiny fraction of the coups that have taken place. While the role of outsiders in defeating coups cannot be ignored, especially for vital third world states, for the foreseeable future, the main line of defense against coups will almost certainly lie within the third world regimes themselves.

The cases we studied demonstrate several strategies that third world regimes can use to prepare for protecting themselves from attempted coups d'état. Militaries can be divided into separate and, to a certain extent, rival commands, because these appear to be less of a threat than their more unified counterparts. Although this kind of division introduces the danger that there will be more sources out of which a coup can be initiated, the benefits of such a move will almost always outweigh the possible costs. The major weakness of coup-prone states lies in their narrow concentrations of power. Insofar as this dangerous concentration can be dispersed by the establishment of countervailing centers of power, the risk of a successful coup will be lessened. It requires no great feat of political evolution or development to divide the military into separate services. Saudi Arabia has successfully done so through the establishment of two distinct forces (the regular army and the National Guard), as well as a third unit (the Royal Guard), whose only function is to provide personal protection for the king. The effectiveness of dividing the armed forces was demonstrated by the suppression of the Imperial Guard's attempted coup in Ethiopia by the combined rival army and air forces.

A third world regime must also be able quickly to mobilize loyalist forces in the capital to deal with coups. The successful countercoups that took place in Ethiopia and the Sudan could not have taken place without the prompt dispatch of loyal troops to challenge the authority of the insurgents and then to overpower them. Deploying troops outside one's country that can be rushed home in case of emergency might also be considered as a reasonable coup-prevention tactic. As the Sudanese case illustrates, troops that are stationed abroad are likely to be free from involvements in conspiratorial plots. Because most coups are backed by a relatively small number of people, the rapid transfer home of loyalist troops from abroad can be decisive in suppressing a coup. Similarly, coup-prone states can encourage the deployment of politically compatible foreign troops in their country. Cuban military advisors acting directly and using their influence with Congolese soldiers preserved the regime of President Massamba-Debat from a coup. American forces stationed in the Dominican Republic proved critical in deterring several coups there from 1965 to 1966. In relation to their own armed forces, third world countries need to be careful to see that they are content. This often will require providing them with ample supplies of arms, high salaries, and control over their autonomy. A discontented military is probably the single greatest danger to the survival of most third world regimes.

Any countercoup launched should communicate to the insurgents exactly for which side they are fighting. A small group of officers intent on overthrowing a government will often enlist the support of other military personnel by telling them that they are defending the existing regime. This deception played a prominent part in the unsuccessful coups in both Ethiopia and the Sudan. In both of these cases, mass defections of insurgents resulted when loyalist forces communicated to them the antigovernment goals of their commanders. Futhermore, the anticoup efforts should consider the use of aircraft and armor to suppress the insurgents, even when these weapons are tactically inappropriate. As was demonstrated in the Ethiopian, Sudanese, and Gabonese cases, the use of sophisticated arms against insurgent troops can have a demoralizing impact out of all proportion to its actual military effect.

Regimes wishing to survive coups need to protect and broaden their leadership. As the cases we studied show, the survival of the actual leaders of the incumbent regime is a critical element in the success of countercoup operations, while the destruction of the leadership elite, as happened in Iraq in 1958, can preclude any attempt to defend or to restore the old government. Moreover, while extraordinary measures for safeguarding heads of state are necessary, they are not sufficient. Because such efforts can never be a guarantee of safety, the regime needs to be broadened to include more than a single individual as its symbol and spokesman, and recognized procedures for political succession should be agreed upon in advance. The Saudi network of several thousand princes, each with a place in the hierarchy of the royal family, is illustrative of this type of measure, even though it is not applicable to most third world states. Many third world leaders will resist such a broadening of the country's leadership out of a reluctance to share even the appearance of power. Nevertheless, by broadening the base of legitimate rule, third world leaders can make certain that a successful coup cannot result from a mere simple assassination. In addition, the likelihood of outside powers intervening to suppress a coup is increased when there are several individuals who have the political stature to request foreign assistance.

The cases in this study demonstrate that where domestic defenses are not adequate, coups can be defeated by prompt, determined foreign intervention. That this is the case should not be surprising. Coups are inherently weak threats that can succeed only when they are confronted with even weaker oppositions. The prospect of outside assistance for defending third world regimes will not bring about the end of coups. It can, however, lessen their frequency and diminish their rate of success.

5

Backing Coups d'État against Third World Regimes

Backing a coup against another sovereign regime is one of the most extreme examples of interference in the internal affairs of another country. The act of conspiring with foreign nationals to help them to forcibly remove their government denies the most basic rights and considerations of national sovereignty. Despite the controversial nature of this kind of action, outside states have backed coups attempting to overthrow existing regimes far more often than they have acted to defend regimes from coups. They have done so because the coup is a swift, inexpensive, and often secret means for replacing a hostile regime with a friendly one. Especially for countries that lack the means to project force against another country in more conventional ways, backing a coup represents an attractive way of defending and asserting their interests. The purpose of this section of this work is to provide an overview of coup-backing efforts, and to assess their effectiveness as an instrument of foreign policy.

Before examining the record of foreign-backed coups, it is necessary to clarify what foreign backing of a coup entails definitionally. Not all actions to topple a third world regime can be considered foreign-backed coups.[1] Countries support invasions, assassinations, insurgencies, and civil wars in order to topple a hostile regime. Direct invasions of target states have also been frequently employed to remove a hostile regime. As significant as these policies have been historically, they are not examples of foreign-backed coups. For a foreign-backed coup to be said to have occurred, an outside state must have supported an actual coup. This means having supported a relatively small group, which already wielded some power in the existing regime or military, in a rapid, forcible, attempted takeover of the government.

In presenting an overview of coup-backing efforts, only cases that resulted in actual coups being backed will be considered. Countries that failed even to bring about a coup attempt, despite reports that they tried to do so, will not be examined. Especially in the third world, accusations against other countries that they are plotting coups are very common and widespread. In the Middle East alone, President Nasser of Egypt was accused of having backed coups in Syria, Lebanon, Iraq, Jordan, Saudi Arabia.[2] In the 1970s and 1980s, Libya's Muammar Khadaffi has been accused of backing coups and plots in the Sudan, Tunisia, Nigeria, Egypt, Ethiopia, Saudi Arabia, North Yemen, and countless other countries. As we discussed in Chapter Two, the United States failed to incite real coups in Chile (1970), Iran (1979), and Libya (1986).

There is little doubt that many of these charges are true and accurate. Nevertheless, to include them in the study would open the examination of coup-backing efforts literally to scores of cases in which one country has been accused of subverting another. Without being able to examine an actual historical coup in order to find possible real foreign involvement, it would be impossible in most cases to separate the facts from politically motivated falsehoods. By focusing only on cases in which an actual coup was launched, the foreign role in determining the success or failure of the coup can best be assessed.[3]

Even focusing on cases in which coups were actually launched, it is often impossible to obtain reliable information on the extent or nature of foreign involvement in these coups. While some regimes might not wish to conceal the role they played in defending a government from a coup, virtually no government wants to reveal that it supported a coup against another regime. At the very least, such a revelation could invite international censure; at the worst, it could provoke a war. Secretly backing a coup is a temptation for some countries precisely because their role in the enterprise can be concealed and denied. This is especially true for communist and authoritarian third world regimes, because they are well-equipped to hide their involvements in such operations. Open societies are far more likely to generate evidence of their involvements in coups than are closed societies.

Moreover, just as false allegations are easily made in connection with plotted coups, so also false allegations can be easily made in connection with actual coups. It is far easier to blame a coup on "foreign aggression" than on fundamental domestic problems, like ethnic divisions, official corruption, or economic difficulties, that might actually have given rise to the coup. Sudan's President Numeiry routinely blamed Libya and Ethiopia for the attempts to overthrow him. While some of the coups against him were backed by these states, others stemmed from the horrendous problems that persist in the Sudan. Significantly, when Numeiry was finally toppled in 1985, outside involvement played no role. It is impossible, consequently, to rely simply on a leader's word that a coup launched against him really had foreign backing.

The difficulties of confirming actual foreign involvement in a coup call for a close study of each successful and abortive coup where such involvement is suspected. For the purposes of this study, the evidence of foreign backing must be quite credible—that is, it must be presented by reliable sources that would not be expected to have altered the facts for political purposes. The reported foreign involvement would have to directly back a specific group in launching a coup rather than simply to incite the military to action through indirect means (e.g., economic sanctions). The alleged foreign involvement would also have to have been significant enough in its impact such that, in its absence, the coup most likely would not have been attempted. Judgments as to what constitutes "credible" evidence and "significant" foreign involvement are unavoidably subjective. Because stringent criteria are employed in making the selections for this study, many coups that have been widely believed to have been backed by outside sources were not included. The cases of foreign-backed coups discussed here are not meant to be all-inclusive. Nevertheless, cumulatively they provide insight into the phenomena of foreign-backed coups.

Successful cases of foreign-backed coups in the third world since 1945 include: the United States and Britain in Iran (1953), the United States in Guatemala (1954), Egypt in North Yemen (1962), the United States in South Vietnam (1963), the United States in Brazil (1964), the United States in South Vietnam (1965), the British in Oman (1970), the United States in Cambodia (1970), Saudi Arabia in North Yemen (1974), Greece in Cyprus (1974), mercenaries in the Comoro Islands (1975 and 1978), the Soviet Union, Cuba, and East Germany in South Yemen (1978), and France in the Central African Republic (1979 and 1981). In all of these cases, the foreign support proved to be critical for enabling the coup successfully to overthrow the existing regime.

Foreign-backed coups that have failed include: Iran in Iraq (1970), the Soviet Union in the Sudan (1971), Libya in the Sudan (1976), Libya in Niger (1976), European and African mercenaries in Benin (1977), Libya in North Yemen (1978), Saudi Arabia in North Yemen (1979), Morocco in Mauritania (1981), and South African–backed mercenaries in the Seychelles (1981). In each of these cases, a coup was launched with the support of outside forces, but it failed to overthrow the government.

These coups, like operations to suppress coups, reveal three principal levels of foreign support (see table 2). First, the outside state provides advice and encouragement to the coup makers. This kind of support is sought by the coup makers from foreign powers who wield substantial influence in the country that is the target of the coup. Because of their influence, such states would be in a position to suppress the coup, if they chose to do so.

Foreign powers are most likely to be asked for their approval of a coup when they deploy large numbers of troops, relative to the indigenous forces, in the country that is the target of the coup. The center of power in that country has then become not the regime or its military, but the foreign presence. Since it is often impossible for indigenous third world forces to defeat a large foreign military presence, a successful coup requires at least the tacit acquiescence of the outside state.

Table 2. Foreign Backing of Third World Coups d'Etat, 1945–1985

Use of Foreign Forces	Material Assistance
United States in Guatemala (1954)	United States and Britain in Iran (1953)
Egypt in North Yemen (1962)	United States in Brazil (1964)
Britain in Oman (1970)	Iran in Iraq (1970) (failed)
Greece in Cyprus (1974)	Saudi Arabia in North Yemen (1974)
Mercenaries in the Comoro Islands (1975) and (1978)	Libya in Sudan (1976) (failed)
Mercenaries (with possible French support) in Benin (1977) (failed)	Libya in Niger (1976) (failed)
USSR, East Germany, and Cuba in South Yemen (1978)	Libya in North Yemen (1978) (failed)
France in the Central African Republic (1979)	Saudi Arabia in North Yemen (1979) (failed)
South African–backed mercenaries in the Seychelles (1981) (failed)	Morocco in Mauritania (1981) (failed)

Advice and Encouragement

United States in South Vietnam (1963)

United States in South Vietnam (1965)

United States in Cambodia (1970)

USSR in Sudan (1971) (failed)

France in Central African Republic (1981)

Note: Included here are only those cases for which there is public and convincing evidence of significant foreign involvement in the backing of a coup. Where several policies were employed to back a coup, the principal means was taken to categorize the coup-backing effort.

For example, the deployment of French troops in the Central African Republic has made getting the approval of Paris a virtual necessity for any coup there. Although the French maintain only thirteen hundred troops in the Central African Republic, that is nearly the size of the country's eighteen-hundred-man army. Consequently, when the head of the military, General André Kolingba, plotted to topple the French-installed regime of David Dacko, it was first necessary to obtain France's approval. Because the French were unhappy with Dacko's inability to cope with guerrilla activity and economic problems, they readily agreed to the coup. The success of Kolingba's September 1981 coup can be traced directly to his knowledge that the French forces would not defend Dacko.

Countries that do not maintain an overwhelmingly large military presence in a state that is the target of coup also support coups with advice and encouragement. American planning allegedly led to the successful coup that replaced Prince Sihanouk with the more pro-Western Lon Nol regime in Cambodia in 1970. (The absence of a large American troop presence in Cambodia was, of course, compensated somewhat by the American forces in neighboring South Vietnam.) American advice and encouragement, however, failed to provoke a coup in Iran in 1979, despite the demand of National Security Advisor Brzezinski that a coup be made.[4] The Soviet Union almost certainly used its influence with Sudanese troops to encourage the unsuccessful coup against Numeiry in 1971. In 1978, the Soviets—with the assistance of the Cubans and East Germans—were able to use their influence with the South Yemeni militia successfully to overpower the South Yemeni army and to overthrow its president, Rubayi Ali. A year later, the Soviets reportedly encouraged a coup against Prime Minister Amin by the more moderate President Taraki in Afghanistan. The failure of the Soviets to initiate a coup led to Taraki's death and to the subsequent Soviet invasion.[5]

A second level of support by foreign powers in backing coups involves providing coup makers with material assistance, such as money or arms. Material assistance serves two goals. It improves the ability of the coup makers actually to carry out the coup, and it provides a tangible symbol of the commitment of the outside state to the success of the coup. This kind of support is especially common coming from third world nations.

The shah of Iran provided weapons and transmitted messages to the Iraqi military officers who launched a coup against their leader, President Saddam Hussein, in January 1970. The failure of the coup nearly led to war at that time between Iran and Iraq.[6] The Saudis reportedly paid $13 million to finance a coup against President Iryani of North

Yemen, which succeeded, but their financial backing failed to lead to the successful overthrow of President Salih of North Yemen in 1979. Both attempts apparently were spurred by Saudi fears of North Yemen drawing closer to South Yemen, thus reducing Saudi influence there.[7] The unwillingness of Mauritania to take a more active stand against the Polisario rebels led to a Moroccan-backed coup attempt there in March 1981. A small group of Moroccan-equipped military exiles joined with about one hundred regular Mauritanian soldiers in a vain attempt to install a government more to the liking of the Moroccan government. The failed coup resulted in strained relations between the two countries.[8]

The United States has provided material support for at least two coups. In 1953, American money helped finance the successful coup against Prime Minister Mossadegh of Iran. In 1964, the United States made available supplies of weapons and petroleum to coup makers attempting to overthrow the leftist president of Brazil, Joao Goulart. The coup succeeded without the insurgents ever having to draw upon the American resources.[9]

One of the countries most active in providing material assistance for coups is Libya under Muammar Khadaffi. In March 1976, Khadaffi allegedly provided weapons to dissident groups for a coup against the government of Niger. Khadaffi reportedly wished to gain control of Niger's rich uranium fields, perhaps for use in the construction of a nuclear weapon. The failure of the coup did not appreciably strain the relations between the two countries. In the same year, Khadaffi trained, transported, and armed a coup force of nearly two thousand mostly Sudanese fighters in an abortive attempt to overthrow the pro-Western President Numeiry in the Sudan. The coup makers, led by exiled politicians and supported by some indigenous forces, succeeded in capturing the airport in Khartoum, where Numeiry had just landed, but the insurgents failed to capture the president and to seize control of the government. Since Numeiry and Khadaffi were already bitter adversaries, the failed coup had little effect on relations between the two countries.[10] In October 1978, Khadaffi struck again when he financed a coup attempt against North Yemen's President Salih. The attempt was designed to support South Yemen in its conflict with North Yemen. The failure of the coup led to the freezing of diplomatic relations between North Yemen and Libya, but they improved a year later.[11]

A third level of outside support for coups involves the direct intervention of foreign personnel in the coup. This kind of support can be distinguished from an invasion when the operation essentially is confined to overthrowing the regime in the capital, relatively few troops are used, the intervention is short in duration, and it acts in support of indigenous groups. The outside state provides foreign forces in the belief that they are needed to give the margin of victory to the domestic coup makers it is supporting.

Small numbers of foreign advisors were employed to support coups in Guatemala and Oman. In Guatemala, CIA pilots allegedly played a pivotal role in the Guatemalan military's overthrow of President Arbenz in 1954.[12] In the Persian Gulf, British officers assisted Omani troops in overthrowing the tradition-bound Sultan and replacing him with his more progressive son in 1970. The British led the assault against the Sultan's palace after the initial Omani effort had failed. By backing the coup against the Sultan, the British hoped to protect Oman from radical subversive forces similar to those that had already emerged in South Yemen.[13]

The list of cases in which organized units of foreign troops have been employed to support coups includes the use of Egyptian forces in a coup against the Imam of North Yemen in 1962. Egyptian troops in North Yemen and troops airlifted into the country from Egypt itself backed North Yemeni forces in a successful coup, which replaced the royalist regime with a republican one more in line with Nasser's pan-Arabist designs. In addition to providing troops, the Egyptians were needed to start the tanks surrounding the Presidential Palace.[14] Greek troops played a critical role in the successful coup in Cyprus against Archbishop Makarios in 1974. Nearly two thousand Greek troops from the Cypriot National Guard, the Greek contingent on Cyprus, and Greek troops flown in from Greece itself participated in the coup. Athens planned and implemented the overthrow because of Makarios's strenuous resistance to Cyprus' union with Greece.[15]

In 1978, over five hundred Cuban and East German (and possibly Soviet) forces played a central role in backing the South Yemeni militia's efforts to overthrow its president, Rubayi Ali. The successful coup removed a leader who had been showing signs of independence from the Soviet Union and a growing affinity for the West.[16] A year later, several hundred French troops from a special long-range strike force in west Africa assisted indigenous forces in bringing off a bloodless coup against Emperor Jean Bokassa of the Central African Republic. The motivation for the coup seemed to come from French displeasure over Bokassa's horrendous human rights abuses, particularly the part he played in ordering a massacre of school children a month prior to the French intervention.[17]

The use of foreign mercenaries constitutes another way by which foreign-backed coups are carried out.[18] The mercenary Gilbert Bourgeaud (alias Bob Denard) successfully overthrew the repressive regime of Ali Solih in the Comoro Islands in 1978. Under Solih, whom Bourgeaud had helped to gain power in a coup in 1975, the Comoro Islands had been terrorized by a brutal militia patterned after the People's Republic of China's Red Guard. Using only fifty men, Denard, probably with the knowledge of the French, captured President Solih in his bed and then quickly took control of the state capital. The army and the militia offered no resistance. A former leader of the Comoro Islands and a supporter of the coup, Ahmed Abdallah, was installed in power, much to the delight of the population.[19] In Benin, approximately one hundred European and African mercenaries attempted to overthrow the government of Mathieu Kerekou in January 1977. The coup was allegedly masterminded by Denard again, and it may have relied upon French and Moroccan resources as well, although their motivations for any such involvement remain murky. The coup makers flew into Benin, seized the airport, and then drove into a nearby town, firing at buildings in a seemingly random fashion. When it became apparent that they were not receiving support from Benin's military, they quickly departed in the same plane in which they had arrived, without having deposed the government.[20] A colleague of Bob Denard's, "Mad" Mike Hoare, reportedly led a South African–backed coup against the socialist leader of the Seychelles, Albert René, in 1981. In South Africa, which had called the Seychelles a "Soviet outpost," Hoare recruited some forty-five mercenaries from Britain, France, West Germany, Zimbabwe, and South Africa itself. They flew to the Seychelles, where customs officers discovered their weapons, reportedly supplied by South Africa, and foiled the coup. After some fighting at the airport, the coup makers hijacked an aircraft and returned to South Africa.[21]

Coup-Backing States and Their Targets

Regimes that are the targets of foreign-backed coups fall into four sometimes overlapping categories. First, regimes that depend on a foreign military presence for their survival are often the targets of foreign-backed coups (e.g., South Vietnam in the 1960s, the Central African Republic in the early 1980s). Outside states backed coups against these regimes when they failed to support their outside interests and because it was relatively easy for them to do so.

Secondly, regimes in countries that are comprised of relatively simple societies with a minimum of meaningful political participation and a maximum of political instability are often tempting targets of foreign-backed coups (e.g., North Yemen, Niger). Outside states recognize that backing a coup against such regimes involves the simple task of neutralizing a small number of individuals.

Third, neighboring countries embroiled in conflict may back coups against each other's regimes. In contrast to a direct invasion, a costly and sometimes impossible undertaking, backing a coup can be an inexpensive and effective alternative for a country for dealing with its regional enemies (e.g., Libya and the Sudan, Iran and Iraq).

Fourth, regimes seeking to distance themselves from a major power, without at the same time canceling that power's influence over their military, also seem to invite a foreign-backed coup. If the third world country is important enough to the stronger power, it will sponsor and support coup machinations among the military as a likely response to problems developing with the political leadership of the country (e.g., the USSR in the Sudan and South Yemen, the United States in Brazil, Chile, and Cambodia).

Outside states have backed different types of coups in order to advance their own interests. Radical states have backed breakthrough coups in order to bring compatible regimes to power. Libya's operations in the Sudan, Niger, and North Yemen (1978) and Egypt's coup-backing actions in North Yemen (1962) fall into this category. Where a leftist regime has failed in the eyes of its sponsors to live up to its revolutionary promise, radicalizing coups have been backed by those sponsors. The USSR's support of coups in the Sudan and in South Yemen stemmed from Moscow's desire to prevent radical regimes from reverting to some sort of moderation. Veto coups have been supported by more conservative countries, such as the United States (in Guatemala, Brazil, and Iran) and Saudi Arabia (in North Yemen). In addition, the mercenary-supported coups in the Comoro Islands in 1975 and 1978 and in the Seychelles in 1981 can be characterized as veto coups. By attempting to topple governments that were trying to bring leftist groups into power, veto coups sought to support or restore the status quo and thus to preserve the interests of the outside power against change. Guardian coups have been employed to deal with regimes that have proved unable or unwilling to govern effectively. The British-backed coup in Oman and the French-backed coup in the Central African Republic were both undertaken to replace incompetent and embarrassing governments with ones better able to control their own countries and thus better able to maintain the outside powers' interests. These and other coup-backing policies illustrate that just as the motivations for backing a coup of an outside state differ, so do the types of coups they will support.

Aside from maintaining interests in other states that they believe could be advanced by coups, there is nothing distinctive about the countries that decide to back coups against foreign regimes. There are differences, however, between the superpowers, the European powers, and the third world countries in the ways in which they prefer to support coups, at least insofar as the public record reveals this support. The most common method of supporting coups employed by the superpowers involves providing advice and encouragement to the coup makers (e.g., the United States in South Vietnam, the Soviet Union in the Sudan). This method reflects the strong degrees of influence maintained by the U.S. and the USSR in the countries where they have backed coups, allowing them to limit themselves to giving advice and encouragement and still produce a successful coup. The superpowers most desire to keep their involvements secret.

The European powers seem to prefer the method of using their own troops in supporting coups. The continuing presence of European forces in their former colonies makes this kind of direct involvement the easiest and most effective choice for them. Because these forces have often already played a crucial role in determining what regime would come to power, their involvement in a coup does not constitute a major deviation from their already-established role.

Third world states tend to back coups by means of material support. By providing money or arms to the coup makers, third world countries make up for their lack of influence with the targeted regime. That kind of influence would have allowed them simply to rely on the kind of encouragement of coups favored by the superpowers. Material assistance does not incur the risks of war that are raised by direct intervention, nor does it entail the logistical problems that a direct intervention would entail.

Third world regimes differ from European countries and from the superpowers in backing coups against regimes that are outside their spheres of influence. The superpowers and the European states tend to back coups against regimes with which they have had both influence and extensive historical contact. Their prior involvement with these countries explains their interest in them in the first place and enables them to back a coup, because that history has linked them with groups seeking the overthrow of the regime. Most of the third world's coups, however, were directed at enemy regimes. Libya's attempts on the Sudan, Niger, and North Yemen are examples, as is Iran's coup attempt against Iraq. All were directed against bitter adversaries.

Too few cases exist to enable us to come to any definitive conclusions about why third world countries differ from the developed states in the kinds of regimes they choose to target for coups, but several possibilities suggest themselves. First, the intensity of conflict between two third world states is often greater than that between a third world state and a developed state. Because of the violence of their sentiments, the extreme measure of initiating a coup against an enemy regime becomes more thinkable to these regimes. In addition, the geographical proximity of some third world states to their adversaries, combined with over-lapping ethnic groups, facilitates their involvement in each other's internal politics. The developed states often do not have a presence in enemy third world countries that would enable them to back a coup there. Common ethnic backgrounds can also motivate coups. Third world states may come to feel that they have a "right" to determine what kind of regime governs "their" people. Furthermore, many of the likely third world targets of the superpowers, especially those of the United States, are not vulnerable to coups (e.g., Nicaragua, Cuba) and thus they are less likely to be targets of a coup-backing effort. Superpower involvement against third world adversaries is also likely to arouse support for the targeted regime among its neighboring states, calling into question whether the coup-backing effort is worth the cost. Most important, many of the possible targets of the major powers are protected by other major powers. If the United States attempted to provoke a coup in Ethiopia or the USSR attempted to launch a coup in South Korea, it could very well bring about a major superpower confrontation. This does not mean that the major powers do not attempt to subvert countries in the other camp. But it means that if they do, they usually behave so cautiously that either no coup results or their involvement is successfully concealed.

Evaluating the Outcomes of Foreign-Backed Coups

There is no significant difference between the rates of success of coups with foreign backing and of all coups. Although the rate of success of foreign-backed coups (63 percent) is higher than the 51 percent rate for all coups, the difference is too small to be significant when it is taken into account that many foreign-backed coups have never been made public and that these figures do not consider failed attempts at inciting coups. Consequently, while specific coups may be benefitted or hurt by foreign backing, not enough reliable data exists for us to be able to make a conclusive statement regarding the effects of foreign involvement on the overall rate of success of coups.

The level of foreign backing that has produced historically the greatest probability of success was the use of outside troops or advisors directly in the coup operations. Eight out of ten foreign-backed coups succeeded when foreign forces were used. The only two failures resulted from mercenary actions. Coups that received only advice and encouragement from an outside state also did well, however, with four out of five of these attempts having proved successful. Only in cases in which foreign backing was limited to giving material assistance did the rate of success fall below 50 percent. In this category, six out of nine attempts failed.

Several reasons for these results emerge from the study of these cases. Coups that used foreign military personnel did well because they were usually launched against weak regimes without broad-based popular support or effective countercoup capabilities. It is not a coincidence that these kinds of regimes were selected as targets of direct foreign intervention. Before an outside state will take the drastic and politically risky step of committing its own forces to a coup against the sovereign government of another state, it wants to ensure that such an action can be carried out quickly and successfully, with a minimum of domestic and international protest. By trying to select weak, unpopular governments, the outside state hopes to reduce the task of the coup makers to the relatively easy one of replacing one small group of individuals with another. Just as few indigenous coups can succeed against determined foreign protection, few indigenous leaders with little domestic support can protect themselves against coups with determined opponents and real foreign support.

Coups backed by the advice and encouragement of an outside state did well largely because of the nature of the regimes that were overthrown. In all of the cases in this category, the survival of the regime that was the target of the coup already depended somewhat on the outside power backing the coup (e.g., the United States in South Vietnam, the French in the Central African Republic). What was critical was not the actual content of the plans provided to the coup makers by the outside power, but the knowledge that the outside power supported their efforts and would support a successor regime. The key predictor of coups of this sort is the amount of influence maintained by the outside power. Where that influence is overwhelming, as it was with the United States in South Vietnam, the chances of success are very high. Where that influence is subordinate to the inherent power of the existing regime, as it was with the Soviet Union in the Sudan, the chances of success are much lower.

Several factors help explain why, as a group, coup makers who received only material assistance fared so poorly. First, the groups that received the support tended to be politically inept and tactically incompetent. While this concurrence in many examples may be a coincidence, it is also true that weak groups would be more likely to seek outside support for their projected coups than those who were well placed to overthrow the government on their own. Since the support they received was not as substantial as foreign personnel, their failures were perhaps predictable. In addition, the outside government that provided the assistance to the coup makers did not in any of these cases have any overwhelming influence over the regime in question. This made its support less critical than it might otherwise have been. Where success with such assistance was achieved, like that of the United States in Brazil and Iran, the material assistance provided was not nearly as critical as the political importance of and promises of continued aid from the major power. Finally, many of the coups in this category were backed by bitter enemies of the countries in which they took place, as was the case with Libya and the Sudan, and Iran and Iraq. This enmity made cooperation with the indigenous military difficult before the coups, and it provoked resistance to the insurgents by the people and the army during the coups.

In sum, the likelihood of a foreign-backed coup succeeding depends on four factors. These are the extent of the dependence of the regime attacked on the state backing the coup, the degree of support for the regime among the populace and the military, the effectiveness of the tactical countercoup measures taken by the regime, and the strength of the coup makers. Foreign-backed coups with the greatest chance of success are those backed by states with overwhelming influence on the threatened regime, those targeted against incompetently defended and unpopular governments, and those that support effective coup makers with their own forces.

It is far more difficult to generalize about the long-term consequences of coups. Much depends on subjective criteria as to what constitutes "success" and what costs are worth paying to achieve it. In terms of the interests of the state backing the coup, such efforts often bring about positive results. Successful coup-backing policies have enabled countries to replace hostile governments with friendly ones at little risk or cost. This is especially true of coup-backing efforts that never became public. When coup-backing efforts do not remain secret, the countries can nevertheless deny their involvement. Explicit denials of complicity in these coups was common to virtually every coup-backing incident considered in this section. Even where convincing evidence exists of outside involvement in a coup, it does not provoke the international censure or demands for retaliation that more overt aggression often generates. With some notable exceptions, the overwhelming number of coup-backing instances considered in this section did not result in any protracted conflict or even in diplomatic censure. As for the future stability of the regimes, there is no evidence that governments placed in power by outside involvements are any less stable or enduring than any other regimes.

Even the failure of a coup-backing effort does not need to produce long-term adverse consequences. Because of the "deniability" factor, failing to overthrow a government does not necessarily result in poor relations between affected states. In some cases (e.g., Libya's abortive coup against Niger) the country that was the target of the foreign-backed coup may publicly accept the disavowals of the aggressor state, so as not to provoke additional attempts. Even repeated failures of coups can eventually produce positive effects for the country backing the coups. Following the 1985 ouster of Numeiry in the Sudan, the new regime sought to mend relations with Libya. Numeiry's successors no doubt judged that they could better protect themselves from Libya's subversive intentions by a policy of appeasement than by one of hostile resistance.

The foreign backing of coups can also, however, entail grave costs. In contrast to the defense of regimes from coups, overthrowing a government carries with it the risk that the new leaders will be no better and might be worse than their predecessors. Dissatisfaction with regimes it placed in power has caused France to back at least two coups in the Central African Republic over a period of just three years from 1979 to 1981. Backing a coup can also undermine whatever political stability exists in a country, making the long-term situation worse for the outside power. The American-assisted overthrow of Diem in 1963 led to a succession of feeble South Vietnamese governments and a weakening of the war effort. When coup-backing efforts become known or strongly suspected, as was the case with the United States in Chile, the international reputation of a country backing them can suffer. This is an especially sensitive issue for democracies.

The foreign support of successful coups can also lead to armed conflict with countries backing the threatened regime. Greece's successful toppling of the Cypriot government of Archbishop Makarios in 1974 led directly to a Turkish invasion of the island, which quickly reversed any Greek gains. Egypt successfully overthrew the Imam in North Yemen in 1962, only to find itself engaged in a costly five-year war with Saudi-backed supporters of the old regime. The Egyptian case also illustrates how removing a regime with popular or military support can lead to a civil war.

Failed efforts to overthrow a regime can also lead to war. Iraq and Iran mobilized troops on each other's borders following Iran's attempt to back a coup against Iraq in 1970. Although this immediate crisis was ultimately defused, armed conflict was a distinct possibility, as it has since become reality. Failing to overthrow a regime can drive it to adopt policies directed against the state that sought to topple it. Numeiry's realignment away from the Soviet Union and toward the West began with an abortive Soviet-supported coup against him in 1971. Reportedly, Soviet efforts against Anwar Sadat of Egypt and Siad Barre of Somalia may have influenced both those leaders also to move away from Moscow.

Balancing the costs and benefits of foreign-backed coups depends on the individual case, the estimate of the consequences of doing nothing, and an assessment of whether those consequences justify the coup-backing effort. Such considerations make it impossible to determine objectively which coup-backing efforts will lead to long-term success. It is interesting to note, however, that with the possible exception of the British involvement in Oman in 1970, no "successful" case of a coup backed by a foreign power has avoided serious long-term problems. Supporting a coup against a foreign government may be the chosen solution to a problem, but it has never been a cost-free one.

Foreign-backed coups are likely to continue so long as coups persist in the third world. The anticipated costs of backing a coup are too small, and the potential for major gains too large, for this type of activity to be halted. If there is a positive side to this assurance, it is that third world regimes that truly command broad support from their people and their military are not likely to provoke foreign-backed coups. Such efforts can too easily produce protracted conflict, canceling out the attraction of making a coup by replacing one small group with another small group. By raising the possibility that it will take more than a coup to deliver the country, the probability of foreign-backed coups is diminished.

6

Prospects for Future American Involvements in Third World Coups

How important is the international dimension of coups likely to be in the future? There are signs that its importance will diminish over time. While they are still an important factor in the politics of the third world, coups are occurring less frequently than they have in the past. For example, between 1955 and 1969 there were over fifteen successful coups in the Middle East and North Africa. Between 1970 and 1984, only six coups succeeded in the same region. Similar declines in the number of successful (and abortive) coups have been reported for other regions of the third world. They reflect an increasing ability on the part of third world states to deter coups. This has been accomplished either by means of more effective suppression capabilities or through the development of stable political systems, either democratic or totalitarian, which make coups unlikely to be attempted.[1]

This decline in the number of coups does not entail, however, a lessening of the importance of the international dimension of coups. Fewer coups does not necessarily mean fewer coups with foreign involvement. On the contrary, the foreign suppression and backing of coups has increased or held steady over this same period of time. Cases of outside involvement in defeating coups have risen from zero in the 1950s to six in the 1960s while dropping slightly to five in the 1970s. Foreign support for coups has increased from two in the 1950s to four in the 1960s to fifteen in the 1970s. Information on the 1980s is necessarily still incomplete, but in the first half of the decade there have already been three cases of foreign efforts to defeat coups and an equal number of foreign-backed coups. While these figures are not all-inclusive, they illustrate that foreign involvements in coups are by no means a relic of the past.[2]

Moreover, there are several developments that point to a continuing if not increasing significance for the international dimension of coups. First, although third world regimes have made some progress in halting coups, the threat or opportunity that coups pose remains very much alive. As long as many third world states are characterized by the rule of a narrow elite, by the absence of legitimate governments, by the primacy of the military in politics, and by the lack of meaningful participation on the part of the general population, coups will dominate third world political life. In addition, the decline we have registered in the incidence of coups may be short-lived. The rising debt crisis and the fall in oil prices could easily create the conditions for a new wave of coups.[3] Furthermore, the large number of authoritarian leaders in power for many years who are likely to die in the coming two decades could very well create the kind of instability that will lead to a greater frequency of third world coups.[4] In the first half of 1985 alone, successful coups in Nigeria, Uganda, and the Sudan, and unsuccessful coups in Thailand and Libya, clearly indicate that coups still play a major role in the politics of third world states.

The development of transnational ties can increase the salience of the international dimension of coups. If states share a sense of community or ideology with other states, they are less likely to be deterred by considerations of sovereignty from meddling in others' affairs. Egypt's Nasser and Libya's Khadaffi have justified their involvements in numerous coups by their commitment to a pan-Arabist ideology that seeks to overthrow "reactionary" regimes and to protect "progressive" ones.[5] Similarly, the rise to power of the Ayatollah Khomeini and the increasing importance of Islamic fundamentalism in the Middle East can increase the importance of the international dimension of coups. As long as leaders appeal to populations over the heads of their government and feel that they have an obligation to make sure that only certain types of regimes are in power, one can expect increased foreign involvement in backing coups and defending against them.

The high cost of conventional warfare, as illustrated by the Iran-Iraq war, is a further incentive for states to attempt to determine the outcome of coups in hostile states. The motivations for both the Iraqi attack and the Iranian counteroffensive lay in the desire to overthrow each other's leaders. The horrendous price being paid by both sides in the conflict may lead other states with similar aims to place more emphasis on backing or suppressing coups than on war to realize their goals. The weakening of norms against interfering in the internal affairs of other states, the deniability of such an involvement, and the ability of many states to act in secrecy may all further contribute to an increase in international involvements in coups.[6]

Most important, the international dimension of coups will continue to be critical as long as outside states can effectively promote their own interests by backing or suppressing coups in the third world at little cost to themselves. They depend on both the weaknesses and strengths of third world regimes. The weaknesses of these regimes allow outside states to play a role in determining their survival and thus their policies. The strengths of these regimes allow them to control the assets that are of such concern to outside powers. As long as the nature of the third world retains this strength/weakness dichotomy, the international dimension of coups will continue to be of major significance in world politics.

An American Response to the International Dimension of Coups

There is a great deal that the United States could do to respond to each of these aspects of the international dimension of coups. While most coups, even those that take place in countries of importance to the United States, do not affect American interests, it is likely that a significant minority will continue to be of major concern to Washington. By putting in power new leaders who often seek to distinguish themselves from their predecessors, coups frequently produce major foreign policy reversals and realignments. A coup can quickly transform a steadfast American friend into an intractable foe, change a moderate regime into a radical one, and change reliable supporters of American economic interests into backers of ideologically motivated economic embargoes. No third world country is free from the threat of coups; no American interest in the third world is either.

It is not the purpose of this study to detail exactly how American policy makers should respond to coups in the third world. Such an analysis would require an examination of the policy making processes of the United States and those of its key allies, and that task is beyond the scope of this work. Specific policy recommendations also depend on the context of the specific coup and the individual country in which it takes place. Nevertheless, by considering the implications of the international dimension of coups that Washington is likely to confront in the coming years, the United States can better prepare itself to cope with the dangers and opportunities that these coups will present.

Defending Third World Regimes from Coups

The United States maintains important interests in the third world that are dependent on friendly regimes being in power in those countries where those interests are represented. In many of these cases, coups are the most likely threat to these regimes and to the American interests they safeguard. While it is not always possible to determine in advance which interests will remain the most important to the United States and which regimes will be threatened by coups, one can highlight certain kinds of situations that are the most likely to provoke American involvements in the defense of governments from coups.

One obvious interest that would likely bring about an American response to try to suppress a coup would involve rescuing a moderate regime, like Pakistan or Brazil, that possesses nuclear weapons from radical coup makers. The implications of a renegade third world country brandishing nuclear weapons are far too horrendous for the United States to allow such weapons to fall into the hands of unstable elements. Other situations that would probably generate American assistance for defensive purposes would include coups directed against key political friends, like El Salvador, Jordan, and Egypt; coups supported by the Soviet Union or by pro-Soviet elements against pro-Western regimes, as possibly in the Sudan; coups against economically critical third world regimes, like Saudi Arabia; and coups likely to pose an immediate threat to American citizens, as occurred in Grenada. The United States may also act to safeguard its long-term interests by protecting newly democratic regimes, especially in Latin America, from coups.

In addition to these kinds of specific interests, there are several factors that have a bearing on the probability of American involvement in coup-defending efforts. First, the coup makers would have to be seen as constituting a threat to American interests if they should gain power for the United States to act to defend the existing regime. In Huntington's terminology, guardian and veto coups would be less likely to provoke an American defensive response, because they are essentially conservative, than breakthrough coups would, because of their revolutionary implications. Coups backed by high-ranking officers and other members of the military or political establishment in a third world state are less likely to bring about the kind of changes the United States fears and are thus less likely to precipitate an American defense of the threatened regime. The chances of an American defensive response are increased when a coup is known to be backed by outside powers hostile to the United States.

The feasibility of U.S. involvement would also help to determine whether and how the United States would respond to a coup. Countries where American troops or advisors are already stationed are more likely to generate an active American role than are countries where a direct intervention would have to be undertaken from scratch. Regimes that require only indirect assistance are naturally more likely to receive it than those that require direct aid. An American involvement would also have a greater chance of coming about if the existing government formally requested U.S. assistance. Furthermore, the prospects of an American involvement are enhanced when a coup does not achieve an immediate success, allowing time for Washington to act.

Most important, the nature of the government to be defended from the coup and the society in which it rules would be of paramount importance for U.S. policy makers in deciding whether to provide assistance. It makes little sense to defend a regime from a coup if the threat is a broadly based one. Such an enterprise, even if it were successful, would simply gain a little time before the next coup. Governments with the support of or at least the acquiescence of their people and their military stand a much better chance of surviving a foreign-backed coup than those whose rule is challenged by powerful elements with popular support in the society. Moreover, regimes whose human rights record is poor (e.g., Mobutu in Zaire) are less likely to be defended by the United States on the pragmatic grounds that such an action would incur both domestic and international censure.

Once the decision is undertaken to defend a third world regime from a coup, ideally there should not be many operational problems in its implementation. In essence, defending a regime from a coup consists of protecting one small group from another—hardly an impossible task in theory for a superpower. In addition, offering protection against a coup when it is requested by the legitimate government safeguards sovereignty rather than undermines it. It is in conformity with international law and Western values.

The preferred method for the United States to safeguard its interests from unfriendly coups is to move third world regimes in the direction of basic economic and political reforms and eventually toward democratic rule. While the prospects of achieving democracy throughout the third world are not encouraging in the short term, actions can be taken to lessen the probability of coups in third world countries by fostering the development of political stability. The United States can use its political and economic influence to encourage third world regimes to diminish large income gaps between the rich and the poor, to establish civilian political institutions to diffuse the power of the military, to broaden bases of popular political participation, limit corruption, halt human rights abuses, and inculcate a civic ethic in the military. Attaining these goals will not be easy, nor is it even possible in many third world states, but this does not relieve the United States of the responsibility of working toward these goals.

It is also in U.S. interests to work toward the deterrence of coups in friendly regimes, like El Salvador and the Philippines. American deterrence of coups is far easier, more effective, and likelier to occur than overt efforts at coup suppression. Many third world countries are dependent on American economic and military aid. An American threat made to the relevant political and military groups that it will withdraw this aid in the event of a coup will often make it sufficiently difficult for potential coup makers to mobilize the support needed to overthrow the government.

A policy of coup deterrence is likely, on occasion, to force Washington to choose between dealing with a friendly regime that came to power through a coup and supporting democracy. As with the American experience with Latin American coups in the 1960s, there will often be a strong temptation for the United States to restore its aid and recognition to a regime that achieved power through a coup, if it adopts a pro-American stance. The Latin American coups of the sixties also demonstrate, however, that failing to punish coup makers who overthrow democratic regimes simply because they are friendly to the United States hurts American credibility in the world, especially in relation to deterring future coups. By withholding aid and diplomatic recognition to groups that have come to power through coups, especially after their having been warned by the United States against taking such an action, Washington will have to suffer some short-term losses. Nevertheless, these losses have to be balanced critically against the potential for long-term gains realized through a more credible deterrent policy and by the protection of democratic regimes in the third world.

Tactically, there is a great deal that the United States can do to defeat coups. Drawing upon the lessons gleaned in Chapter Four, an American approach to defending third world regimes from coups would include giving assistance to third world countries to counter coups on their own, providing logistical support for European and third world states willing to intervene to protect pro-Western regimes from coups, and encouraging the formation of regional pacts in the third world whereby larger pro-Western states would protect smaller ones from coups. More direct American assistance would involve training diplomatic and military personnel for coup contingencies, preparing in advance for the use of secure communications facilities by beleaguered leaders, and upgrading the intelligence capabilities of third world countries to help them determine when coups are likely to occur and which potential coup makers are hostile to their own and American interests.

It is also possible that the United States could find it necessary to intervene with its own troops in an effort to defeat an ongoing coup attempt. This kind of action would most likely be taken only under the most extreme circumstances. A direct American countercoup intervention would seek to defend a friendly regime of critical importance to the United States against a coup backed by groups hostile to American interests. In order to avoid transforming a countercoup intervention into a counterrevolutionary intervention, Washington would have to be very careful that it is not defending a regime that lacks broad social and military support from a broadly based threat.

If the United States should decide that it must intervene, the lessons of past coups demonstrate that speed is essential to the success of the mission. Any delay in sending troops into the target country could result in the success of the coup. This would change the mission of the intervention from a defense of the existing regime to the much more difficult and politically sensitive one of overthrowing a newly "established" government. Tactically, therefore, it is far preferable to send in several hundred troops within a day of the coup than to wait a week—at which point it may be too late—to send in an armored division.

The vast majority of coups will obviously not provoke such a drastic reaction as a direct American intervention. It would be prudent, nevertheless, for Washington to focus its analysis on regimes that might justify and require this kind of involvement in order to prepare for this kind of American action, should it become necessary. The Pakistani regime of Zia ul-Haq, for example, is suspected of possessing nuclear weapons. Zia, who came to power via a coup himself, is very vulnerable to coups, as is evidenced by the uncovering of a serious coup plot against him in January 1984.[7] If a coup were to be launched against Zia by fundamentalist elements allied with the Ayatollah Khomeini in Iran, for example, a direct American response might well be called for, if Washington believed that this was the only way to keep nuclear weapons out of the hands of the coup makers. Similarly, the key strategic role played by Saudi Arabia in the Middle East makes the active defense of that regime from a coup a real possibility. As long as the coup makers came from the royal family or did not appear to threaten American interests, direct American involvement would remain a remote possibility. But if radical opponents of the regime attempted to launch a coup and if the existing Saudi leadership requested American assistance, it is probable that such assistance would be given. Protecting the regime of Hosni Mubarak in Egypt is another instance where the United States might become involved in a countercoup. As one of the key countries of the Middle East, Egypt is of great concern to Washington. Mubarak's pro-Western government is threatened by a host of problems, including Islamic fundamentalism, exploding population growth, and a deteriorating economy exacerbated by the decline in oil prices. Should any of these factors (or some others) provoke a coup that threatens to place a radical, anti-American leadership in power, the United States might be required to defend the existing regime with substantial support.

If the United States does indeed find it necessary to intervene to defend a vital regime from a radical or pro-Soviet coup, such an action would probably not be opposed by American public opinion. Since World War II, the American people have not been against direct United States involvements in other countries per se, but rather they have been opposed to any American involvement that is protracted and waged on behalf of ambiguous ends. An intervention undertaken by the United States to defeat a coup and not some broader threat would necessarily be swift—a few days at most—and presumably it would be taken on behalf of interests generally recognized as vital. Moreover, assuming that an American intervention was requested by the government in power, it would not be counted as an unwarranted interference in the internal affairs of another state. Just as the United States is prepared to defend the Pakistanis, the Saudi Arabians, and the Egyptians from aggression, so should it be prepared as well to defend its friends from coups.

Coping with the Absence of Coups

Not all coups threaten American interests. When important third world countries are led by regimes hostile to the United States, coups against those regimes can support American interests. Coups in Ghana (1966), Mali (1968), and Oman (1970) were all generally understood as being helpful to the West. Similarly, there is little doubt that the United States would welcome any pro-Western coup against Libya's Muammar Khadaffi, Iran's Ayatollah Khomeini, or Nicaragua's Daniel Ortega. It is the eventual result of a coup and not the idea of the coup itself that determines whether it is in American interests.

Whatever the potential benefits of mounting coups against anti-American regimes, it is becoming increasingly difficult for such operations to be mounted successfully. This is true both for indigenous and for foreign-backed coups. Nowhere is the difficulty of launching coups more striking than among Soviet clients. As described in Chapter Three, there have been no pro-Western coups in regimes protected by the USSR since the 1960s. The development of vanguard parties, the establishment of secret police forces, the political control of the military, the mobilization of the masses, and the personal protection afforded by Cuban and East German forces explain much of the Kremlin's success in this regard. As the Soviets gain additional experience in the third world, their efforts at protecting friendly regimes from coups should become even more effective. Moreover, regimes that are not in the Soviet sphere of influence have also become less vulnerable to coups. Whether that relative invulnerability is due to increasingly successful means of repression or to greater mass support for a regime itself, many third world countries of importance to the United States, like Iran, are becoming less susceptible to coups.

One has only to contrast the American experience in the 1950s with more contemporary efforts to see how regimes can become more resistant to foreign-backed coups. In 1954 the United States was able to successfully back a coup against the mildly leftist government of Jacobo Arbenz in Guatemala with little effort. In the early 1980s, the Reagan administration has been unable to topple a much more anti-American and pro-Soviet government in Nicaragua. The very fact that Washington finds it necessary to support a "contra" army against the Nicaraguan regime, despite the domestic and international criticism this support has engendered, shows that it does not believe that the far less costly and protracted option of an American-supported coup could be achieved. In 1953 the United States had little trouble in backing a coup against Prime Minister Mossadegh of Iran. In 1979, when confronted with a much greater threat to American interests, the United States proved unable to initiate a coup to prevent the Khomeini regime from taking power.

Although they are very different, the regimes in Nicaragua and Iran have both taken similar steps to make the prospect of a coup in either place highly remote. Both regimes have placed the military under civilian control, mobilized the support of large numbers of people, and neutralized many of their opponents. Moreover, the use of communist ideology by the Sandinistas and Islamic fundamentalism by Khomeini has legitimized their regimes to a degree not found in many other third world states. As a result, it is unlikely that either a domestic group or a foreign power such as the United States will be able to remove either regime through a coup.

How should the United States respond to the increasing invulnerability to coups of hostile third world regimes? To a great extent, the American response must depend on the specifics of the situation. More generally, American responses can be divided between policies that do not aim at the overthrow of the hostile regime and policies that do.

The effectiveness of countercoup efforts in third world regimes may encourage more American actions to try to stop anti-American forces before they seize power. This is especially true in relation to pro-Soviet groups. As long as governments friendly to Moscow were vulnerable to pro-Western coups, the United States could view the expansion of Soviet influence in the third world with some complacency. If Soviet gains are inherently short-lived, the fact that the Soviets might secure a temporary foothold in a given third world state is not cause for undue alarm. But should Soviet gains come to be protected effectively from coup-induced reversals, it would be more difficult for Washington to accept the establishment of pro-Moscow regimes with equanimity.

If the United States cannot depend on coups to reverse pro-Soviet and other anti-American directions of third world regimes, it must focus more of its efforts on weaning existing leaders away from the other blocs. Since the 1960s, the major Soviet setbacks in the third world have come not from changes of leadership but from changes of mind. Egypt's Sadat, Sudan's Numeiry, Somalia's Siad Barre, Guinea's Sekou Touré, and (most important) China's Mao all realigned themselves and their countries away from the USSR because of dissatisfactions with the Kremlin's policies. Promoting other realignments will likely provide Washington with its best opportunities for extending its influence in a Soviet camp largely free from coups.

Convincing pro-Soviet third world leaders to turn toward the West will not be easy. The Kremlin has learned from past defections and has taken steps to make future realignments very difficult. Surrounded by Cuban bodyguards and an internal security apparatus controlled by the East Germans, these third world leaders would find any decision that moves in a direction against the wishes of the Kremlin dangerous to take. This is especially true in the "transition" stage of the transfer of influence, when Soviet influence is still strong and the United States has yet to establish itself. As we saw in Chapter Three, Soviet efforts to back coups have focused on leaders already within Moscow's sphere of influence. If the United States wants to entice these leaders away from the USSR, it must first convince them that it will ensure their short-term survival, as well as meet their long-term needs.

Another implication of the decline in the number of coups launched against anti-American regimes is that U.S. support for insurgency movements and even direct U.S. military involvements will be considered more seriously than they have been in the past to remove hostile governments from power. When coups no longer function as avenues for producing indigenous change and when democratic means of replacing governments are lacking, outside military intervention or even invasion may be the only way to reform or replace existing governments that pursue policies contrary to American interests. This is especially true when the incumbent regime either was placed in power or is protected in power by foreign assistance. The temptation to aid indigenous groups in trying to overthrow these regimes is shown by recent American behavior. In the mid-1980s, the United States has publicly supported insurgent movements in Afghanistan, Nicaragua, and Cambodia, while holding out the prospect of aiding other insurgencies in Ethiopia and Angola. The American invasion of Grenada in 1983 marked the first time the United States has invaded a third world country to remove its government since World War II. However one feels about these American actions, they indicate that direct, public, and protracted U.S. involvement in attempting to overthrow third world regimes may be on the increase, due in part to the declining utility of American coup-backing efforts.

Backing Coups

One policy that the United States is likely to consider, despite its limitations, to cope with the permanence of certain anti-American regimes is to support coups against these governments. This approach falls somewhere in between the drastic measure of launching a direct invasion and the often ineffectual policy of imposing economic sanctions or diplomatic censure. In theory, American assistance for coups could compensate for the increasing effectiveness of third world regimes, often with foreign assistance, in suppressing coups. By supporting indigenous groups in the overthrow of their governments, the United States can exercise the possibility of removing a hostile regime at far less risk or cost than a protracted military operation would entail.

It must be emphasized that an American policy of supporting coups against hostile regimes would be of only limited utility in the third world. American-backed coups will necessarily suffer from the same inhibiting factors that have curtailed indigenous coups in third world states: existing regimes, especially pro-Soviet ones, are better able to defend themselves now against threats to their leadership in many ways. American concern for deniability and secrecy also limits the possible extent of Washington's support, and third world states are better able to protect their regimes by means of increasingly effective policies of repression and mobilization.

An American coup-backing policy would suffer from an inability to moderate hostile regimes. Economic sanctions, support for indigenous insurgents, and diplomatic bargaining can all be manipulated gradually to increase or decrease threats to a government. A coup, however, is an event quickly over, which either succeeds or fails. Perhaps the United States could exploit a reputation as a coup-making power to attempt to intimidate existing third world leaders. President Carter tried to use the threat of an American-backed coup to coerce support for the Bakhtiar government in Iran. Carter's failure demonstrated, however, that in order for intimidation to be effective, the United States would have to be able to convince the relevant groups that it had the will and the capability directly to launch a coup. Cultivating such a reputation is possible for the USSR; it is highly unlikely and ultimately undesirable for the United States.

Most important, backing coups against foreign governments would be difficult for the United States because these are such controversial actions. Instead of protecting the sovereignty of third world regimes, the United States would be undermining their sovereignty. International and domestic norms against interfering in the internal affairs of other states are likely to remain formidably operative for the United States. Moreover, the problems that open societies such as the United States have in pursuing covert actions also limit the effectiveness of any coup-backing policy. That such a policy would be morally and politically repugnant to many Americans stands as a further constraint on its utility.

American prohibitions against backing coups can be overcome when vital interests are at stake. However, if truly vital interests are threatened and time is a factor, supporting a coup would often be too risky a policy on which to rely. The extreme delicacy required for backing a coup and the need to rely on others make this often a dubious policy in terms of effectiveness. The time needed to prepare the operation would also often preclude it as a policy choice. In most cases, if the threat to American interests is critical enough to justify trying to topple a regime, it is also critical enough to justify an open invasion by American or allied forces, as in Grenada, to directly remove the offending regime.

Under what conditions then would the United States best consider backing coups? To a great extent, those conditions would mirror the conditions for an American involvement in defending a regime from a coup. The major difference between the two different kinds of involvement is that the controversial policy of backing a coup would require even more favorable conditions than the less objectionable policy of protecting a third world regime from a coup.

The first condition for American involvement in a coup-backing effort is that important interests should be at stake. Before supporting a coup, Washington would have to have concluded that critical American interests were involved and that these interests would be threatened by the continued rule of the existing regime. Whether such an involvement had a reasonable chance of success and whether it could be kept secret would also be critical factors influencing American decision makers.

These considerations in turn would have to be based on the extent of support for the regime among the military and the people in that country. In general, the United States probably would not choose to assist a coup against a government that commands the allegiance of broad groups in the society and the military. While the initial coup might be successful, ensuring the survival of the new government would be likely to lead to protracted difficulties, as the Egyptians learned in Yemen. Conversely, leaders who do not enjoy the support of the military and the people, and particularly leaders who engage in human rights violations (e.g., Emperor Bokassa of the Central African Republic), are the most vulnerable to having the United States support coups against them.

The nature of the opposition to the existing regime must also play a role in any decision on the part of Washington to become involved in a coup. Obviously, the United States should only support potential coup makers who will respect and further American interests once they have seized power. It would also be far easier to justify American involvement in a coup if the coup makers are genuinely committed to the support of American values, such as democratic rule. While any American involvement in a coup is bound to have negative repercussions, the replacement of a dictatorship by a democracy should mitigate some of the criticism that would follow any American coup-backing effort.

Once Washington decides to back a coup, there are several policies that it can employ. The United States has already helped to bring about coups through the cultivation of a "coup climate," which helps to provoke an otherwise reluctant military to act—in Chile in 1973 and in Guatemala in 1954. The United States has also made material support available to coup makers, as in Brazil in 1964, has introduced coup makers into the indigenous military, as allegedly in Cambodia in 1970, and has also planned actual coup operations, as in Iran in 1953. Other states have taken an even more active role in assisting coups by committing relatively large numbers of troops to the coup, as France did in the Central African Republic in 1979, and as Egypt did in North Yemen in 1962. Depending on the situation, any or all of these policies can be utilized by the United States in the coming years.

The most likely approach for the United States to follow would be to confine itself to encouraging or approving of the plans of coup makers. This policy has proved successful in the past in the short term, as in South Vietnam in 1963 and 1965, and in Brazil in 1964. By limiting its involvement to encouraging or approving the actions of others, the United States stands the best chance of avoiding the embarrassment and censure that a more interventionary participation in a coup would surely bring. Even when more direct and open American participation is requested, there is a good chance that Washington will nevertheless choose not to become involved in a coup directly. The ultimate unwillingness of the United States to assure potential Iranian coup makers in 1979 of tangible military support reflected Washington's reluctance to become deeply and publicly involved in a coup-making effort, even when critical interests were at stake.

An American policy that limits itself to encouraging coups is likely to focus on regimes where the United States already maintains considerable influence. It is of course impossible to back a coup by any means without having some influence among the members of the power structure who are attempting the regime's overthrow. Moreover, if all the United States is prepared to do is simply to encourage or approve the plans of indigenous coup makers, it will have to wield a substantial degree of influence in the country involved, if it is to be confident of success. Consequently, a coup-backing policy is far more likely to be used against friends (or former friends) than against enemies. The history of coup-backing efforts by the United States and the other major powers has demonstrated this overwhelming bias for aiding coups against regimes that are already within the coup-backing state's sphere of influence. There is nothing to indicate that this trend will be changed in the foreseeable future.

This is not to suggest that countries hostile to the United States would never be the target of American coup-backing efforts. Regimes that present a direct threat to U.S. interests, a threat serious enough to justify the removal of the instigator but not so serious as to warrant an American invasion, are likely objects of U.S. coup-backing efforts. The regime of Libya's Muammar Khadaffi and its support of terrorism fall readily into this category. Efforts to back coups against enemy regimes, such as Libya's, are likely to remain rare, however, because the United States will usually lack close ties with opposition groups in the country (especially among the military) that are necessary for a successful coup. When such efforts are undertaken, they will probably be designed to create a climate for a coup so that the indigenous military will be provoked to act against the regime. Exacerbating the country's economic woes, assisting the coup-backing efforts of countries that do maintain ties with opponents of the regime, and even directly attacking elements of the military that support the existing leadership (all of which have been done against Libya) are likely policies for the United States to follow.

There are several situations that could provoke the United States to become involved in a coup-supporting effort against a country within its sphere of influence. Any regime of vital importance to the United States that is overthrown by groups hostile to the United States might provoke an American-backed coup to try to restore it to its pro-Western alignment. The overthrow of regimes, for example, in El Salvador, Pakistan, Saudi Arabia, or Egypt could all provoke American support for a coup to restore the status quo. This is especially true where the United States has retained its influence among the armed forces supporting the overthrown regime.

Coups against countries of less than vital importance (as well as countries of vital importance) could also provoke an American-supported coup if the new regime has not yet had time to legitimize or establish itself firmly. Once a coup has overthrown a regime, a counter-coup to restore the original leadership can be seen as a defensive action supportive of sovereignty. Because it is likely to incur less domestic and international censure, this kind of countercoup policy would be more likely to be pursued by Washington than some others. Although it was accomplished through an invasion, the quick American overthrow of the government in Grenada following a leftist coup there shows Washington's belief in the need and the justifiability of acting quickly once a government has been illegally replaced.

The United States is most likely to back a coup against an existing pro-Western leader if he is losing his ability to cope with anti-American threats to his regime. American policy makers have long been accused of having backed leaders far longer than was justified in terms of their support among key elements in their society. It has been argued that by the time the United States distances itself from these leaders, a radical anti-American opposition has already emerged, precluding the consolidation of a moderate pro-Western alternative. Examples of leaders in relation to whom this mistake allegedly was made include the shah of Iran, Somoza in Nicaragua, and Batista in Cuba.

Whether this argument is valid in relation to these or other cases need not concern us here. What is germane is that the United States will likely be confronted in the future with leaders who no longer command their people's support and yet will not step down or submit to democratic rule. While the days of engineering coups against such leaders are probably over, it is probable that military groups in countries supported by the United States will seek a signal from Washington or even its outright approval before launching a coup against the leadership. By supporting the military in this kind of "guardian" coup, the United States would increase the possibility of a regime coming to power that could both effectively govern and preserve American interests.

Although they did not involve coups, American actions in Haiti and the Philippines in 1986 demonstrate the way the United States may become involved in coup-supporting efforts in the future. In both of these countries, the United States used its influence and especially the threat of withholding aid to support opposition elements and to encourage the existing leaders to step down. Facilitating the American effort was the fact that both Duvalier of Haiti and Marcos of the Philippines had lost the support of, and were rapidly losing control of their ability to rule, large portions of their citizenry and the armed forces. Crucial to these American successes was the understanding that if the leaders would not relinquish power, the United States would not assist them against the popular and military threats against their position. Moreover, it is possible that the United States informed military officials of its intention to support a successor government (including the provision of increased military and economic aid) to encourage their efforts. If so, the United States at least held out the possibility of supporting a coup against these leaders if they refused to give up power on their own.

Similar situations could easily arise in relation to other leaders who are within the American sphere of influence, but whom the United States sees as liabilities. In South Korea and Chile, for example, rulers opposed to democracy hold power in defiance of broad groups in their countries. It is at least possible that a situation may arise in which American support is sought by opposition forces seeking to launch a coup to restore democratic rule in these and other pro-Western countries. Preparing to respond to these contingencies is a critical requirement for United States policy makers.

In deciding how to respond to requests for American support for coups, each situation must be treated on a case-by-case basis. Nevertheless, in general terms it will frequently be tempting to use a coup as a means of replacing a head of state who has become an embarrassment and a threat to American interests with a democratic or even a military leadership dedicated to preserving pro-Western interests and suppressing anti-American threats. And yet, before Washington attempts to use coups as a way of solving its problems with developing countries, a word of caution is in order. It must be remembered that the apparent successes of the United States in removing leaders in Haiti and the Philippines were achieved due to a broad-based mandate for change in both of these countries without the United States having to back an actual coup. Where the United States has backed coups, any gains achieved have proven to be short-lived. Coups beget coups, they damage the reputation of the United States, and they involve Washington in the internal political problems of another state that it may well prefer to avoid. While coups hold out the possibility of providing time for needed reforms, they also can legitimize an unstable form of succession and make democracy less likely to be achieved, both of which work against American long-term interests. It would be foolhardy to argue that it is never in American interests to back coups. It would be equally foolhardy to believe that Washington could rely on such a policy to meet its fundamental needs in the third world.

Notes

Introduction

1. Some of the standard works on coups are: S. E. Finer, *The Man on Horseback: The Role of the Military in Politics* (New York: Praeger, 1962); Samuel DeCalo, *Coups and Army Rule in Africa* (New Haven: Yale University Press, 1971); Eric Nordlinger, *Soldiers in Politics: Military Coups and Governments* (Englewood Cliffs, N.J.: Prentice-Hall, 1977); Samuel P. Huntington, *Political Order in Changing Societies* (New Haven: Yale University Press, 1968); Morris Janowitz, *The Military in the Political Development of New Nations* (Chicago: University of Chicago Press, 1964); John J. Johnson, ed., *The Role of the Military in Underdeveloped Countries* (Princeton: Princeton University Press, 1962); and Edward Luttwak, *Coup d'Etat: A Practical Handbook* (Cambridge: Harvard University Press, 1979).

2. These figures are principally based on *The New York Times Index, 1945–1985*. Assistance in tracking down coups came from a list compiled by Edward Luttwak and updated by George Schott, which can be found in Luttwak's *Coup d'Etat*, 195–207, and from an unpublished list of coups compiled by Phillip J. Borinsky, for a research project sponsored by The Georgetown Center for Strategic and International Studies entitled *Military Coups World-Wide, 1969–1983: The How and Why, Causes of Success and Failure*. These two sources are especially helpful in assessing the broad scope of coup occurrences, broken down by states and regions. Nevertheless, since my definition of a coup differs slightly from those of both Borinsky and Luttwak, and since both of these lists contain omissions, my totals of coups do not correspond with their figures exactly.

3. The quotation is from "The Melian Dialogue," in Thucydides, *The Peloponnesian War* (Middlesex: Penguin Books, 1975), 402.

4. For a similar point, see Luttwak *Coup d'Etat*, 19–21.

5. The focus on third world coups is not meant to suggest that coups that occur in developed societies are not important. On the contrary, successful and abortive coups in Greece, Portugal, Spain, and elsewhere have had enormous international repercussions. Because this study rests exclusively on third world cases, I have not offered judgments about coups in the de-

veloped world. Nevertheless, it is probable that many of the more general conclusions I have reached with regard to coups in the third world would also apply to coups elsewhere.

Chapter One. The Coup d'État and American Interests

1. S. E. Finer, *The Man on Horseback: The Role of the Military in Politics* (New York: Praeger, 1962), 154.
2. For a similar formulation, see Edward Luttwak, *Coup d'Etat: A Practical Handbook* (Cambridge: Harvard University Press, 1979), 24–26.
3. For a similar description of coups, see Samuel P. Huntington, *Political Order in Changing Societies* (New Haven: Yale University Press, 1968), 218.
4. Finer, *Man on Horseback*, 4–7.
5. Some view the loss of governmental legitimacy as the most important factor that causes military coups. See Eric Nordlinger, *Soldiers in Politics: Military Coups and Governments* (Englewood Cliffs, N.J.: Prentice-Hall, 1977), 93.
6. See, for example, Lucian W. Pye, "Armies in the Process of Political Modernization," in *The Role of the Military in Underdeveloped Countries*, ed. John J. Johnson (Princeton: Princeton University Press, 1962), 69–89.
7. Nordlinger, *Soldiers in Politics*, 63, 71.
8. Finer, *Man on Horseback*, 39–49.
9. Samuel DeCalo, *Coups and Army Rule in Africa* (New Haven: Yale University Press, 1971), 14–15, 21.
10. Huntington, *Political Order*, 196–97.
11. Nordlinger, *Soldiers in Politics*, xi, 6.
12. Finer, *Man on Horseback*, 87, 72.
13. Samuel P. Huntington, "The Renewal of Strategy," in *The Strategic Imperative*, ed. Samuel P. Huntington (Cambridge, Mass.: Ballinger Publishing Co., 1982), 45.
14. For a good account of the problems created by "micro" states, see George Quester, "Trouble in the Islands: Defending the Micro-States," *International Security* 8, no. 2 (1983):160–175.
15. This section draws heavily on Huntington's descriptions of "breakthrough," "guardian," and "veto" coups as found in Huntington, *Political Order*, 198–237.
16. Of approximately five million barrels of oil imported by the United States each day, only 625,000 come from the Arab OPEC states. For more details, see the *Annual Energy Review*, 1983, Energy Information Administration (Washington, D.C.: Government Printing Office, 1984), especially 85.
17. The United States Central Command can draw on some 300,000 troops and substantial air and sealift capabilities. Nevertheless, interservice rivalry and the lack of a truly unified command structure can impede its effectiveness. See, for example, Edward Luttwak, *The Pentagon and the Art of War: The Question of Military Reform* (New York: Simon and Schuster, 1984), 84–86.
18. It has been reported that former Secretary of Defense Harold Brown informally discussed the use of American troops for suppressing coups with the Saudi leadership. Whether anything developed from these talks is not

public knowledge. See Donald Zagoria, "Into the Breach: New Soviet Alliances in the Third World," *Foreign Affairs* 57, no. 4 (1979):745.

19. Samuel P. Huntington, "The Renewal of Strategy," 46.

20. Gabriel Kolko, *The Roots of American Foreign Policy: An Analysis of Power and Purpose* (Boston: Beacon Press, 1969), 50.

21. Michael Shafer, "Mineral Myths," *Foreign Policy*, no. 47 (1982): 156–157.

22. For an account of the ways that nuclear proliferation can relate to coups d'état, see Lewis A. Dunn, "Military Politics, Nuclear Proliferation, and the 'Nuclear Coup d'Etat,' " Hudson Institute Paper 2392/2–P (Croton-on-Hudson, N.Y.: Hudson Institute, 1976).

23. For a forceful argument that the only purpose of nuclear weapons is the deterrence of other nuclear weapons, see Robert McNamara, "The Military Role of Nuclear Weapons," *Foreign Affairs* 62, no. 1 (1983):59–80.

24. Some have argued that strong conventional forces are needed to make a nuclear threat credible. See Barry M. Blechman and Douglas M. Hart, "The Political Utility of Nuclear Weapons: The 1973 Middle East Crisis," *International Security* 7, no. 1 (1982):132–156.

25. For an excellent analysis of the command, control, and communications problem, see John D. Steinbruner, "Nuclear Decapitation," *Foreign Policy*, no. 45 (1981/82):16–28.

26. Chapters Two and Three develop this point in greater detail.

27. For an eloquent expression of this point of view, see Robert W. Tucker, *The Radical Left and American Foreign Policy* (Baltimore: Johns Hopkins University Press, 1971), 138–45.

28. Robert W. Tucker makes this point in "The Purposes of American Power," *Foreign Affairs* 59(1980/81):270–73.

Chapter Two. The United States' Experience with Third World Coups

1. For a provocative account of why development will not bring about democracy, see Elie Kedourie, "The Development Delusion," *The New Republic*, November 17, 1984, 13–18.

2. *New York Times*, March 19, 1964.

3. For an argument that the Mann doctrine was not a departure from President Kennedy's policies, see Robert A. Packenham, *Liberal America and the Third World* (Princeton: Princeton University Press, 1973), 75.

4. *New York Times*, March 19, 1964.

5. Central Intelligence Agency, *Handbook of Economic Statistics* (October 1978):71–73; Central Intelligence Agency, *Handbook of Economic Statistics* (October 1980):72, 87, 102, 107.

6. Harry F. Young, *Atlas of United States Foreign Relations*, United States Department of State, Bureau of Public Affairs, Office of Public Communication (Washington, D.C.: Government Printing Office, 1982).

7. Samuel P. Huntington, *Political Order in Changing Societies* (New Haven: Yale University Press, 1968), 193. Successful coups in Ethiopia (1974), in Liberia (1980), and in the Sudan (1985) support the contention that U.S. assistance does not inhibit the military from intervening in third world politics.

8. Young, *Atlas of United States Foreign Relations*, United States Department of State.

9. As I will discuss in the following section, the U.S. Navy has helped to deter coups in the Dominican Republic and in Guatemala.

10. The Reagan administration has amassed a great deal of political credit by claiming that no pro-Soviet or Marxist regimes have come to power during its first term, in contrast to the many reverses that took place under President Carter. What the Reagan administration has not explained is what different actions it would have taken to prevent some of the Carter "losses," such as the leftist coups in Ethiopia, the Seychelles, Grenada, Suriname, and South Yemen.

11. For an elaboration of this point, see Edward Luttwak, *Coup d'Etat: A Practical Handbook* (Cambridge: Harvard University Press, 1979), 38–45.

12. Stephen Schlesinger and Stephen Kinzer, *Bitter Fruit: The Untold Story of the American Coup in Guatemala* (New York: Doubleday and Co., 1982), 238–239.

13. Jerome N. Slater, "The Dominican Republic, 1961–1966," in *Force Without War: U.S. Armed Forces as a Political Instrument*, ed. Barry M. Blechman and Stephen S. Kaplan (Washington, D.C.: Brookings Institution, 1978), 292–299.

14. John Bartlow Martin, *Overtaken by Events: The Dominican Crisis From the Fall of Trujillo to the Civil War* (New York: Doubleday and Co., 1966), 570; Abraham Lowenthal, *The Dominican Intervention* (Cambridge: Harvard University Press, 1972), 29.

15. See Chapter Four for details concerning the American role in the Dominican rebellion.

16. For an account of the Wessin episode, see Theodore Draper, *The Dominican Revolt* (New York: Commentary, 1968), 189–193.

17. *New York Times,* June 7, 1981, and December 21, 1981.

18. *Baltimore Sun,* November 2, 1984.

19. For an account of why the United States failed to prevent coups in spite of having tried to do so in the early 1960s, see Edwin Lieuwen, *Generals vs. Presidents: Neomilitarism in Latin America* (New York: Praeger Publishers, 1964), 115–119.

20. Ibid., 118–119.

21. For a further elaboration of these points, see Arthur M. Schlesinger, Jr., *A Thousand Days: John F. Kennedy in the White House* (Boston: Houghton Mifflin Co., 1965), 786–87; and Lieuwen, *Generals vs. Presidents,* 116–118.

22. See Chapter Four for more details on American involvement in this coup.

23. Jerome Slater, "The Dominican Republic," 298; G. Pope Atkins, *Arms and Politics in the Dominican Republic* (Boulder, Co.: Westview Press, 1981), 13.

24. *Newsweek,* September 3, 1973; *New York Times,* August 27, 1973.

25. *New York Times,* July 6, 1984.

26. The following account is based principally on reports in the *New York Times* from May 16 to May 19, 1961

27. Reference to American assistance for Indonesian and Tibetan rebels can be found in Victor Marchetti and John D. Marks, *The CIA and the Cult of*

Intelligence (New York: Dell, 1980), 26, 36, 37, 101. There are many accounts of the U.S. support of the Bay of Pigs invasion. For a clear explanation of the interpretation that its purpose was not so much to initiate a coup as it was to set off a general rebellion, see Schlesinger, Jr., *A Thousand Days*, 234, 237, 247, 264.

28. For more on alleged American involvements in assassinations, see *Alleged Assassination Plots Involving Foreign Leaders*, November 20, 1975, Senate Intelligence Committee, Select Committee to Study Government Operations with Respect to Intelligence Activities, 94th Cong., 1st Sess., Senate Report 94–465, 13098–8.

29. This list is not meant to be exhaustive. As I discussed in Chapter Five, conclusive proof rarely comes to light that an outside state attempted to back a particular coup. This is especially true if no coup attempt developed from outside machinations. The cases included all have produced allegations of substantial American involvement supported by credible, public sources. Nevertheless, especially in the area of American involvement in trying to provoke coups, other cases in addition to the two discussed in this chapter could have been included.

30. For a sometimes inadvertent illustration of why covert actions are difficult to keep secret, see U.S. Congress, Senate, *Hearings Before the Select Committee to Study Governmental Operations with Respect to Intelligence Activities*, 94th Cong., 1st Sess., vol. 7, "Covert Action" (Washington, D.C.: GPO, 1975).

31. For two accounts of the American role in the 1953 Iranian coup, see Kermit Roosevelt, *Countercoup: The Struggle for the Control of Iran* (New York: McGraw-Hill, 1979); and Barry Rubin, *Paved With Good Intentions: The American Experience in Iran* (New York: Oxford University Press, 1980).

32. The principal source for this account is: Schlesinger and Kinzer, *Bitter Fruit*.

33. The best account of American involvement in the Diem coup can be found in *The Pentagon Papers: The Defense Department History of United States Decisionmaking on Vietnam*, The Senator Gravel Edition, vol. 2 (Boston: Beacon Press), 201–276; an additional treatment of these events and their aftermath can be found in Stanley Karnow, *Vietnam: A History* (New York: Penguin Books, 1983), 270–311.

34. Karnow, *Vietnam*, 297.

35. Ibid., 384–386.

36. For an examination and analysis of the Brazilian political situation that led to the coup, see John W. F. Dulles, *Unrest in Brazil: Political Military Crisis, 1955–1964* (Austin: University of Texas Press, 1970); Alfred Stepan, *The Military in Politics: Changing Patterns in Brazil* (Princeton: Princeton University Press, 1971); Thomas E. Skidmore, *Politics in Brazil, 1930–1964: An Experiment in Democracy* (New York: Oxford University Press, 1967). For a well-researched, concise treatment of the 1964 coup, see Phyllis R. Parker, *Brazil and the Quiet Intervention, 1964* (Austin: University of Texas Press, 1979).

37. This section draws principally from Seymour Hersh, *The Price of Power: Kissinger in the Nixon White House* (New York: Summit Books, 1983), 184–202, and Henry A. Kissinger, *White House Years* (Boston: Little, Brown and Co. 1979), especially 457–468.

38. Kissinger, *White House Years*, 463.
39. There is a great deal of material on the U.S. role in Chile. Some of the best accounts include: U.S. Congress, Senate, *Covert Action in Chile, 1963–1973*, Staff Report of the Select Committee to Study Governmental Operations with Respect to Intelligence Activities (Washington, D.C.: GPO, 1975); Kissinger, *White House Years*, 653–684; Hersh, *The Price of Power*, 258–296; and Nathaniel Davis, *The Last Two Years of Salvador Allendé* (Ithaca: Cornell University Press, 1985), especially chapters 12 and 13.
40. Henry Kissinger, *White House Years*, 653.
41. Nathaniel Davis, *The Last Two Years*, 308.
42. For a persuasive argument to the effect that the United States did not plan the 1973 coup and probably could not have stopped it even if it had wanted to, see ibid., 345–366.
43. The following account of the U.S. involvement in Iran comes from these sources: Zbigniew Brzezinski, *Power and Principle: Memoirs of the National Security Adviser, 1977–1981* (New York: Farrar, Straus and Giroux, 1983), 377–398; Cyrus Vance, *Hard Choices: Critical Years in America's Foreign Policy* (New York: Simon and Schuster, 1983), 335–341; William H. Sullivan, *Mission to Iran* (New York: W. W. Norton, 1981), 228–239, 241–253; Gary Sick, *All Fall Down: America's Tragic Encounter With Iran* (New York: Random House, 1985), 137–145, 151–156; Michael Ledeen and William Lewis, *Debacle: The American Failure in Iran* (New York: Alfred A. Knopf, 1981), 173–187, 193–194; Jimmy Carter, *Keeping Faith* (New York: Bantam, 1982), 442–450.
44. Vance, *Hard Choices*, 334–338; Sullivan, *Mission to Iran*, 228, 238.
45. Brzezinski, *Power and Principle*, 377–398.
46. Carter, *Keeping Faith*, 443.
47. Ledeen and Lewis, *Debacle*, 178.
48. Sullivan, *Mission to Iran*, 238–239.
49. Ledeen and Lewis, *Debacle*, 182.
50. Brzezinski, *Power and Principle*, 387.
51. Sick, *All Fall Down*, 156.
52. Vance, *Hard Choices*, 341; Sullivan, *Mission to Iran*, 253.
53. Lisa Anderson, "Qadhdhafi and His Opposition," *Middle East Journal* 40, no. 2 (Spring 1986): 229–231.
54. *New York Times*, April 17, 1986.
55. *New York Times*, April 29, 1986.
56. *New York Times*, April 18, 1986.
57. *Boston Globe*, April 19, 1986.
58. *New York Times*, April 15, 1986.
59. *New York Times*, April 19, 1982.
60. *Economist*, September 19, 1981.
61. It is noteworthy that the French, using the Foreign Legion to prevent an incursion into Zaire in 1978, encountered far fewer domestic problems than the Belgians, who also participated in the intervention. For more on the events in Zaire, see Peter Mangold, "Shaba I and Shaba II," *Survival*, May/June 1979.
62. Many of these coups will be treated in greater detail in Chapter Five.
63. Helen Kitchen, "Africa: Year of Ironies," *Foreign Affairs, America and the World, 1985* 64, no. 3 (1985): 580; *Economist*, September 19, 1981, 44.

64. Alvin J. Cottrell, Robert J. Hanks, and Frank T. Bray, "Military Affairs in the Persian Gulf," in *The Persian Gulf States: A General Survey,* ed. Alvin J. Cottrell (Baltimore: Johns Hopkins University Press, 1980), 161–169.

65. The Gambian and Omani coups are discussed in Chapters Four and Five, respectively.

66. See Chapter Four for a detailed analysis of the failed Egyptian countercoup.

67. Nadav Safran, *From War to War* (Indianapolis: Bobbs-Merrill, 1969), 86.

68. David Blumberg, *Bilateral Relations in the Absence of Diplomatic Ties: Africa and Israel in the Post-1973 Era,* Senior thesis, Harvard University, 1981, 31; Ignacio Klich, "Israel Returns to Africa," *Middle East International,* June 4, 1982.

69. Reports of the Israelis replacing the East Germans come from personal interviews with Israeli academics and military officials who have chosen to remain anonymous; see also Seth O. Kaye, *Israeli Arms Sales and American Interests in the Third World,* unpublished paper, Johns Hopkins University, Spring 1983, 17.

70. *New York Times,* December 3, 1982.

71. Paul Quinn-Judge, "Israel Sells Arms to Asia Discreetly, Even Secretly," *Christian Science Monitor,* December 27, 1982.

72. See Chapter Four for more details of the Senegalese intervention.

73. *Africa Contemporary Record: Annual Survey and Documents 1979–1980,* ed. Colin Legum (New York: Africana Publishing, 1981), B430. Moroccan troops were required to execute the leader of the former regime, President Francisco Macias Nguema, because troops from Equatorial Guinea refused to do so out of fear that Macias held mystical powers.

74. See Chapter One for a description of veto, guardian, and breakthrough coups.

Chapter Three. The Soviet Experience with Third World Coups

1. Adam B. Ulam, *Dangerous Relations: The Soviet Union in World Politics, 1970–1982* (New York: Oxford University Press, 1983), 153–154, 311–12.

2. Mark Katz, *The Third World in Soviet Military Thought* (Baltimore: Johns Hopkins University Press, 1982), 27.

3. Eric Nordlinger, *Soldiers in Politics: Military Coups and Governments* (Englewood Cliffs, N.J.: Prentice-Hall, 1977), 76.

4. The effort of the Indonesian Communist Party to eliminate the army leadership was not, strictly speaking, a coup because it was not directed at the head of state. Nevertheless, since it is almost always referred to as an "abortive coup," and since the Soviets treated it as such, the Indonesian case is included with other examples of coup-induced setbacks. For more on this point, see Harold Crouch, *The Army and Politics in Indonesia* (Ithaca: Cornell University Press, 1978), Chapter Four, especially 78.

5. Nordlinger, *Soldiers in Politics,* 74.

6. G. I. Mirskiy, *The Army and Politics in the Countries of Asia and Africa* (Moscow: Izdatel'stvo Nauka, 1970), 4, quoted in Stephen Hosmer and Thomas Wolfe, *Soviet Policy and Practice Toward Third World Conflicts* (Lexington: Lexington Books, 1983), 28.

7. Katz, *Third World,* 52, 53.
8. Ibid., 81.
9. David Albright, "Vanguard Parties in the Third World," in *The Pattern of Soviet Conduct in the Third World,* ed. Walter Laqueur (New York: Praeger, 1983), 211.
10. Katz, *Third World,* 81.
11. V. Solodovnikov and N. Gavrilov, "Africa: Tendencies of Non-Capitalist Development," *Mezhdunarodnaya zhizn',* no. 2 (February 1976): 35, quoted in Hosmer and Wolfe, *Soviet Policy,* 40.
12. Francis Fukuyama, "A New Soviet Strategy," *Commentary,* October 1979.
13. Katz, *Third World,* 89, 104, 107.
14. Albright, "Vanguard Parties," 212.
15. Ibid., 213, 217.
16. Ibid., 216; COPWE became an approved vanguard party after the publication of Albright's article.
17. For a similar view, see Francis Fukuyama, *The New Marxist-Leninist States in the Third World,* The Rand Paper Series (Santa Monica, Calif.: Rand Corporation, 1984), 33, 41.
18. Excluded from this list of Soviet arms transfers are deals with Cuba, Vietnam, and North Korea.
19. Hosmer and Wolfe, *Soviet Policy,* 17, 23.
20. Walter Laqueur, "Introduction," in *The Pattern of Soviet Conduct in the Third World,* ed. Laqueur, 33.
21. Hosmer and Wolfe, *Soviet Policy,* 75.
22. U.S. Congress, House of Representatives, Report for the House Subcommittee on Foreign Affairs, *Changing Perspectives on U.S. Arms Transfer Policy,* 97th Cong., 1st Sess. (Washington, D.C.: Government Printing Office, 1981).
23. Central Intelligence Agency, *Communist Aid Activities in Non-Communist Less Developed Countries, 1979 and 1954–1979,* ER 80–10318U (Washington, D.C.: Government Printing Office, 1980), 15–16.
24. Central Intelligence Agency. *Arms Flows to LDCs: U.S.–Soviet Comparisons, 1974–1977* (Washington, D.C.: Government Printing Office, 1980), ii–5.
25. For a chart of Soviet recipients of arms, see Hosmer and Wolfe, *Soviet Policy,* 74.
26. *The Politics and Economics of Aristotle,* transl. Edward Walford (London: Henry G. Bohn, 1853), 196.
27. William J. Durch, "The Cuban Military in Africa and the Middle East: From Algeria to Angola," *Studies in Comparative Communism* 11, nos. 1 and 2 (1978): 48.
28. Laqueur, "Introduction," in *The Pattern of Soviet Conduct,* 14.
29. Durch, "The Cuban Military," 58.
30. Roger E. Kanet, "East European States," in *Communist Powers and Sub-Saharan Africa,* ed. Thomas H. Henriken (Stanford, Calif.: Hoover Institute Press, 1981), 46.
31. Melvin Croan, "A New Afrika Korps?" *The Washington Quarterly* 3 (Winter 1980): 31.

32. "U.S. National Security," in Harry F. Young, *Atlas of U.S. Foreign Relations,* United States Department of State, Bureau of Public Affairs, Office of Public Communication (Washington, D.C.: Government Printing Office, 1982). The Madagascar reference can be found in *Newsweek,* December 17, 1984,

33. Ulam, *Dangerous Relations,* 251.

34. Hosmer and Wolfe, *Soviet Policy,* 62–63.

35. *Africa Contemporary Record: Annual Survey and Documents, 1979–1980,* ed. Colin Legum (New York: Africana Press, 1981), B428–434.

36. See Chapter Four for a more detailed treatment of this case.

37. Legum, *Africa Contemporary Record, 1980–81,* B55.

38. *New York Times,* May 9, 1984; *New York Times,* November 4, 1985. The number of coups launched against Khadaffi may be even higher than is indicated in the text. For an account of the threats to Khadaffi's rule see Lisa Anderson, "Qadhdhafi and His Opposition," *Middle East Journal* 40, no. 2 (Spring 1986): 225–238.

39. Bradford Dismukes, "Soviet Employment of Naval Power For Political Purposes, 1967–1975," in *Soviet Naval Influence: Domestic and Foreign Dimensions,* ed. Michael MccGwire and John McDonnel (New York: Praeger Publishers, 1977), 486–490.

40. Ibid., 486–489.

41. James Cable, *Gunboat Diplomacy, 1919–1979: Political Applications of Limited Naval Force* (New York: St. Martin's Press, 1981), 165.

42. Hosmer and Wolfe, *Soviet Policy,* 58.

43. Michael Doyle, "Grenada: An International Crisis in Multilateral Security," in *Escalation and Intervention,* ed. Arthur Day and Michael Doyle (Boulder, Co.: Westview Press, forthcoming 1986).

44. Paul Henze, *Russians and the Horn: Opportunism and the Long View,* European American Institute for Security Research, The EAI Papers, no. 5, (Marina del Ray, Calif.: European American Institute, 1983), 34.

45. David and Marina Ottaway, *Ethiopia: Empire in Revolution* (New York: Africana Press, 1978), 168.

46. Hosmer and Wolfe, *Soviet Policy,* 110–111.

47. For an argument that the Soviets were surprised by the coup, see Raymond L. Garthoff, *Détente and Confrontation: American-Soviet Relations from Nixon to Reagan* (Washington, D.C.: Brookings Institution, 1985), 897.

48. Theodore Eliot, Jr., "Afghanistan After the 1978 Revolution," *Strategic Review* 7 (Spring 1979): 58.

49. Hosmer and Wolfe, *Soviet Policy,* 110–111; Fukuyama, *The New Marxist-Leninist States,* 14.

50. *Arab World Weekly,* July 1, 1978.

51. *Middle East Economic Digest,* June 2, 1978.

52. Nimrod Novik, *On the Shores of Bab Al-Mandab: Soviet Diplomacy and Regional Dynamics,* Monograph no. 26 (Philadelphia: Foreign Policy Research Institute, 1979), 18.

53. *Newsweek,* July 10, 1978.

54. Faris Glubb, "The Yemens: The Pot Boils," *Middle East International* 86 (1978): 16.

55. Ibid., 16.

56. Robin Bidwell, *The Two Yemens* (Boulder, Co.: Westview Press, 1983), 279; Novik, *On The Shores*, 19.

57. Donald S. Zagoria, "Into the Breach: New Soviet Alliances in the Third World," *Foreign Affairs* 57 (1979): 737.

58. Alvin Rubinstein, "The Soviet Union and the Arabian Peninsula," *World Today* 35, no. 11 (1979): 443–452.

59. Fukuyama, *The New Marxist-Leninist States*, 28.

60. Bidwell, *The Two Yemens*, 280.

61. There is of yet no evidence that the Soviets knew about or encouraged the 1986 purge and subsequent civil war in South Yemen. It is noteworthy, however, that despite all of the confusion and chaos, there was never much doubt that whatever leadership emerged would retain South Yemen's pro-Soviet alignment.

62. Some would argue that the Soviet invasion of Afghanistan represents a successful coup. However, if we accept the definition of a coup as necessarily involving a "small group," the nearly one hundred thousand Soviet troops required to bring down the old Afghan regime and protect the new one would not qualify. Moreover, since the Afghan government was toppled almost entirely by outside forces, the internal dimension required for a coup was absent.

63. For more on the Ali Sabri affair, see: Mohammed Heikal, *The Sphinx and the Commissar: The Rise and Fall of Soviet Influence in the Arab World* (London: Collins, 1978), 220; Anwar el-Sadat, *In Search of Identity: An Autobiography* (New York: Harper and Row, 1978), 215; P. J. Vatikiotis, "Egypt's Politics of Conspiracy," *Survey* 18, no. 2 (1972): 89; Alvin Z. Rubinstein, *Red Star on the Nile: The Soviet-Egyptian Influence Relationship Since the June War* (Princeton: Princeton University Press, 1977), 149.

64. For more on the various plots against Sadat, see: *U.S. News and World Report*, June 7, 1976; *Middle East Intelligence Survey*, May 1, 1973; April 15, 1974; November 15, 1974; October 1, 1975; and March 15–31, 1975; Pedro Ramet, *Sadat and the Kremlin*, The California Seminar on Arms Control and Foreign Policy, Student Paper Number 885, University of California at Los Angeles, February 1980, 6; *New York Times*, July 29, 1984.

65. For a detailed account of the abortive Sudanese coup, see Chapter Four.

66. For details on the 1976 coup, see *Africa Contemporary Record, 1976–1977*, ed. Colin Legum, B107; for the 1977 attempt, see ibid., B114; Zagoria, "Into the Breach," 736–737.

67. For possible Soviet involvement in the Somali coup, see Zagoria, "Into the Breach," 736–737; the Negede Gobeze affair is described by Paul Henze, *Russians and the Horn: Opportunism and the Long View*, EAI Papers, no. 5, Summer 1983, 45.

68. *Africa Contemporary Record, 1976–1977*, B496.

69. David Birmingham, "The 27th of May: An Historical Note on the Abortive 1977 Coup in Angola," *African Affairs* 77 (October 1978): 560.

70. *Africa Contemporary Record, 1977–1978*, B510.

71. Birmingham, "The 27th of May," 563.

72. William LeoGrande, "Cuban-Soviet Relations and Cuban Policy in Af-

rica," *Cuban Studies/Estudios Cubanos* 10, no. 1 (January 1980): 16–17; Hosmer and Wolfe, *Soviet Policy,* 86.

73. LeoGrande, "Cuban-Soviet Relations," 16–17.
74. *Africa Contemporary Record, 1977–1978,* B509.
75. Birmingham, "The 27th of May," 562.
76. Not all observers believe Lin ever planned a coup against Mao. Questions about the validity of the coup plans and Lin's involvement in them are raised by Jurgen Domes, "The Chinese Leadership Crisis: Doom of an Heir?" *Orbis* 17 (1973): 869–873.
77. Ying-mao Kau and Pierre M. Perrolle, "The Politics of Lin Piao's Abortive Military Coup," *Asian Survey* 14, no. 6 (June 1974): 562–565.
78. Kau and Perrolle "The Politics of Lin Piao," 561.
79. Ibid., 571; *A Great Trial in Chinese History* (New York: Pergamon Press, 1981), 25.
80. According to one report, the Soviets were contacted about the coup, but they chose not to respond. See Yao Ming-le, *The Conspiracy and Death of Lin Biao* (New York: Alfred A. Knopf, 1983), 81–82.
81. Garthoff, *Détente and Confrontation,* 923.
82. *Strategic Survey, 1979* (London: International Institute of Strategic Studies, 1979), 49; Garthoff, *Détente and Confrontation,* 907; Garthoff says it was a "near certainty that Taraki had acted to remove Amin at Soviet urging."
83. Zalmay Khalizan, "Afghanistan and the Crisis in American Foreign Policy," *Survival* 22 (July–August 1980): 155.
84. Henry S. Bradsheer, *Afghanistan and the Soviet Union* (Durham, N.C.: Duke University Press, 1983), 115–116.
85. Hosmer and Wolfe, *Soviet Policy,* 114–115.
86. Ibid., 114–115, 117.

Chapter Four. Defending Third World Regimes from Coups d'État

1. Edward Luttwak, *Coup d'Etat: A Practical Handbook* (Cambridge, Mass.: Harvard University Press, 1979), 64.
2. Peter Mangold, "Shaba I and Shaba II," *Survival,* May/June 1979, 114.
3. For an account of the East African mutinies, see *The New York Times,* January 21, 24, 25, 1964; an excellent analysis of mutinies can be found in Elihu Rose, "The Anatomy of Mutiny," *Armed Forces and Society* 8, no. 4 (1982): 561–574.
4. A good account of the American intervention in Lebanon can be found in William Quandt's "Lebanon, 1958," in *Force Without War: U.S. Armed Forces as a Political Instrument,* ed. Barry Blechman and Stephen Kaplan (Washington, D.C.: Brookings Institution, 1978), 222–257.
5. Ibid., 248.
6. For a comprehensive treatment of the U.S. intervention in the Dominican Republic, see Abraham Lowenthal, *The Dominican Intervention* (Cambridge, Mass.: Harvard University Press, 1972). For a more concise analysis see Jerome Slater, "The Dominican Republic, 1961–1966," in *Force Without War,* ed. Blechman and Kaplan, 289–342.
7. Slater, "The Dominican Republic," 289.

8. See Chapter Two for more on American efforts to protect the government of the Dominican Republic from coups.

9. The following draws on an account found in *Africa Contemporary Record, 1971–1972,* ed. Colin Legum (New York: Africana Press, 1972), B680–682.

10. See Chapter Three for more on how the East Germans and Cubans have helped defend regimes from coups.

11. This account of the Grenada operation is based on news reports from the following: *New York Times,* October 26–November 14, 1983; and *Newsweek,* October 31 and November 7, 1983.

12. The American intervention did not proceed as smoothly as it was initially thought. For an account of the problems encountered in Grenada, see Edward N. Luttwak, *The Pentagon and the Art of War: The Question of Military Reform* (New York: Simon and Schuster, 1984), 52–58, 237–238.

13. *Africa Contemporary Record, 1981–1982,* B55, B69. See also *New York Times,* September 23, 1985, and Roger Faligot and Pascal Krop, *La Piscine: Les Services secrets français, 1944–1984* (Paris: Editions du Seuil, 1985), 346–348.

14. *Middle East Contemporary Survey, 1976–1977,* ed. Colin Legum (New York: Holmes and Meier, 1978), 498–499 and 512–513.

15. *Newsweek,* December 26, 1960; Margery Perham, *The Government of Ethiopia* (Evanston, Ill.: Northwestern University Press, 1969), 86; personal interviews conducted by the author with Ethiopian students and officials in Addis Ababa in February of 1973.

16. Christopher Miniclier, "Military Aid and the Ethiopian Revolt," *The New Republic,* August 21, 1961.

17. Christopher Clapham, *Haile Selassie's Government* (London: Longmans Press, 1969), 25.

18. Richard Greenfield, *Ethiopia: A New Political History* (New York: Praeger Publishers, 1965), 412.

19. Ibid., 414.

20. Miniclier, "Military Aid," 16.

21. Greenfield, *Ethiopia,* 422.

22. Miniclier, "Military Aid," 16.

23. *New York Times,* February 24, 1964.

24. For more justifications of the coup, see Brian Weinstein, *Gabon: Nation Building on the Ogooué* (Cambridge: MIT Press, 1966), 178.

25. *New York Times,* February 20, 1964.

26. *New York Times,* February 21, 1964.

27. Gordon C. McDonald et al., *Area Handbook for People's Republic of the Congo* (Washington, D.C.: Government Printing Office, 1971), 102.

28. William J. Durch, "The Cuban Military in Africa and the Middle East," *Studies in Comparative Communism* 11, nos. 1 and 2 (Spring/Summer 1978): 48.

29. Durch, "The Cuban Military," 48.

30. McDonald, *Area Handbook of the People's Republic of the Congo,* 103; *New York Times,* October 20, 1966.

31. *New York Times,* June 29, 1966.

32. Harold D. Nelson et al., *Area Handbook for the Democratic Republic of Sudan* (Washington, D.C.: GPO, 1973), 183.

33. *New York Times,* July 23, 1971.
34. *Time,* August 2, 1971.
35. Arnold Hottinger, "The Great Powers and the Middle East," in *The World and Great-Powers Triangles,* ed. William E. Griffith (Cambridge: MIT Press, 1975), 135.
36. Peter Bechtold, *Politics in the Sudan* (New York: Praeger Publishers, 1976), 270; Stephen T. Hosmer and Thomas W. Wolfe, *Soviet Policy and Practice Toward Third World Conflicts* (Lexington, Mass.: Lexington Books, 1983), 49.
37. Much of the material for this section came from an excellent series of articles written by Leon Dash in *The Washington Post* during the week of July 30, 1981, and from interviews with State Department personnel who requested anonymity.
38. Malcom Kerr, *The Arab Cold War: 1958–1967* (London: Oxford University Press, 1967), 14.
39. Ibid., 28–34.
40. *Newsweek,* October 9, 1961.
41. *New York Times,* September 30, 1961.
42. These cases are covered briefly in Chapter Two.
43. For lessons on the U.S. failure in South Korea, see Chapter Two.
44. *Newsweek,* October 9, 1961.

Chapter Five. Backing Coups d'État against Third World Regimes

1. See Chapter Two for a discussion of American-backed coups.
2. See, for example, Nadav Safran, *From War to War: The Arab-Israeli Confrontation 1948–1967* (Indianapolis, Ind.: Bobbs-Merrill, 1969), especially 57–88.
3. This is not to imply that all plots simply entail the word of one leader against another. There is overwhelming evidence, for example, that Iran backed a coup plot against Bahrain in December of 1981. For an account of this Iranian operation, see *Middle East Contemporary Survey, 1981–82,* ed. Colin Legum (New York: Holmes and Meier, 1984), 490–491. Because of the extreme "softness" of coup-plot allegations, however, it was deemed preferable to concentrate only on those cases in which actual verifiable coups were launched.
4. See Chapter Two for more details on these cases.
5. See Chapter Three for more details on these cases. The Soviet effort to incite a coup in Afghanistan in 1979 is not on this list of failed coups because Taraki was not able to launch a coup.
6. For more on the Iranian involvement in the Iraqi coup, see Majid Khadduri, *Socialist Iraq: A Study in Iraqi Politics Since 1968* (Washington, D.C.: Middle East Institute, 1978), 53–56.
7. For possible Saudi involvement in the 1974 coup, see Robin Bidwell, *The Two Yemens* (Boulder, Colo.: Westview Press, 1983), 296; for the 1979 coup, see *Middle East Contemporary Survey, 1978–1979,* 895.
8. For more on this coup, see *Africa Contemporary Record, 1981–82,* B475.
9. See Chapter Two for more on this coup.
10. See *Africa Contemporary Record, 1976–1977* for more on this attempted coup, B107–108. Egyptian troops may have played a role in suppressing the July 1976 coup in the Sudan. See *New York Times,* April 29, 1986.

11. Bidwell, *The Two Yemens*, 205.
12. See Chapter Two for more on the American role in these Guatemalan events.
13. J. E. Peterson, *Oman in the Twentieth Century: Political Foundations of an Emerging State* (London: Croom Helm, 1978), 202.
14. Bidwell, *The Two Yemens*, 197.
15. For an account of this coup, see Taki Theodoracopulos, *The Greek Upheaval* (New Rochelle, N.Y.: Caratzas Brothers, 1978); Pierre Oberling, *The Road to Bellapais: The Turkish Cypriot Exodus to Northern Cyprus* (New York: Columbia University Press, 1982), especially 154–170.
16. See Chapter Three for more on the South Yemeni coup.
17. *Africa Contemporary Record, 1979–1980*, B400–401.
18. Mercenary-backed coups are to be distinguished from outside invasions by the relatively small numbers of foreign forces used, by their focus on overthrowing the regime, and by their support of indigenous forces. The first two conditions were clearly met in each of the cases in this section. Support from indigenous elements could not always be confirmed, but in each of the cases studied here such support was strongly suspected.
19. For more on this intriguing coup, see *Jeune Afrique* (Paris), June 21, 1978; *Le Monde* (Paris), June 4–5, 1978; the *Observer* (London), June 25, 1978; and *Africa Contemporary Record, 1978–79*, B187–192.
20. *Africa Contemporary Record, 1977–1978*, B616–617.
21. *Africa Contemporary Record, 1980–1981*, B295–296, B777.

Chapter Six. Prospects for Future American Involvements in Third World Coups

1. For an insightful but brief analysis of the implications of the decline in third world coups, see Charles Waterman, "Decline in Coups Around the World is a Mixed Blessing," *Christian Science Monitor,* January 10, 1985.
2. Figures come from Chapters Four and Five. The reasons why these figures are not all-inclusive, that is, they report only cases for which there is reliable and persuasive public information, can also be found in both chapters.
3. For a brief account of how the debt crisis promotes coups, see *New York Times,* April 14, 1985; for an interesting analysis of the instabilities produced by Arab migrations resulting from declining oil production, see *New York Times,* October 6, 1985.
4. Richard K. Betts and Samuel P. Huntington, "Dead Dictators and Rioting Mobs," *International Security* 10, no. 3 (1985/86): 130–131.
5. For the role pan-Arabism played in Nasser's involvements with other Arab states, see Nadav Safran, *From War to War: The Arab-Israeli Confrontation 1948–1967* (Indianapolis, Ind.: Bobbs-Merrill, 1969), 68–70.
6. For an account of how norms against interfering against sovereignty are eroding in Africa, see S. Neil MacFailane, "Africa's Decaying Security System and the Rise of Intervention," *International Security* 8, no. 4 (1984): 146–149.
7. "Pakistan is on the Threshold of Developing a Nuclear Device," *Christian Science Monitor,* February 21, 1985, 21.

Index

About the Author

Steven R. David is assistant professor of political science at the Johns Hopkins University. He is the author of many publications on third world security issues.

Third World Coups d'Etat and International Security

Designed by Ann Walston

Composed by Brushwood Graphics in Sabon
with display lines in Optima Black

Printed by BookCrafters on 50-lb. Glatfelter Offset and
bound in Holliston Roxite A